Unsafe for Democracy

❖ STUDIES IN AMERICAN ❖
THOUGHT AND CULTURE

Series Editor

Paul S. Boyer

Margaret Fuller: Transatlantic Crossings in a Revolutionary Age
Edited by Charles Capper and Cristina Giorcelli

Observing America:
The Commentary of British Visitors to the United States,
1890–1950
Robert P. Frankel

Picturing Indians:
Photographic Encounters and Tourist Fantasies
in H. H. Bennett's Wisconsin Dells
Steven D. Hoelscher

Cosmopolitanism and Solidarity:
Studies in Ethnoracial, Religious, and Professional Affiliation
in the United States
David A. Hollinger

Seaway to the Future:
American Social Visions and the Construction of the Panama Canal
Alexander Missal

Unsafe for Democracy:
World War I and the U.S. Justice Department's Covert Campaign
to Suppress Dissent
William H. Thomas Jr.

Unsafe for Democracy

*World War I and the U.S.
Justice Department's Covert Campaign
to Suppress Dissent*

William H. Thomas Jr.

THE UNIVERSITY OF WISCONSIN PRESS

This book was published with the support of
the Evjue Foundation, Inc., the charitable arm of *The Capital Times*, and
the Anonymous Fund of the College of Letters and Science
at the University of Wisconsin–Madison.

The University of Wisconsin Press
1930 Monroe Street, 3rd Floor
Madison, Wisconsin 53711-2059

www.wisc.edu/wisconsinpress/

3 Henrietta Street
London WC2E 8LU, England

1   3   5   4   2

Printed in the United States of America

Library of Congress Cataloging-in-Publication Data
Thomas, William H., Jr.
Unsafe for democracy : World War I and the U.S.
Justice Department's covert campaign to suppress dissent /
William H. Thomas, Jr.
p.   cm.—(Studies in American thought and culture)
Includes bibliographical references and index.
ISBN 978-0-299-22890-3 (cloth: alk. paper)
1. World War, 1914–1918—Protest movements—United States.
2. Peace movements—Government policy—United States.
3. United States Bureau of Investigation.
4. Freedom of speech—United States.
I. Title. II. Series.
D639.P77T56   2008
940.3′1—dc22   2008011973

To my grandparents

The world must be made safe for democracy.

from President Woodrow Wilson's
2 April 1917 speech to Congress
requesting a declaration of war
against Germany

Contents

Illustrations

Acknowledgments

Many years ago, Ellis Hawley read my proposal for research in Justice Department records from the First World War, and his advice steered me toward this project. Allen Steinberg skillfully helped me convert this initial blueprint into a completed dissertation at the University of Iowa. This work has also benefited greatly from the generosity and expertise of Kenneth Cmiel, Shelton Stromquist, Herbert Hovenkamp, Linda K. Kerber, T. Dwight Bozeman, Anuj Desai, Athan Theoharis, and Michael Pfeifer, all of whom read the work in progress, in whole or in part, and offered their thoughtful recommendations. Colin Gordon provided me with judicious evaluations of my chapters, and Arthur McEvoy helped me sharpen and refine my arguments. I wish to thank my editors at the University of Wisconsin Press, Gwen Walker, Adam Mehring, and Paul Boyer, for their enthusiastic support and their expert guidance, which have made this a better book. I am also indebted to my copyeditor, Mary Sutherland, for her meticulous review of the manuscript.

Librarians and archivists at a number of institutions provided generous assistance: the State Historical Society of Iowa, the University of Iowa Libraries, the Ann Arbor District Library, the Bentley Historical Library at the University of Michigan, the Marnie and John Burke Memorial Library at Spring Hill College, the Baltimore County Historical Society, the Archives and Rare Books Division of the University of Cincinnati, the John B. Sears Law Library at the University of Buffalo, the Wisconsin Historical Society, the University of Wisconsin Libraries, the University of Wisconsin Archives, the Max Kade Institute of the University of Wisconsin, the Georgetown University Library, the Moorland-Spingarn Research Center at Howard University, the Northeastern University Libraries Archives and Special Collections Department, the

Rhode Island Historical Society, the John D. Rockefeller Library at Brown University, the Schlesinger Library of the Radcliffe Institute for Advanced Study at Harvard University, the Tulane University Library, the Texas/Dallas History and Archives Division of the Dallas Public Library, and the Public Library of O'Fallon, Illinois. The archivists at the Diocese of Superior and at the Archdiocese of Milwaukee lent their expertise and went to considerable lengths to find documents relating to the history of the Roman Catholic Church in Wisconsin during this era. The staff at the National Archives in Washington, D.C., and in College Park, Maryland, provided me with valuable guidance. Clara Rolen of the National Archives Great Plains Region branch in Kansas City, Scott M. Forsythe of the National Archives Great Lakes Region branch in Chicago, George P. Young of the National Archives Northeast Region branch in Waltham, Massachusetts, and Gregory Plunges and John Celardo of the National Archives Northeast Region branch in New York City tracked down valuable records for me. FBI historian John Fox as well as Debbie Lopes and Loren Shaver of the FBI's Freedom of Information Act office also helped me locate important materials.

The Paul L. Murphy Award from the American Society for Legal History enabled me to conduct research at the University of Buffalo and the University of Cincinnati. The J. Willard Hurst fellowship at the University of Wisconsin Law School's Institute for Legal Studies provided me with the opportunity to research in the holdings of the Wisconsin Historical Society and the University of Wisconsin Libraries, and also offered me the chance to draw on the insights and encouragement of Arthur McEvoy. At the University of Wisconsin, the translation skills of Gregor Mieder proved invaluable.

Kurt Vorndran, Martin Murray, Douglas Baynton, and Katy Stavreva kindly offered me places to stay when I came to Washington, D.C., to do research. Scott Grau and John and Bridgett Williams-Searle provided intellectual and moral support time and again. Countless thanks go to my parents, Barbara Thomas and William Thomas Sr., who went to great lengths to help me out as I tried to juggle parenting, writing, and teaching simultaneously. My sisters Jenny and Sarah were always sources of encouragement. I am deeply grateful to Helen Patterson for her generosity and good humor. My wife, Martha Patterson, is a constant source of love and inspiration, and she offered a keen editorial eye. Finally, I would like to thank my sons, Mark Robert and Walter Clark, who demonstrated considerable patience with their father.

Author's Note

In quoting from Justice Department documents, I have let stand the misspellings and grammatical errors that appeared in the original, but I have corrected minor punctuation and typographical mistakes.

Unsafe for Democracy

Prologue

> After the first six months of the War, it would have been
> difficult for fifty persons to have met for any purpose, in
> any place, from a Church to a dance hall in any part of
> the United States, without at least one representative of
> the Government being present. I doubt if any country
> was ever so thoroughly and intelligently policed in the
> history of the world.
>
> Thomas Watt Gregory,
> speaking in August of 1919,
> several months after his retirement
> as attorney general

While the public efforts of the U.S. Department of Justice to repress opposition to the First World War have received significant attention from historians, who have generally focused on the prosecutions of dissenters under the wartime sedition statutes, relatively little attention has been paid to the Justice Department's covert campaign to silence antiwar dissent.[1] An examination of the records of the Justice Department's Bureau of Investigation reveals that in 1917 and 1918 the department engaged in a massive and largely secret effort, unprecedented in American history, to suppress opposition to the war. In countless cases, department detectives paid cautionary visits on suspected opponents of the war, advising them to stop talking about the war or demanding that they support the war effort. Targets of the department's investigations included pacifists, isolationists, Socialists, union organizers, clubwomen, ministers, German Americans, and African Americans. Homes, schools, workplaces, churches—all came under the scrutiny of the Justice Department, which also deployed undercover operatives in the hopes of eliciting unguarded comments by Americans regarding the war.

Department detectives saw nothing wrong with trying to intimidate critics of the war into silence, and many investigators displayed an expansive notion of what constituted disloyalty, in some cases treating radical criticism of economic or racial inequalities as unpatriotic. Investigators often feared immigrant disloyalty and wished that the foreign-born would assimilate into American culture. And yet, Justice Department detectives did not share a uniform ideology. Some investigators displayed tolerance toward Socialists, while others did not regard those born abroad as automatically suspect; some, in fact, recognized that certain immigrant groups favored the Allied cause.

Based on the perceived threat they posed, certain groups were singled out for investigation. The nation's pastors—who outnumbered college presidents and professors by a ratio of more than seven to one in the early twentieth century—played a vital role in shaping public attitudes and consequently were subjected to particular scrutiny.[2] The nation's churches generally backed the war effort, often enthusiastically, but some ministers were suspected of opposing the war. In April 1918 John Lord O'Brian, the special assistant to the attorney general for war work, warned the chair of the House Judiciary Committee that "the most dangerous type of propaganda used in this country is religious pacifism, i.e., opposition to the war on the ground that it is opposed to the word of God. . . . The statements used in it generally consist of quotations from the Bible and various interpretations thereof."[3] The Justice Department conducted extensive efforts to monitor and intimidate recalcitrant pastors, including using undercover informants and appealing to the Catholic Church's leadership to corral seemingly unpatriotic priests.

The Justice Department also focused much of its attention on the Left. Shortly after the congressional declaration of war, a Socialist Party conference in St. Louis condemned American entry into the conflict, resolving that, "The American people did not and do not want this war. . . . They have been plunged into this war by the trickery and treachery of the ruling class of the country."[4] Public opinion makers vilified the party's stand. "Every socialist who still clings to the socialist party," declared an Illinois newspaper, "is a Hun within the gates."[5] Many suspected the radical labor union, the Industrial Workers of the World (IWW), of trying to impede the war effort. Former president Theodore Roosevelt claimed that "organizations like the I.W.W. are criminally aiding German propaganda in this country."[6] Under the federal wartime sedition laws, prominent Socialists and IWW members were prosecuted and imprisoned. The Justice Department harassed less famous members of these organizations as well. Nativist sentiments reinforced the department's animosity toward the Left, but at the same time investigators, on occasion, recognized that Socialists often viewed the German government with hostility or believed that disputes between labor and management did not always require the department's intervention.

The department conducted wide-ranging investigations in Wisconsin—a state that, perhaps more than any other, suffered from a reputation for harboring disloyal elements. The state's senior senator, Robert M. La Follette, one of the most prominent critics of the decision to enter the conflict, was scorned by Theodore Roosevelt as "the most sinister enemy of democracy in the United States."[7] Fervent war supporters found the state's ethnic composition and political tendencies worrisome. As of 1910, about one third of the state's residents were either German-born or claimed at least one German-born parent.[8] The state's largest city, Milwaukee, boasted a thriving Socialist Party, which in 1910 had sent Austrian-born Victor Berger to the U.S. House of Representatives and in 1916 had captured the mayor's office. In the spring of 1918, concern about the state's loyalty escalated during a special election to fill the seat of deceased senator Paul Husting. Vice President Thomas Marshall, visiting the state in support of the Democratic nominee, remarked, "your State of Wisconsin is under suspicion" and accused the Republican candidate of angling for support from the disloyal.[9] In 1917 and 1918 Justice Department investigators examined the state's newspapers, churches, and citizens for disloyalty. Not simply top-down, the department's efforts relied heavily on tips from a variety of sources—cooperative clergy, educators, local government officials, and even from the state's largest-circulation newspaper, the *Milwaukee Journal*. In the process the department became woven into the political life of the state.[10]

At the same time, across the nation, the Justice Department competed with an alternative system of justice—vigilantism. From the spring of 1917 on, patriotic mobs subjected suspected opponents of the war to all kinds of punishments—forcing some to kiss the flag, tarring and feathering others, and running many out of town. In 1917 Montana vigilantes murdered Frank Little, an IWW organizer, and a mob lynched an allegedly pro-German mineworker in southern Illinois the following spring. Apologists for extralegal violence of the late nineteenth and early twentieth centuries argued that such methods were more rapid and just than a legal system, which in their minds tilted in favor of criminal defendants.[11] During the war, many interpreted the patriotic mob violence as an attempt to compensate for the failure of federal officials to crack down effectively on disloyalty. Justice Department employees, both high and low, responded to the challenge of extralegal violence. To discourage vigilantism, the Justice Department pushed for stricter laws forbidding disloyal speech, while its agents in the field occasionally tried to curb vigilante activity.

The larger project of the Justice Department during the war years represented a logical fulfillment of the progressives' faith in government. Just as early-twentieth-century reformers had sought to expand the power of government to regulate business conduct and to provide for the common welfare, progressives tried to extend the power of government in an attempt to guarantee public support for the war effort. And just as progressives sought to enlighten the immigrant as to how to live in a modern, urbanizing America, Justice Department investigators viewed their admonitions to immigrants as civics lessons. Likewise, the department's efforts to supplant vigilante mobs with professional detectives reflect the progressive confidence in the value of trained experts.

Indeed, the wartime experience laid the groundwork for the permanent establishment of a federal office for the suppression of disloyalty. The covert methods of surveillance and harassment used against the Left and against advocates of racial equality in subsequent decades had their origins in 1917 and 1918. During the post–World War I "Red scare," Attorney General A. Mitchell Palmer and his young assistant J. Edgar Hoover directed the mass roundups of immigrants suspected of belonging to radical political parties.[12] The department also closely monitored black radicals and civil rights organizations.[13] Hoover was appointed to head the Bureau of Investigation in 1924—a position he would hold until his death in 1972 (the bureau went through various name changes, eventually becoming the Federal Bureau of Investigation in 1935). Hoover's FBI showed little concern for the Bill of Rights. In the 1940s and 1950s, during the cold war, Hoover's bureau devoted immense resources to monitoring and harassing radicals and members (or former members) of the Communist Party while working to drive suspected Communist sympathizers from academia.[14] In the 1960s the FBI, fearful of Communist influence in the civil rights movement, placed the Reverend Martin Luther King Jr. under electronic surveillance, wiretapping his telephone line and bugging his hotel rooms.[15] In the same decade, the bureau monitored and sought to disrupt student antiwar and protest movements.[16]

In the wake of the terrorist attacks of September 11, 2001, the FBI's surveillance powers increased dramatically. With the passage of the USA Patriot Act in October 2001, the FBI received expanded authority to monitor electronic communications and to deploy National Security Letters (NSLs). The FBI issues NSLs, which are akin to subpoenas but do not require the approval of a judge, to demand the records of individuals from institutions such as telephone companies and banks. Telephone records, for example, obtained in this manner would allow the bureau to keep track of what numbers a person had called. The annual number of such letters issued has surged from roughly 8,500 in 2000 to around 47,000 in 2005. Because NSLs do not require a judge's approval, the FBI typically must merely attest that the NSL relates to an inquiry "to protect against international terrorism or clandestine intelligence activities." Although recipients of such letters may seek legal counsel, they are usually barred from telling others that they have received an NSL.[17] The Justice Department's inspector general alarmed many when he testified before Congress in March 2007 that his office's inquiry into the NSL program had uncovered "widespread and serious misuse." He added, however, that such problems were typically due to factors such as "carelessness" or "lack of training."[18] Federal authorities also appear interested in expanding their surveillance capacities in other ways. In the summer of 2007, ABC News reported that the FBI was planning on increasing its use of undercover informers in the United States.[19]

And, although the Bush administration has emphasized that these new powers will be deployed in the fight against terrorism, there is a danger that this expanded authority will be used to monitor and intimidate dissenters. Indeed, some evidence suggests that the FBI is once again conducting political surveillance. Documents released under a recent Freedom of Information Act request reveal that the FBI monitored an antiwar and social justice organization, the Thomas Merton Center (named after a pacifist Roman Catholic theologian), in Pittsburgh, Pennsylvania. As early as 2002, an FBI memo, characterizing the center as "a left-wing organization advocating, among many political causes, pacificism," noted that a special agent had taken pictures of Merton Center "leaflet distributors." Other released FBI documents suggest that the bureau used an undercover informant to monitor the group. Heavily redacted reports from 2004 and 2005 begin with the following sentences, "Source, who is not in a position to testify, provided the following information: . . ."[20] The Freedom of Information Act can offer us some glimpses into the inner workings of today's FBI, but it may be decades before we learn the true nature and scope of the bureau's current surveillance efforts. After all, the public gained ready access to the bureau's massive collection of investigative reports from the First World War only after the FBI provided a microfilmed set of the files to the National Archives in 1976.[21]

1

Setting the Stage

In 1915, the town of Pomeroy in Calhoun County, Iowa, numbered 935 residents. One of the town's more prominent leaders was the Reverend Wilhelm Schumann, pastor of the Pomeroy Evangelical Synod church. Schumann gave the benediction at the June 1915 program honoring the graduates of Pomeroy High School, and the following year was elected president of the local German society. As the presence of such a society might suggest, there was a sizable German American community in Calhoun County. In 1910, more than 8 percent of the county's residents had been born in America to German parents, and an additional 5 percent of the population had been born in Germany.[1] During the period of American neutrality, the German-born Schumann, it appears, was sympathetic to the German cause. The *Pomeroy Herald* reported that in September 1915, Schumann was making plans to attend a Chicago embargo conference (the "Friends of Peace" congress), backed by prominent German and Irish Americans, and which called for U.S. neutrality toward the European war.[2]

Schumann's prominence in the community may help explain how he became embroiled in a controversy over the war. As far back as 1914, there was evidence that Pomeroy's residents were divided about the war in Europe. In August of that year, as German and Allied forces clashed on the western front, the *Pomeroy Herald* reported that "A battle was fought last Sunday, in the northwest corner of the Railroad park between Germany and England. It ended in a tie, for each side's voice grew so hoarse that they had to stop and postpone it to another day."[3] As early as March 1917, even before America had entered the war, railroad depot agent F. Robinson of Pomeroy wrote to the U.S. secretary of state to warn him "of the disloyalty to our government of a majority of the Germans around here." The Germans, he maintained, "often gather at end of depot during several days of the week when weather will permit and can tell by their heated expression on their faces that they are roasting the United States although it is all in German which I dont understand. Also understand that a number has made statements that they would not take up arms against Germany if US was drawn into war." The situation, Robinson felt, merited a government response. "Seems to me," he suggested, "secret service men could render valuable service in and around this vicinity if there is any law to prevent this kind of practice." The allegations were forwarded to the Justice Department and from there to the department agent at Omaha, Marshal Eberstein.[4] Later that year the department received allegations about Schumann from those who lived in or around Pomeroy, including an accusation from the local postmaster, Edwin Wattonville. A department report dated 3 November 1917 noted that "The postmaster at Pomeroy writes us that Rev. Schuman is absolutely without doubt pro-German in sympathies but that he is a shrewd, careful man and although the Mayor of the town, T. S. Johnson and himself have tried to get the goods on him have been unable to get testimony to convict him."[5]

Later that month, Marshal Eberstein, the department agent at Omaha, received a report from Werner Hanni, a twenty-four-year-old native of Switzerland who was employed by the department as an undercover informant. Hanni recommended that Schumann be arrested for disloyalty, even as he assured the department of his own discretion. "I consider my work in this town completed and my advise is that Rev. Schumann should be put under arrest immediately," he wrote, adding, "the Postmaster and the Mayor of Pomeroy are the only men who know my work." Hanni accused the minister of using church services to spread seditious ideas:

> The following report is an extract from his sermon he preached last Sunday morning in his church. There were about 70 persons present, including myself, and I swear to God, that every word I report here is a true translation of what Schumann said from his pulpit. England and Russia started this war because they wanted to rule whole Europe and the whole world. . . . God sent Luther to the Germans that they may become leaders in Christianity and that they give the world civilization

and Kultur. . . . This war is for the capitalist only and the Liberty Bond is a great humbug. . . . The mayor of Pomeroy asked me to tell you people to contribute money to the Y.M.C.A. Now I do not advise you to give your money to that organization. I don't want our Lutheran sons to go into this Y.M.C.A. buildings.[6]

Eberstein directed investigator John F. McAuley to take Schumann into custody. Arriving in Pomeroy on 1 December 1917, McAuley interviewed Schumann. According to McAuley's report, Schumann denied having told his church to reject war bonds, but he did admit telling them not to support the Red Cross or YMCA. According to McAuley, Schumann also defended the sinking of the *Lusitania* and accused President Wilson of partiality toward England. McAuley escorted Schumann to Sioux City, Iowa, where the pastor was charged with violation of the federal Espionage Act.[7] Schumann's arrest warrant claimed that the pastor had "unlawfully and willfully made use of treasonable and seditious language in a sermon to his congregation."[8] Freed on bond, Schumann returned home to Pomeroy, but the arrest may have only intensified suspicions. On 3 December 1917, a crowd of some 150 youngsters and residents appeared at Rev. Schumann's home, and the pastor complied with a demand to salute the American flag.[9] Three days later, the *Pomeroy Herald* warned that if the government failed to penalize the minister adequately, Schumann would face the wrath of local residents: "Pomeroy citizens are loyal, and are doing all in their power to suppress dis-loyalty, and about the surest way for the federal authorities to force them to take the law in their own hands, would be to maintain an easy going punishment, or light fine in this case."[10] On 20 December, the *Herald* asserted that the community's resentment of the pastor was growing:

Schumann has been asked by men in authority to leave Pomeroy, and he has replied that he would leave when he got ready. And, when warned as to his danger in remaining in Pomeroy, he stated that he was prepared for the worst. The sentiment of Pomeroy is strung to about its greatest pitch, and if word should be received in Pomeroy, that one of our Pomeroy soldiers have been killed by a Hun, Schumann would leave Pomeroy very quietly, according to present indications. Its up to Schumann as to whether he leaves Pomeroy, in a quiet and peaceful way, or whether he takes his chance of being forceably ejected. From all indications, he will not be given a great deal of time to decide, either.[11]

About a week and a half after this article appeared, on the night of 31 December 1917, Schumann's church, the First Evangelical, was burned to the ground. Various explanations circulated as to the cause of the blaze. One newspaper suggested that the cause may have lain in a furnace that had gotten too hot. Some local residents suspected arson, and some wondered if Schumann, attempting to demonstrate that he was the victim of oppression, was somehow responsible for the fire.[12]

In any case, as the *Herald* had predicted, Schumann was soon compelled to flee Pomeroy. On 8 January 1918, a crowd confronted the pastor in a store and warned him to leave town. One press account claimed that after the confrontation in the store, two groups had formed, one seeking to drive Schumann from Pomeroy, the other seeking to guard the minister. Of those trying to protect Schumann, the report noted, many also tried to persuade him to flee.[13] Arriving on the scene, county deputy sheriff Harry Smerdon sensed that trouble was brewing, and, according to one press account, "observed that a mob was collecting in the business part of town, and it didn't look good to him. Some things he overheard gave him the impression that there were weapons in the crowd and that there was a spirit among the men which boded no good to the alleged Kaiser-lover." Deputy Smerdon tracked down Schumann and escorted him out of Pomeroy.[14] In a later telephone interview with a local newspaper, Pomeroy mayor Theodore Johnson concluded that "I am sure that if Rev. Schumann stays away there will be no more trouble. Of course, he has a legal right to be in Pomeroy, but many of the citizens do not think so. If he comes back, serious consequences are sure to result."[15]

At some point after this incident, Schumann apparently returned to town, for in May 1918 Iowa governor William Harding personally asked the pastor to leave Pomeroy. The *Coon Rapids Enterprise* reported that the possibility of vigilantism had led Pomeroy residents to alert the governor, and that Governor Harding then had sent a state marshal to escort Schumann to the town of Coon Rapids. At Coon Rapids, Harding met with the pastor and requested that he leave Pomeroy. Schumann refused. According to the *Enterprise,* the governor then instructed a marshal to escort Schumann to Des Moines and to keep him there until the trial.[16]

Schumann's Espionage Act trial began in June 1918. U.S. attorney F. A. O'Connor and assistant U.S. attorney Seth Thomas served as prosecutors, while attorney C. H. Van Law represented Schumann. The prosecution called as its first witness Werner Hanni, who declared that it was his job "to investigate reports of pro-Germanism in this country." Hanni testified that he had attended Schumann's sermon of 11 November 1917 and had heard the minister declare that England and Russia were to blame for the war and that war bonds were "great humbug."[17] Defense attorney Van Law responded by trying to call Hanni's credibility into question. Schumann's church belonged to the Evangelical Synod, a sect separate from the Lutheran church, and Van Law was able to demonstrate that Hanni mistakenly believed that Schumann's church was Lutheran.[18] The defense attorney set his trap as follows:

> Q [Attorney Van Law]: Now you said something about he didnt want the Lutheran boys out there to become members of the Y.M.C.A?
>
> A [Hanni]: He didnt say to become members, he say he didnt want them to go in the Y.M.C.A. huts.
>
> Q: In the Y.M.C.A. huts?
>
> A: Yes, over in France.
>
> Q: In connection with the army and the cantonments?
>
> A: Yes sir.
>
> Q: He wanted them to stay where?
>
> A: He wanted them to stay away from there.
>
> Q: That is because he wanted to keep them Lutherans?
>
> A: Yes sir, that is what he said.
>
> Q: Now Mr. Hanni are you sure that he said Lutherans?
>
> A: Yes sir.
>
> Q: And are you sure that he said "we Lutherans?"
>
> A: Yes sir.
>
> Q: You are sure of that are you?
>
> A: He said we dont want our Lutheran boys.
>
> Q: Dont you know as a matter of fact Mr. Hanni that that isnt a Lutheran Church at all?
>
> A: Which?
>
> Q: Why the one where you heard this sermon?
>
> A: It wasnt?
>
> Q: No.[19]

Hanni's accusations became a major focus of the rest of the trial. The prosecution called two local residents who had attended Schumann's sermon, one of whom testified, "Well, as far as I recollect that he said it was a capitalistic war." The prosecution also raised the question of what Schumann had told John McAuley. Taking the stand, McAuley stated that during his talk with Schumann, the pastor had tried to justify the *Lusitania*'s sinking and had claimed that America had entered the war because of its financial ties to England.[20]

On taking the stand, Schumann defended himself against Hanni's charges. In reference to the 11 November sermon, he denied having stated that England and Russia had entered the war to govern the globe but did acknowledge that he had referred to the war in the course of his description of Martin Luther's work. Schumann testified that he had compared the Reformation to recent European events and he recounted his sermon to the courtroom:

> The Pope had the only power in those days, and as long as the Pope was in power, only the Catholic Church, everything was in peace, everything was peaceful, but then came Martin Luther and—and started the Reformation, and this peace was disturbed, and Dr. Martin Luther was called the Beast of Wittenberg, an outcast of Hell, and all kinds of names, and I said it is something like in our days, in our days England and Russia had the power, were world powers, and they had divided the world among themselves and—and the German commerce, and Germany wanted a place in the sun also, and then Germany was called the disturber of the peace, and all those names you read about in the paper.[21]

Schumann's sermon had indeed used an analogy that to his Protestant congregation would have cast Germany in a heroic light.

The prosecution grilled Schumann about his conversation with John McAuley. Since Schumann, at the time of his arrest, had discussed the causes and justification for the war with McAuley, it became easier for the prosecution to question Schumann about his opinions of the war. The prosecutor asked the pastor whether he now believed that it had been within Germany's rights to have sunk the British ocean liner and what his views regarding the origin of the war had been at the time of his arrest. The minister answered that at the outbreak of the war in 1914 his loyalties had been with Germany, but that he felt a reluctant duty to support the American cause: "Well, I am not in favor of war, and when the war started in 1914 I worried a great deal for I am not in favor of wars at all, and then my sympathies went with Germany, that is the country of my birth, and I considered the cause of Germany right, and then when we entered this war it was a very hard feeling for me, and we consider Germany our mother and we consider America our bride, and it isnt a normal state of affairs when mother and bride are in quarrel, and if I—well I—I just the same considered it my duty to support this country, and even if I had to support it with bleeding heart, for we as Christians we know we have to be—have to be obedient to the Government."[22]

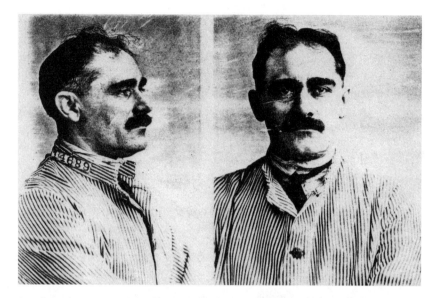

A prison photograph of the Reverend Wilhelm Schumann, an Iowa pastor convicted of violating the Espionage Act. Schumann spent approximately two years in the federal penitentiary in Leavenworth, Kansas, before receiving a presidential pardon in December 1921. (Federal Bureau of Prisons)

After deliberating for fewer than thirty minutes, the jury delivered a guilty verdict. The judge sentenced Schumann to five years in prison and fined him $250 and costs. Schumann's lawyer filed an appeal, while the pastor returned to Pomeroy, where his presence again evoked conflict. On 2 November 1918, Schumann was overseeing the reconstruction of his church when postmaster Edwin Wattonville, accompanied by a Hans Weygandt, appeared at the building site. Schumann, it appears, may have warned the two men to leave; in any case, the pastor threw a brick that struck a wooden two by four not far from where Wattonville was. A fight then erupted. "For a while a lively time ensued," reported the *Pomeroy Herald*, adding, "an armistice was finally forced by the contractors in charge of the building." The postmaster later filed assault charges against the pastor, and the following January a jury found Schumann guilty of assault with intent to inflict great bodily injury.[23] The pastor's appeals of his Espionage Act conviction fared poorly as well. In May 1919, the federal appellate court in St. Louis refused to hear Schumann's case, and a further appeal to the U.S. Supreme Court was rejected that autumn. The *Pomeroy Herald* reported that "With the coming of darkness on

Monday night, after the news of the supreme court's refusal to review Rev. Wilhelm Schumann's case, a bonfire was built in front of his church and parsonage, and the ringing of bells and firing of shot guns made one think that peace had again been declared."[24] Schumann began serving his sentence at the federal penitentiary at Leavenworth, Kansas, in November 1919 and was pardoned by President Warren Harding in December 1921.[25]

The experience of Wilhelm Schumann is but one example of the massive effort of the U.S. Department of Justice to repress domestic opposition to the First World War. Worried about the impact of dissent on morale, the department prosecuted many American citizens for speaking out against the war effort. To ascertain the true opinions of suspected disloyalists regarding American intervention in Europe, the government deployed undercover investigators and informers. In addition, the department engaged in a quiet campaign to intimidate critics of the war into remaining silent. Justice Department investigators visited countless Americans, warning them to avoid criticizing the war or, on other occasions, recommending that they more actively support the war effort. The targets of these efforts ranged across the ideological spectrum. The Socialist Party and radical labor unions came under attack, as did isolationists, pacifists, German Americans, and African Americans. Clergymen of a wide variety of denominations faced harassment as well—the leadership of the Russellites (forerunners of the Jehovah's Witnesses) faced federal prosecution—and pastors were interviewed by Justice Department investigators, who cautioned them to eschew disloyalty and to uphold the flag.

The Justice Department's wartime crusade paved the way for a new federal role in suppressing dissent, serving as a trial run for a decadeslong struggle to monitor and harass critics of America's foreign and domestic policies. The department's work, too, provides an example of the less pleasant legacies of the progressive heritage—namely, how the centralized bureaucracies favored by many progressives as an solution to civic problems could be deployed in the service of intolerance.

The outbreak of war in Europe set in motion a course of events that led to the Justice Department's campaign against dissent. From the summer of 1914 on, Americans felt deeply divided over the events unfolding across the Atlantic. Reactions generally fell along ethnic lines, for while Americans of British descent tended to favor the Allied cause,

Americans of German ancestry were often suspicious of the Allies and sympathetic to the Central Powers. Many German Americans endorsed a proposal to cut off supplies of munitions to the European combatants. Such a move would have been to Germany's advantage, given that it was already being blockaded by Allied navies. Embargo advocates, however, suffered from the charge of serving the German cause, and efforts by German Americans to assert their political influence were met with suspicion and scorn. A January 1915 conference of German American political activists in the nation's capital led the *New York Times* to warn that "never since the foundation of the Republic has any body of men assembled here who were more completely subservient to a foreign Power and to foreign influence, and none ever proclaimed the un-American spirit more openly."[26]

Attempts by the governments of the Central Powers to influence matters to their advantage in the United States backfired disastrously and in the process inflamed suspicion toward immigrants. In August 1915, the U.S. Secret Service snatched the briefcase of Heinrich Albert, a German attaché in New York City. The contents of the briefcase, leaked to the press by the Wilson administration, contained documents suggesting that Germany was trying to subsidize propaganda in the United States.[27] Subsequent disclosures of efforts by Austria-Hungary to influence its citizens employed in the United States fostered concerns about immigrant loyalties. A confidential note written by Konstantin Dumba, the Austro-Hungarian ambassador to America, indicating his approval of plans to foment discontent among workers in American industrial plants, was obtained by British authorities in August 1915 and released to the public. The ambassador's explanation of his efforts to the American press only made matters worse. "There are thousands of workingmen in the big steel industries, natives of Bohemia, Moravia, Carniola, Galicia, Dalmatia, Croatia, Slavonia, and other peoples of the races from Austria-Hungary," observed the ambassador,

> who are uneducated and who do not understand that they are engaged in a work against their own country. In order to bring this before them, I have subsidized many newspapers published in the languages and dialects of the divisions mentioned, attempting in this way to bring the felonious occupation to their attention. But this has been difficult. In some of the great steel plants of Pennsylvania these uneducated men of my country are nothing more or less than slaves. They are even being

worked twelve hours a day, and herded in stockades. It is difficult to get at these workers except en masse, and a peaceful walkout of these work-ingmen would be of the greatest advantage to my Government.

The diplomat's candid admission struck a nativist nerve. The *New York Sun* asked, "Were the United States to engage in war, would it be possible for its enemy, or Powers in sympathy with that enemy, to demoralize even temporarily the industrial plants on which we should depend for ammunition by inducing workingmen to quit their benches?" The paper wondered, "could a system of sabotage, directed by aliens, be established under which imperfect and undependable products might be served to our fighting forces?" The Wilson administration requested the recall of the ambassador, who soon departed American shores.[28]

The years 1915–17 also saw the exposure of multiple conspiracies to hinder the flow of war materials to the Allies. In December 1915, the Justice Department charged several individuals, including a German naval officer who had been living in the United States, Franz Rintelen, with acting in restraint of foreign trade. The indictment accused the defendants of conspiring to block the shipment of munitions to the Allies by instigating strikes in both the transportation sector and in plants producing war materials.[29]

Other conspiracies were more violent. In February 1915, for example, a would-be saboteur named Werner Horn detonated an explosive charge on a railroad bridge linking Canada and Maine. The blast did negligible damage, and Horn, quickly apprehended, proclaimed himself to be a German citizen.[30] That autumn, federal authorities charged several men with having conspired to sabotage ships departing America bound for the Allies, and the following May a jury found three defendants, whose number included a self-described German army veteran, guilty.[31] In December 1915 the government announced that it had uncovered a plot to attack a Canadian canal, and in the following April indicted Franz von Papen, the former German military attaché in the United States, for his role in the affair. The indictment was largely symbolic, given that the Wilson administration, suspecting Papen to be something of a machinator, had already ejected him from the country. Later that summer, the allegations behind Papen's indictment received corroboration when one of the principals in the Canadian canal plot testified in federal court that Papen had discussed sabotage with him and had supplied him with money.[32] The spring of 1916 also brought the arrests and indictments of several men, including sailors from a German liner, on charges of conspiring to plant firebombs on cargo ships bound for the Allies.[33]

The disclosures of these plots heightened nativist sentiments and deeply colored subsequent political rhetoric. In the summer of 1915, federal investigators were hard at work unraveling German conspiracies, and it appears that their findings may have shaken President Wilson, who noted in early August, "I am sure that the country is honeycombed with German intrigue and infested with German spies. The evidence of these things are multiplying every day."[34] Soon Wilson's concern over foreign influence began to seep into his public statements. In October 1915, Wilson suggested, in an appearance before the Daughters of the American Revolution, that there be "an opportunity to have a line-up and let the men who are thinking first of other countries stand on one side . . . and all those that are for America, first, last, and all the time on the other side." Not to be outdone, former president Theodore Roosevelt shortly thereafter spoke out against what he termed "hyphenated Americanism."[35] In December, presenting the State of the Union address, President Wilson railed against foreign disloyalty: "There are citizens of the United States, I blush to admit, born under other flags but welcomed under our generous naturalization laws to the full freedom and opportunity of America, who have poured the poison of disloyalty into the very arteries of our national life; who have sought to bring the authority and good name of our Government into contempt, to destroy our industries wherever they thought it effective for their vindictive purposes to strike at them, and to debase our politics to the uses of foreign intrigue."[36]

With both Wilson and Roosevelt publicly raising the specter of immigrant disloyalty, it is not surprising that many German American political activists sought other choices for the 1916 presidential contest, eventually turning to Supreme Court Justice Charles Evans Hughes, a former New York governor. But their support for Hughes, both before and after his nomination as the GOP contender, allowed Democrats to paint him and his party as agents of German influence. Less than a week after the conclusion of the Republican convention, Wilson, speaking to a Flag Day gathering in Washington, warned that America was under siege and delivered an implicit attack on Hughes: "There is disloyalty in the United States, and it must be absolutely crushed. It proceeds from a minority, a very small minority, but a very active and subtle minority. It works underground, but it also shows its ugly head where we can see it; and there are those at this moment who are trying to levy a species of blackmail, saying, 'Do what we wish in the interest of a foreign sentiment or we will wreak our vengeance at the polls.'"[37] Wilson hammered the theme of immigrant subversion again in September, claiming that "the passions and intrigues of certain active groups and combinations of men amongst us who were born under foreign flags injected the poison of disloyalty into our most critical affairs, [and] laid violent hands upon many of our industries."[38] Xenophobic rhetoric could also be found coming from Republican Theodore Roosevelt, who, in the course of backing his party's nominee, blasted "those professional German-Americans who seek to make the American President in effect a viceroy of the German Emperor."[39] The presidential campaign of 1916 reinforced the fear among Americans that the nation was riddled with those whose sympathies lay with a foreign power.[40]

Events soon pushed the Wilson administration into abandoning its neutrality. On 31 January 1917, Germany announced that it would commence unrestricted submarine warfare, which meant that American ships in the vicinity of the British Isles would be considered fair game for German U-boats. Earlier that month, German foreign minister Arthur Zimmermann secretly instructed the German ambassador in Mexico via telegram that, if it became evident that America would enter the war against Germany, he should ask Mexico to go to war against the United States. The British intercepted the message and turned it over to the Wilson administration, which in turn made the contents public on 1 March 1917. Later that month, German U-boats sent a number of American cargo ships to the bottom of the Atlantic, and on 2 April 1917 Wilson appeared before a joint session of Congress to ask for a declaration of war against Germany.[41] Wilson contended that Germany posed a threat to America's domestic security and insinuated that opposition to the war bore a foreign stamp. While praising the patriotism of the bulk of German Americans, the president, in an echo of his peacetime pronouncements, declared that Germany's government "has filled our unsuspecting communities and even our offices of government with spies and set criminal intrigues everywhere afoot against our national unity of counsel, our peace within and without, our industries and our commerce." Ironically, Wilson, in his earlier careers as history professor and college president, had advocated freedom of expression, and his writings, too, had reflected an understanding that war could erode civil liberties. But by April 1917, the role of unscrupulous alien conspirators in stoking domestic discord rendered dissent less legitimate and more dangerous. Declaring that "if there should be disloyalty, it will be dealt with with a firm hand of stern repression," Wilson foreshadowed the Justice Department's campaign against the expression of antiwar ideas. On 4 April 1917, the Senate voted for war, 82 to 6, and two days later, the House voted likewise, 373 to 50.[42]

Despite the lopsided congressional votes in favor of war, it is not clear to what extent Americans embraced the president's call to arms—especially given that accurate methods of polling public opinion through random sampling would not be developed until well after the war.[43] Evidence suggests that at the very least there were substantial pockets of resistance to entering the conflict. In Wisconsin, a referendum held in Monroe shortly before the congressional vote revealed that 954 voters cast their ballots against going to war, while 95 voted in favor.[44] As the House of Representatives debated the president's war resolution on 5 April, a Minnesota congressman noted that he had submitted the question of going to war to his constituents and claimed that the results, though not yet final, indicated that an overwhelming majority of respondents opposed going to war.[45]

Many Americans were hesitant about embarking on a crusade against Germany. During the period of American neutrality, for example, there had been a good deal of sympathy for Germany in some quarters of the Swedish American community. Right up until the congressional vote in favor of war in April 1917, the German-language press had generally opposed American military intervention.[46] The American Left was divided over the question of going to war. While a few Socialists lent their support to the war effort, the Socialist Party, meeting in an emergency conference in St. Louis shortly after the congressional declaration of war, approved by wide margins a platform denouncing the decision to enter the conflict.[47]

The imposition of the draft may have further fueled opposition to the war. Some Americans expected that America's primary role would be to guard the Atlantic and to supply the Allies with money and arms rather than to send an expeditionary force to Europe.[48] The congressional votes on imposing conscription suggest that the draft was less popular than had been the decision to go to war. In the House, 199 congressmen voted in favor, 178 were opposed, with fifty-two congressmen abstaining from voting. Sixty-five senators voted in favor of conscription, eight were in opposition, and twenty-three senators did not vote.[49] Instances of popular opposition to conscription were not hard to find. In Butte, Montana, marchers demonstrated against the draft, while in New Ulm, Minnesota, thousands flocked to an antidraft protest, where they listened to speeches by, among others, the head of a local Lutheran college.[50] In New York City, large crowds turned out for a rally at Hunt's Point Palace, which the *Times* described as "a very lame denunciation of the Government, of militarism which, all the speakers said, was about to grip America about the throat, and utterances along similar lines."[51] Former Populist Tom Watson of Georgia lambasted the war as being fought on behalf of J. P. Morgan and other wealthy interests; when Watson issued a call for funds for a constitutional challenge to conscription, he received roughly $100,000 in donations.[52] Many rural southern whites had little interest in leaving their homes to fight in a foreign war. On occasion, officials attempting to enforce the draft in Appalachia were met with gunfire from those who had no intention of serving in an army of conscripts.[53] Oklahomans opposed to compulsory military service organized the "Green Corn Rebellion," in which armed Sooners banded together for a protest march on Washington. Drawing its name from the plan of the participants to eat corn on the way to the nation's capital, the revolt was quickly quashed. More than 180 suspects were put on trial for their alleged roles in the affair, and roughly 150 were found guilty.[54]

In an effort to win the sympathies of those hostile to or ambivalent about the war, the Wilson administration formed the Committee on Public Information (CPI). Headed by progressive author and reformer George Creel, the CPI created a masterful advertising campaign aimed at stoking patriotic fervor. Across the nation, thousands of "four-minute men," orators commissioned by the CPI, addressed theater audiences. In its effort to build support for the war, the CPI charged that German conspiracies within American borders threatened the nation's safety. A CPI advertisement appearing in the *Saturday Evening Post* in August 1918 claimed that "German agents are everywhere, eager to gather scraps of news about our men, our ships, our munitions." Such espionage, observed the ad, could result in "death to American soldiers and danger to American homes." In emphasizing the threat of German subversion, the CPI reinforced fears that dissent stemmed from foreign influences. The ad urged readers to "report the man who spreads pessimistic stories, divulges—or seeks—confidential military information, cries for peace, or belittles our efforts to win the war," and to "send the names of

Spies *and* Lies

German agents are everywhere, eager to gather scraps of news about our men, our ships, our munitions. It is still possible to get such information through to Germany, where thousands of these fragments—often individually harmless—are patiently pieced together into a whole which spells death to American soldiers and danger to American homes.

But while the enemy is most industrious in trying to collect information, and his systems elaborate, he is *not* superhuman—indeed he is often very stupid, and would fail to get what he wants were it not deliberately handed to him by the carelessness of loyal Americans.

Do not discuss in public, or with strangers, any news of troop and transport movements, or bits of gossip as to our military preparations, which come into your possession.

Do not permit your friends in service to tell you—or write you—"inside" facts about where they are, what they are doing and seeing.

Do not become a tool of the Hun by passing on the malicious, disheartening rumors which he so eagerly sows. Remember he asks no better service than to have you spread his lies of disasters to our soldiers and sailors, gross scandals in the Red Cross, cruelties, neglect and wholesale executions in our camps, drunkenness and vice in the Expeditionary Force, and other tales certain to disturb American patriots and to bring anxiety and grief to American parents.

And do not wait until you catch someone putting a bomb under a factory. Report the man who spreads pessimistic stories, divulges—or seeks—confidential military information, cries for peace, or belittles our efforts to win the war.

Send the names of such persons, even if they are in uniform, to the Department of Justice, Washington. Give all the details you can, with names of witnesses if possible—show the Hun that we can beat him at his own game of collecting scattered information and putting it to work. The fact that you made the report will not become public.

You are in contact with the enemy *today*, just as truly as if you faced him across No Man's Land. In your hands are two powerful weapons with which to meet him—discretion and vigilance. *Use them.*

COMMITTEE ON PUBLIC INFORMATION
8 JACKSON PLACE, WASHINGTON, D. C.

George Creel, Chairman
The Secretary of State
The Secretary of War
The Secretary of the Navy

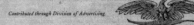

Contributed through Division of Advertising   United States Gov't Comm. on Public Information

This advertisement from the Committee on Public Information, a federal agency, appeared in the *Saturday Evening Post* in August 1918. (courtesy of University of Iowa Libraries)

such persons, even if they are in uniform, to the Department of Justice, Washington."[55]

At the federal level, the task of muffling opponents of the war fell largely to the Department of Justice, which as of 1917 had almost no recent experience in monitoring and punishing dissent. At the federal level, there was some precedent for the policing of opinions. During the presidency of John Adams, as the nation skirted close to an open war with France, the Federalist Party authored the Sedition Act, under which critics of the president were prosecuted.[56] During the Civil War, both the Union and Confederate governments took measures to repress antiwar feeling on their respective home fronts.[57] In 1903, roughly a year and a half after the assassination of President William McKinley by an anarchist, Congress passed a law barring adherents of anarchism from entering the nation.[58] Additionally, the post office, through an 1873 law, had punished those who purveyed materials relating to sex through the mails. Leading this anti-vice effort was Anthony Comstock, who served as special agent from 1873 to 1915 and whose targets included literature criticizing the institution of marriage.[59] Before 1917, however, all federal efforts at censorship had been of limited duration or scope.

Despite the dearth of federal powers to police expression in the late nineteenth and early twentieth century, there was plenty of precedent at the local level of government for attempting to silence controversial opinions. In the half-century leading up to 1917, the most persistent agents of repression were local law enforcement agencies. Police departments harassed or broke up protest gatherings, such as meetings of the unemployed, and arrested radical street orators. In the wake of the Haymarket bombing of 1886, Chicago police waged a war of harassment against anarchists and other radicals.[60] In 1914 Edward A. Ross lamented the state of civil liberties in America: "During the last dozen years, the tales of the suppression of free assemblage, free speech and free press by local authorities or by the State operating under martial law have become so numerous as to have become an old story. These rights . . . are attacked at the instigation of an economically and socially powerful class, itself enjoying the full advantages of free communication but bent on denying them to the class it holds within its power. . . . The constitutional rights of free communication have been denied to socially insignificant persons."[61]

The courts of the time did little to guard controversial expression from such intrusions. As David M. Rabban has shown, judges prior to

World War I often accepted the "bad tendency" test for speech—that is, the notion that the government had the right to punish speech that had a propensity to injure society in some fashion. The bad tendency test did not require that the government demonstrate the specific damage wrought by a particular speech but instead allowed the authorities to criminalize speech that would presumably have the effect of undermining society or government. Time and again, courts upheld laws and prosecutions aimed at curtailing or punishing certain kinds of expression. "The overwhelming weight of judicial opinion in all jurisdictions before World War I," writes Rabban, "offered little recognition and even less protection of free speech interests."[62]

The Justice Department's campaign against dissent would also draw on practices that had evolved in the nineteenth and early twentieth centuries among the nation's private detective agencies. Undercover operatives from such firms had often been retained by employers eager to monitor and disrupt labor organizations and strikes. For example, operatives of the Pinkerton National Detective Agency, masquerading as union members, reported the activities of worker organizations to employers. In 1917 and 1918, the Justice Department would likewise use informants working incognito, such as Werner Hanni, to spy on suspected opponents of the war.[63]

The Justice Department's wartime crusade was in many ways a reflection of progressive philosophy. Progressives often believed that the solution to the nation's economic and social problems lay in the creation of professionally staffed federal agencies.[64] The Bureau of Investigation, founded in 1908 during the Theodore Roosevelt administration as an investigative arm of the Justice Department, was a prime example of such an agency. Headed since 1912 by Alexander Bruce Bielaski, the bureau investigated a wide variety of federal offenses, including violations of antitrust, banking, and peonage laws.[65] After passage of the Mann Act of 1910, which made it illegal to transport women from state to state for corrupt purposes, the bureau also targeted the sex trade. U.S. attorneys in turn used the information garnered by the bureau to build prosecutions. To a substantial extent, the bureau's agenda overlapped with that of the progressive movement, which had long called for action against monopolistic practices and organized prostitution.[66] And in keeping with the progressive emphasis on expertise, bureau investigators were often well educated. Most had attended at least some high school and some had attended a trade or professional school as well.

Alexander Bruce Bielaski served as chief of the Justice Department's Bureau of Investigation from 1912 to 1919. (Federal Bureau of Investigation)

Many of the department's detectives had college degrees, often in law. By comparison, a college diploma was relatively rare among the general population; according to one estimate, by 1920 fewer than one in twenty Americans had spent at least four years in college.[67]

Many Americans, progressive-minded or otherwise, had long attributed the ills plaguing industrial cities to the supposed ignorance or immorality of the foreign-born.[68] One moderate progressive, the prominent attorney John Lord O'Brian, believed that immigrants were at least partly to blame for the problems bedeviling his hometown of Buffalo. In an interview late in his career, in 1952, O'Brian asserted that in the early twentieth century, "conditions locally in Buffalo had become very deplorable. Both of the party organizations were pretty much to blame. As I said before, the foreign element in Buffalo were sort of a permanent millstone around our necks. They were very difficult to deal with for either party. Conditions had grown very bad. There was a lot of gossip about scandalous contracts. The school situation was deplorable. The Democratic administration had neglected them. The Democratic mayor had narrowly escaped indictment on a charge of corruption." The situation had been so dire, O'Brian claimed, that many "good citizens" appealed to him to run for mayor of Buffalo in 1913, a race he subsequently lost.[69] As director of the Justice Department's War Emergency Division in 1917 and 1918, O'Brian would play a leading role in the war on dissent.

The Justice Department's wartime efforts reflected a belief held by many progressives that government had a special responsibility to hasten the assimilation of immigrants. Much of the poverty and illness in urban neighborhoods, progressives believed, could be alleviated by educational programs that would simultaneously enlighten and Americanize immigrants. In the era of the First World War and in the decade following, many progressives supported programs for instructing immigrant families about proper diet, child care, and sanitation. Underlying such efforts was the assumption that to a large extent education and assimilation overlapped. Dietary education programs, for example, often warned that certain aspects of immigrant cuisine were unhealthy.[70]

The key leaders of the wartime Justice Department were moderate progressives, including Attorney General Thomas Watt Gregory and the director of the War Emergency Division, John Lord O'Brian, and O'Brian's assistant, Alfred Bettman. The Mississippi-born Gregory had received a bachelor of laws degree from the University of Texas in 1885, and, while later working as a lawyer in Austin, had helped bring antitrust

charges against an oil firm. Active in Texas politics, Gregory had supported Woodrow Wilson at the 1912 Democratic presidential convention, and, after a stint as a special assistant to the attorney general, had
been appointed to head the Justice Department in the summer of 1914.[71]
Gregory's chief assistant for national security matters, the Republican
lawyer John Lord O'Brian, was a moderate progressive as well. A native
of Buffalo, O'Brian, while a student at Harvard in the 1890s, had been
profoundly impressed when he witnessed Theodore Roosevelt speak on
the importance of public service. Returning to his hometown after grad-
uation, O'Brian later won election to the New York State Assembly,
where he lent his backing to Governor Charles Evans Hughes, a reform-
minded Republican. O'Brian later remarked that as an assemblyman
he had been regarded "as sort of a half reformer and Good Government Republican who could not be relied on to go along on party measures always and who occasionally voted with Al Smith and his followers
on tenement house legislation."[72] O'Brian's progressivism was militant
in one sense; like Roosevelt, he was committed to strengthening America's armed forces. He approved of the Plattsburg scheme, under which
privately operated camps offered military training to volunteers during
the period of American neutrality.[73] O'Brian, too, had become much
more aware of the German government's undercover efforts within this
country when he was appointed by the department to help prosecute
German naval officer Franz Rintelen for his efforts to slow the shipment
of supplies to the Allies. The trial concluded in May 1917 with the conviction of Rintelen and other defendants, and in October of that year
O'Brian was appointed as the special assistant to the attorney general
for war work.[74] The chief assistant to O'Brian was Cincinnati lawyer
Alfred Bettman, whose most notable contribution to the progressive heritage, perhaps, came after the war. An advocate of urban planning, Bettman in 1926 prepared a brief for a Supreme Court case deciding the
constitutionality of an Ohio town's zoning ordinance; his argument appears to have helped convince the Court that zoning was permissible
under the Constitution.[75]

During the war, Gregory and O'Brian tried to solve the problem of
antiwar dissent in true progressive fashion by expanding the Department of Justice and its Bureau of Investigation. Some of the bureau's
work before 1917 had related to foreign affairs, and they had, for example, monitored Mexican revolutionaries who were using the United
States as a sanctuary from where they could work to topple Mexico's

Thomas Watt Gregory served as attorney general during World War I. (Center for American History, University of Texas–Austin, CN 03570, Prints and Photographs Collection)

government.[76] In addition, the bureau had investigated violations of federal law that were connected to the European war. In April 1916, bureau agents, together with New York City police, arrested several Germans for their alleged roles in a conspiracy to plant bombs in vessels destined for Allied ports.[77] To some extent, the Justice Department's expansion after American entrance into the war was justified as a means of curbing further efforts by Germany at espionage and sabotage—and the department performed other tasks useful to the war effort, such as regulating the conduct of alien enemies.[78] But in 1917 and 1918, a large portion of the department's time was simply spent policing the opinions of Americans.

The Espionage Act of 15 June 1917 provided the department with a new and sweeping weapon in its war on dissent. Under the terms of the law,

> Whoever, when the United States is at war, shall willfully make or convey false reports or false statements with intent to interfere with the operation or success of the military or naval forces of the United States or to promote the success of its enemies and whoever, when the United States is at war, shall willfully cause or attempt to cause insubordination, disloyalty, mutiny, or refusal of duty, in the military or naval forces of the United States, or shall willfully obstruct the recruiting or enlistment service of the United States, to the injury of the service or of the United States, shall be punished by a fine of not more than $10,000 or imprisonment for not more than twenty years, or both.

Under the act, prosecutors charged critics of the war with having interfered with the war effort.[79] An even more draconian amendment passed in May 1918, commonly known as the Sedition Act, went so far as to forbid the deliberate expression of "any disloyal, profane, scurrilous, or abusive language about the form of government of the United States, or the Constitution of the United States, or the military or naval forces of the United States, or the flag of the United States."[80] Between 15 June 1917 and 1 July 1919, more than 850 Americans were convicted of violating the Espionage or Sedition Acts.[81] Just as significantly, these laws provided the Justice Department with a tool for discreetly threatening vocal opponents of the war into silence.

2

Methods and Ideology

For more than half a century after the end of the First World War, the bulk of the records of the Justice Department's Bureau of Investigation was closed to researchers. Not until 1976 did the FBI release to the National Archives "The Investigative Case Files of the Bureau of Investigation, 1908–1922," a collection of hundreds of reels of microfilm, much of which is composed of war-related reports and memoranda from the years 1917 and 1918.[1] In the years since their unveiling to the public, however, relatively few researchers have tapped this resource to examine the Justice Department's wartime activities, and as a result, historians have only a limited understanding of the nature and scale of that department's crusade against antiwar sentiment. These files reveal that prosecutions were only the visible tip of a massive iceberg of federal suppression of dissent. Only a small proportion of the Justice Department's investigations ever resulted in an indictment or trial. Far more typically, investigators admonished those they suspected of disloyalty to be more patriotic or told them to remain silent about the war. These reports, too, indicate the methods used by undercover investigators and by informants—techniques that paved the way for the department's assault on subversion in subsequent decades.

These files, too, reveal that the Justice Department's investigators mirrored contemporary society's views of immigrants, African Americans, and women. Sometimes, investigators treated ethnicity as an arbiter of loyalty. Detectives had similar concerns about the patriotism of African Americans and sometimes regarded criticism of Jim Crow as

31

tantamount to sedition. Women who came under investigation were typically viewed through the lens of traditional gender roles. The department worried that female critics of the war were tainting their children's minds with disloyalty. Female dissenters compounded their transgression by asserting their views in an unfeminine and aggressive fashion.

In 1917 and 1918, many Americans feared that the country was rife with subversion. "Every German or Austrian in the United States, unless known by years of association to be absolutely loyal, should be treated as a potential spy," declared the *Providence Journal* of Rhode Island in 1917. "Keep your eyes and ears open," the newspaper implored, "Whenever any suspicious act or disloyal word comes to your notice communicate at once with the Bureau of Investigation of the Department of Justice." America, the *Journal* warned, was endangered by foreigners in its midst: "We are at war with the most merciless and inhuman nation in the world. Hundreds of thousands of its people in this country want to see America humiliated and beaten to her knees, and they are doing, and will do, everything in their power to bring this about. Take nothing for granted. Energy and alertness in this direction may save the life of your son, your husband or your brother." The *Journal's* entreaty was reprinted in newspapers in Connecticut, Pennsylvania, Florida, Missouri, North Dakota, and New Mexico. A similar announcement from Justice Department official George C. Kelleher in the *Lowell Sun* of Massachusetts in June 1918 asserted, "It is your patriotic duty to report disloyal acts, seditious utterances and any information relative to attempts to hinder the United States in the prosecution of the war, to the United States Department of Justice, Bureau of Investigation, 45 Milk Street, Boston, or Federal Building, Concord, N.H."[2]

Allegations of disloyalty flooded the Justice Department. As the attorney general's *Annual Report* for 1918 observed, "every day hundreds of articles or passages from newspapers, pamphlets, books, or other printed matter, transcripts of speeches, reports of private conversations, etc., have been reported to officials of the department for decision as to whether or not the matter justified prosecution under the espionage act."[3] The demands of wartime swamped the department, which, in addition to suppressing antiwar dissent, was charged with monitoring alien enemies and with handling allegations of sabotage and draft evasion.[4] The special agent in charge in Portland, Oregon, noted in a letter to the head of the Bureau of Investigation in the fall of 1918: "I have eight agents and employees here. On Saturday last the filing clerk made

60 files and the same on Monday. These agents cannot keep abreast of the work. For the last few days they have been called as witnesses in Court and Grand Juries and the work lags during their absence and it is impossible for me to keep abreast of demands."[5] As the special agent's letter suggests, the Justice Department lacked the resources to bring charges against every disloyalist. A successful prosecution for speaking out against the war required tracking down reliable witnesses who could provide specific accusations as to what the suspect had said. Finding secondhand allegations of a suspect's disloyalty was one thing, but firsthand, detailed, and credible assertions that someone had clearly and unambiguously spoken out against the war were harder to obtain.

For example, in Coushatta, Louisiana, in the summer of 1918, investigator Max M. Schaumburger decided that he lacked sufficient proof to take three men suspected of socialism and subversive statements to court. "No one," wrote Schaumburger, "could recall any definite remark which had been made by any of the parties named." The suspects themselves rejected accusations of disloyalty: "When subjects were located at their favorite fishing places, about fifteen miles from Coushatta, they of course, denied that they had ever been against the Government, etc. and protested that they were good, patriotic loyal democrats."

Hence, the department's detectives frequently opted to meet with an alleged dissenter and to caution him or her to avoid criticizing the war. Such informal warnings could be issued quickly, leaving the investigator free to pursue other cases, and before issuing a warning, a detective would not have to meet the same standard of proof that would be required for a prosecution. In the case of the Louisiana suspects, Schaumburger, acting on the advice of the U.S. attorney, "explained to them, as per suggestion of United States Attorney Moore, that under present conditions, any seditious talk would be followed by punishment on the part of the United States Government."[6]

Across the country, investigators delivered similar warnings. In Milwaukee, an alleged disloyalist "was severely reprimanded and warned [to] never be guilty of making remarks that would necessitate another investigation by this department."[7] A man from Racine, Wisconsin, confronted by an investigator "was warned that any further report of seditious behavior on his part, will lead to serious trouble," while another resident of the city "was warned that any further report of seditious talk or behavior would mean serious trouble for him."[8] A Texan of supposed German sympathies was administered "a severe lecture on

Americanism and what will be expected of him in the way of his future remarks and actions," while a resident of Storm Lake, Iowa, thought to have made antiwar remarks, was informed "that such talk made him liable to imprisonment and he didn't seem to realize that he was doing any wrong to express his opinion." In any case, the Iowan "promised, however, to keep his mouth shut henceforth."[9] An African American woman of Richmond, Virginia, was advised "that if she had been making any unpatriotic remarks, that she was not to repeat them, under the penalty of being arrested."[10] In Connecticut, one investigator recounted the reprimand he had delivered to a schoolteacher: "I cautioned Miss Albanesius against any extreme remarks on her part, depicting the embarrassment which such remarks might cause her. She stated that she would endeavor to refrain from discussing the War question again."[11] Two Chicago women received "an intelligent warning, and they promised not to discuss any War situation and to be loyal and patriotic as they have always been in the past."[12] A Californian suspected of venting his sympathies for Germany was visited by an investigator, who subsequently reported that "I gave him a good talking to and I do not think he will offend again."[13] Despite his protestations of innocence, a Herman Frick of Norfolk, Virginia, who had been reported as having expressed himself against the war, was given an ultimatum by an investigator, who noted the following in his report: "I informed Frick that whether he had made the statement in question or not, my visit would be a warning to him, and if we ever had any further reports about him along this line, things would go hard with him."[14]

In New York City, investigator L. S. Perkins was especially aggressive in confronting alleged subversives. He called on Joseph Mushotsky, "a Russian Hebrew" who supposedly had expressed unpatriotic sentiments. As Perkins recorded it,

> I found him asleep in his room at No. 2 west 118th street, had him waked up by the landlady, and interviewed him as he lay in bed. He was apparently pretty badly frightened, when I explained the nature of my errand to him, and said: "Mushotsky, you are reported, on good authority, to have made ugly remarks about the United States, reflecting upon our government and its institutions, calling other men 'slaves of the government,' and declaring that you were going to say just what you pleased, as this is a free government, etc. How about that?" Mushotsky sat up in bed and denied vigorously that he had ever used such

language. When I told him there were three witnesses to it, he said he had had trouble with a letter carrier, and supposed the latter had told a story about him. He said he was a native of Russia, and had been here about five years, and had taken out his first citizenship papers. I then said to him: "You are a citizen of a country that is friendly to the United States, but you are likely to be arrested for disloyal talk, and if you use any more such talk you will be taken in hand, for your name is listed, and you will be carefully observed. So your only safety lies in strictly behaving yourself and keeping your disturbing talk to yourself." Mushotsky seemed greatly relieved at being allowed to remain free, but I made it plain to him that next time he would not fare so well.[15]

After chastising another suspect, this one "a very ignorant native Russian," Perkins reported, "I finally told him he could go, if he could behave himself; but that if he was ever caught saying ugly things against this Government any more, it would go hard with him."[16]

Sometimes, detectives noted how shaken a suspect appeared by their interrogations or reprimands. In Alabama, investigator Mark Hanna recounted his reproach of a man alleged to have made disloyal comments: "I gave him a good strong call-down, and told him that if there was a repetition of the report against him, that in all probability he would be taken into custody, as he is of <u>German descent</u>." The suspect, "with a trembling voice," promised "that he would never discuss the war situation again."[17] One Los Angeles woman questioned about statements she had supposedly made "appeared to be greatly humiliated by the interview and broke down and cried."[18] An Illinois man, interviewed by an investigator about allegations that he had disparaged certain aspects of the war effort, "begged like a baby that he would never say anything again or do anything that would get him or anybody else in any trouble, and that he was very sorry for the remarks he made."[19]

If detectives were unable to meet with the suspect, they sometimes asked a member of the suspect's family to pass along a warning. When investigator J. P. Folsom was unsuccessful in his attempt to meet with a woman in Chicago accused of subversiveness, he contacted her husband, who declared that while his wife was a bit high-strung, she was by no means a German sympathizer. Wrote Folsom, "He was sure that his wife could not and did not attack this government or its President, in so far as conducting the war is concerned, or the handling of the draft." Still, Folsom's visit appeared to have accomplished its purpose, since the husband "stated upon his return home he would admonish her, and as agent suggested, caution her to be careful hereafter in regard to any of her expressions relative to our country in this war."[20]

Some of those interviewed were told to remain silent on the topic of the war. One Virginian was told that "the American Government demanded of him, that he keep his mouth shut."[21] From others, the department solicited public affirmations of patriotism. A professor at the University of Southern California, questioned in regard to allegations that his lectures favored the German cause, defended his loyalty by offering "several excerpts from his lecture, all of which are of a highly patriotic nature." Nevertheless, the professor "was cautioned that whenever he delivered a speech of any kind to be sure he delivered it in such ringing American terms that no one would question his loyalty."[22] In Wisconsin, investigator John E. Burke may have nudged his interviewees into promises to support the war enthusiastically. When Burke met with Julius Gausche of Racine, an immigrant reported to have made comments sympathetic to Germany, Gausche responded by claiming that "anything he may have said about Germany, was meant only as a joke." Such questioning did elicit a pledge to be more vigorously American, as the investigator noted that Gausche "realizes, however, that this is a rather poor time to make such jokes and that in the future he will be careful to show his real attitude by actively patriotic talk."[23] Another reported disloyalist Burke met with recognized "the necessity of precluding suspicion by actively demonstrating his loyalty to this country," while another alleged dissenter told Burke "that in the future he will so act and speak that there will be no doubt of his active support of the government."[24] Impartiality toward the war was unacceptable. In Oklahoma City, investigator Donald D. Lamond interviewed a woman who supposedly had rejected entreaties to join the Red Cross. The woman responded that she "had her own individual way of giving," which she preferred to donating via any kind of formal group. When Lamond asked her how she felt about the war, she answered "that she is neutral," to which he retorted that "we could not be neutral."[25] The department could be intolerant of any failure—even in difficult circumstances—to properly display a patriotic attitude. Shortly after the armistice in November of 1918, investigator E. D. Kirk received a report that the staff at a San Francisco hospital had neglected to rearrange a flag that had become twisted and tangled. The city had been suffering from the great flu epidemic of 1918, but this was of little concern to Kirk, who asked the chief hospital custodian, Charles Schmidt, why the colors hadn't been tended to. Kirk recounted that: "SCHMIDT started to deny that this was true, and stated how busy he and the balance of the people were about the Hospital on account of the Influenza, there being so many patients. but as these explanations did not seem sufficient excuse for neglect of the Flag, I instructed SCHMIDT to see that the Flag was straightened out and kept straightened out, and told him that the first report that we got that the Flag was not in proper condition I would come up to the Hospital and take him in custody."[26]

The Justice Department's auxiliary, the American Protective League (APL), provided a substantial amount of assistance. Founded in 1917, the APL was composed of volunteer detectives who collected allegations and passed them on to the Justice Department.[27] One APL member provided the names and addresses of twenty-seven "people who read nothing but German books at the Toledo Library."[28] On other occasions, APL volunteers escorted Justice Department employees as they made their inquiries.[29] The APL also conducted investigations on behalf of the department. At its request, an APL member began checking into the activities of Seventh-Day Adventists in Connecticut.[30] In June 1918, one APL member, E. F. Warner, prepared a report on an acquaintance of his, the writer H. L. Mencken. Warner defended Mencken's loyalty, noting that the author's parents were American-born.[31]

On the whole, the APL offered a good deal of help to the Justice Department—the historian Joan Jensen, for example, found that the APL performed four-fifths of the Bureau of Investigation's labors in Cleveland, Ohio.[32] Not everyone in the department, however, appreciated the league's efforts. A Justice Department investigator in Illinois questioned the motives of one APL detective, writing, "I am of the opinion that McGill the head of the A.P.L. is very desirous of securing a job with the government and therefore is very active. I have investigated many reports of he and his men and found them all nothing to worry about."[33]

For more than two years before the congressional declaration of war, Americans had freely discussed the European conflict as well as the virtues and vices of the belligerents. After America's entry into the war, however, the Justice Department sought to curb a wide variety of speech about it. Attacks on the justification for American intervention, dismal portrayals of life on the front lines, pessimistic predictions as to the duration of the war, expressions of sympathy for Germany, or criticism of the government or of war auxiliaries—all such remarks could run afoul of the department.

Investigators sought to silence any challenge to the legal or moral rationales for the American declaration of war. In Wisconsin, for example, investigator Charles E. Woida looked into a story that a Richard Erles had damned international law and had asserted that it was a German prerogative to attack American ships. After some investigation, Woida was also told that the man had used epithets to describe Americans. Woida confronted an apologetic Erles, who, by Woida's account "admits that on June 23, 1918, he said . . . that Germany had a right to blow up ammunition boats, and that Americans were warned to keep off the seas; that this country had no business to declare war." Erles also acknowledged "that he was not sober when he made these statements . . . and promises never again to talk in that way." Woida chastised Erles and was "satisfied with subject's sincerity in this matter."[34] In Los Angeles, a New Zealand-born woman confessed to having previously stated that nations which were opponents of Germany had committed brutal deeds in previous conflicts. The detective "informed her that this was a very poor time for a British subject to be attempting to justify Germany in any of her acts."[35]

The department's detectives wanted to inhibit the spread of defeatism among soldiers and potential soldiers. For example, detective C. E. Argabright visited a Kansas woman who allegedly had advised a young man departing for camp that he should not fight and should give himself up to the German side. At first, the woman disputed these allegations, Argabright recounted, "but upon being told that it was known that she had done this she began to cry and said she might have said it but if she did she did not remember about it, and that she had not meant to be disloyal, but just wanted the war to stop."[36] As part of this policy, the department tried to suppress negative depictions of warfare or gloomy forecasts as to the duration of the conflict. Thus, investigator W. A. Weymouth set out to interview a Frank Besson, who allegedly had been describing the experience of combatants in frightening terms. Supposedly, Besson had said "in the presence of men of draft age that the average life of an aviator was less than forty hours, that the trench life was very bad, and that he had seen body lice crawl off of dead bodies onto the men fighting, and other remarks of the same character." When confronted by the detective, Besson defended his loyalty, asserting he was a veteran of the Canadian army and that he had served on the western front. Besson maintained that his comments had been an attempt to answer the questions posed by others, "that he had never made any remarks derogatory to the warfare at the front," and that he had been trying to demonstrate that "the Infantry was more desirable than the other branches." Weymouth seems to have accepted Besson's version of events but nevertheless "warned him to be careful and not say anything which would serve to cause men of draft age to hesitate about going to France because of conditions there."[37]

Forecasts of a lengthy conflict were similarly suspect. Investigator John Burke, responding to a report of disloyalty, visited Fred Dunnebacke, a pessimistic Wisconsin businessman. Dunnebacke proclaimed his support for the war but asserted that no one realized how difficult it would be to defeat Germany. Dunnebacke, wrote Burke, believed that it was his duty to alert others to "the strength and resources of Germany in an effort to wake people up." Dunnebacke asserted that his wife had warned him that such talk could lead to difficulties with the authorities, but, noted Burke, Dunnebacke thought that his spouse was "down on them [the Germans] too much." Burke told Dunnebacke that "his wife is right" and "that he is bound to get into trouble if he continues to talk as he had just talked." Those in authority recognized the seriousness of America's circumstances, maintained the investigator, who told Dunnebacke that he ran the risk of winding up on trial if he continued to express such opinions. The businessman replied by pledging "to limit his activities to patriotic deeds in the future."[38]

Expressions of admiration or sympathy for Germany were discouraged as well. In interviewing a Los Angeles man suspected of "pro-German talk and activities," investigator C. L. Keep "cautioned him concerning any activities on his part that could be construed as pro-German."[39] Responding to a complaint that a Cincinnati library carried a copy of a book about the Kaiser, investigator W. H. Valentine looked into the matter, concluded that the text "would tend to incite sympathy of the reader for the German Empire," and consulted a library staff member, "who stated that all publications of any German tendency had been taken from the shelves, and placed in a box under lock and key, and accordingly same would be done with this publication, which was done in the presence of this agent."[40] In April 1918, Alfred Bettman, special assistant to the attorney general, advised A. Bruce Bielaski, head of the Bureau of Investigation, of allegations that a New York playhouse "is presenting pro-German plays and other things which lampoon the habits and customs of the people of the United States." Bettman suggested that if such allegations proved accurate, "the manager of that Theatre should be gently warned to exercise very careful discretion in the plays to be performed." Subsequently, an investigator met with a manager of the theater, who said that his playhouse had avoided acts that might offend American sensitivities and had also lent its support to the war-loan drive.[41]

To some investigators, almost any manifestation of German culture was a cause for suspicion. In Philadelphia, a detective, on finding that a department store was selling socks that bore the word "GERMANY," advised the store to stop selling this item.[42] In New York City, another investigator, Paul Hofherr, noted that during his visit to Pabst's Casino he "did not hear the band play the Star Spangled Banner during the entire evening." Hofherr thought that "no German music should be allowed to be played" in this or other similar venues and suggested that other institutions should be so advised.[43]

Remarks denigrating the armed services likewise drew the attention of the Justice Department. In October 1917, for example, a Minnesota man, who reportedly had impugned the virtue of the female residents of St. Paul and had blamed their behavior on the local servicemen, was called in for an interview, where he was advised "that he be more discreet in his remarks in the future, and on account of him having a bad temper that he discontinue the discussion of the war entirely."[44]

Speaking out against war bonds could earn a reprimand as well, even before the Sedition Act of 16 May 1918 made it illegal to "say or do anything, except by way of bona fide and not disloyal advice to an investor or investors, with intent to obstruct the sale by the United States of bonds or other securities of the United States."[45] In April 1918, an investigator rebuked a worker who had allegedly hurled his bond to the floor and trod on it, "and let him go with a warning that if he is brought in again he will be dealt with more severely."[46] In North Carolina in late May 1918, special agent Denver Graham interviewed a Mr. Griffin, who supposedly was opposed to war bonds. When Griffin told the agent he favored taxation as a means of generating revenue, Graham "explained why the Government did not care to raise the taxes unless compelled to do so." Graham told "Griffin that he was violating the law of the United States when he talked against the sale of Liberty Bonds which occurred in the 2nd and 3rd Liberty Loan Campaign." On finding that Griffin had not bought any Liberty Bonds, he advised "Griffin to get busy and make a purchase else his friends and the business men that he delat with would be down on him."[47]

Some investigators inquired of suspects if they had purchased war loans, as a means of gauging their loyalty. In Milwaukee, an investigator asked a suspect why he had not bought war bonds.[48] In North Carolina, when Denver Graham questioned an allegedly disloyal minister and his wife if they had invested in war loans, the pastor had a ready answer for the agent: "the Rev. Wilson stated if I could tell him how a man with 12 childred drawing $800 a year could clothe, feed them, and buy Liberty Bonds, he would appreciate it."[49] In Texas, investigator A. E. Farland pressed a recalcitrant bank employee to purchase bonds. Earlier, Farland had met with a lawyer who was upset over the fact that some hadn't contributed money to the war effort, and who said that he "wanted Employe to try and throw a scare into them." The lawyer mentioned several names, including a bank employee who had not purchased bonds or stamps. Farland and the local assistant U.S. attorney visited the employee, who thought that "he did not feel that he could afford to buy Liberty Bonds, because if he did so he would have to go into debt. However, he stated that if we insisted he would borrow the money and buy them. We told him that we were not insisting on anything. That if he claim to be a good loyal American citizen we thouhht it would be no more than right that he should at least own one Liberty Bond." The bank employee responded that he would quickly prepare to purchase war securities. However, Farland seems to have realized that such aggressive salesmanship might violate the Justice Department's guidelines. Although the patriotic lawyer had supplied other names, Farland decided against visiting them, "as it looked as though this was being done as a threat to make these people buy Liberty Bonds and War Stamps, and Employe did not think it was the policy of this Department to scare anyone into buying Liberty Bonds and War Stamps if they did not feel disposed so to do."[50]

Likewise, critics of war auxiliary organizations, such as the Red Cross, found themselves being interrogated. In Covington, Louisiana, investigator Max M. Schaumburger responded to allegations that an H. J. Smith had failed to donate to the Red Cross and had characterized that organization as wasteful. Schaumberger met with Smith, who claimed that he had donated forty dollars to the Red Cross and that he was acting within his rights to comment on the organization. Schaumburger "tried to explain to Smith that the Red Cross should be considered the same as the government, and nothing should be said which might interfere with the success of a campaign." Smith promised to use more caution, and Schaumburger indicated the case "is considered closed for investigation," though he thought that the matter should be brought to the attention of the U.S. attorney.[51]

Some detectives believed that criticism of Woodrow Wilson, the Democratic president, was forbidden, or at least grounds for suspicion. In interrogating a J. J. Crowe, who was suspected of expressing disloyal sentiments, investigator Willard N. Parker asked, "Have you anywhere at any time, criticised the Wilson Administration, Mr. Crowe?"[52] In December 1918, a Margaret Rice of Delaware was questioned after having earlier commented in a letter to a friend in Mexico that the president was dishonest. When interviewed by a detective, Rice acknowledged that her spouse was Republican but contended that her remarks were not illegal. "[W]hen I wrote the letter criticizing the President," she maintained, "I felt that I had a right to do so owing to the fact that in my opinion the President was making false statements through the newspapers." The investigator informed Rice of the risks she ran in critiquing the nation's chief executive: "When Mrs. Rice was cautioned to the effect that she may get into serious trouble if she persisted in criticizing the President of the United States, she replied, 'Well, you can rest assured that I will not do any more criticizing, either through letters or word of mouth.'"[53] In Chicago, George W. Ellis, an African American political candidate for municipal court judge, was interrogated for supposedly having claimed that President Wilson was unfaithful to blacks. Ellis himself was not a typical Chicago politician. He was an intellectual who had authored scholarly articles on Liberia, where he had served as an American diplomat. He was also a prominent lawyer who served as general counsel of the *Chicago Defender* and as an assistant corporation counsel for the city of Chicago. A figure of some note in local Republican politics who was committed to equal rights for African Americans, Ellis had signed the previous December a telegram beseeching President Wilson and Congress "to suppress mob violence." At the same time, Ellis backed the war effort, for the telegram also argued that "the whole-hearted devotion and service of every citizen are now needed to win this war for democracy and to make the world safe against the further aggressions of the Prussian autocracy."[54] The investigator in this case, F. M. Sturgis, "was of the opinion that subject was using the old policy platform, that the negro race should be in favor of Republican politics as in many of the platforms they state that the Republican party is the only party who ever did anything for their race." Wilson's treatment of African Americans was to be off-limits to criticism during the war. Sturgis "reprimanded subject and told him that in these times this office would hold him to account for any statements which would be made of an insulting nature to the president."[55] In short, Justice Department agents encouraged Americans to censor their opinions on a wide range of topics.

Justice Department detectives were likewise on the lookout for immigrant disaffection from the war effort. Indeed, the Bureau of Investigation owed some of its expansion in the prewar era to fear of immigrants, particularly on the role allegedly played by foreign-born procurers in urban prostitution networks. The belief that sexual immorality—much of it foreign in origin—threatened the nation helps to explain the passage of the Mann Act of 1910, which reaffirmed an already existing prohibition on importing women for illicit reasons from other countries and made it illegal to transport women from state to state "for . . . prostitution or debauchery, or for any other immoral purpose." Enforcement of the act was assigned to the fledgling Bureau of Investigation.[56] In 1917 and 1918, the Justice Department became especially concerned about the loyalty of German Americans, many of whom prior to the declaration of war had expressed sympathy for their country of origin. In the spring of 1918, Justice Department official Charles De Woody publicly charged that pro-Germans had appealed to immigrant communities as part of their propaganda campaign. De Woody warned of "the propagandist machine which directs the sending the hundreds and thousands of telegrams to public officials and persons of influence urging them to do this or that 'in behalf of our country.' On their face these telegrams appear to be real expressions of individual opinion, but investigation nearly always shows that they are a part of a concerted movement directed by friends of Germany and paid for with German money. This kind of propaganda is, as a rule, directed from various headquarters in what may be termed the strategic centres of the more thickly populated sections, particularly those in which there is a large foreign-born voting strength." Efforts by German immigrants to retain their cultural heritage were suspect, he cautioned: "We should not forget that kind of propaganda which agitates for the maintenance of the German language in our schools and seeks to maintain a German spirit in our very home life. The singing of German songs in schools in some parts of the country and the teaching of history which is clearly of a pro-German tendency are features."[57]

For some investigators, ethnicity was a convenient measure of loyalty. In San Francisco, investigator N. H. Castle examined allegations that the dining room of a Bertha Gnepper was decorated with German nationalist ornamentation. Accompanied by an APL investigator, Castle paid a call on Gnepper and discovered "several small German Flags, Pictures of the Kaiser and German placards." The investigators questioned Mrs. Gnepper as to her choice of decorations, advising her "that this was a poor way to display American citizenship."[58] Justice Department investigator T. A. Matheson was astonished over the failure of some South Dakota Germans to assimilate. Visiting one town, Matheson felt as if he had been transported across the Atlantic: "Employee noticed with keen interest the visages of old Europe, in the actions and customs of the towns people." German, not English, was the language of choice, and Matheson "observed many of the youths, and the young ladies, standing on the different street corners conversing in the tongue of their previous home." Indeed, he noted, "the community in general seems defiant in thier adherance to the mother tongue."[59]

To some extent, the suspicions aimed at Germans extended to immigrants in general. A detective observing a rally in San Francisco noted that he had "carefully looked over this audience and was impressed with the fact that the greater percentage of the audience were foreigners," and grew alarmed when a speaker who spent his time "arraigning capital" drew a favorable response: "Agent considers it very unfortunate for the country at a critical time like this when the nation is involved in war for a wild and intense harangue as this speech was to be delivered to an audience mostly foreign-born, and he seemed to arouse the audience up to a great pitch of enthusiasm, and they drank in his prejudice."[60]

Detectives sometimes felt that measures were required to keep the foreign-born in check. In Connecticut, detective Raymond Littell judged that a native of Hungary had been guilty of making disloyal comments. Both Littell and a fellow investigator felt that steps needed to be taken to curb disloyalty: "Because of the numerous complaints made against Austrian and Hungarian subjects in this city," both detectives agreed "in recommending that affirmative action be taken in this instance."[61] In New Orleans, one investigator claimed that three Latin American men (one of whom was employed by the Cuban consulate and two of whom were from Honduras) "are, like most Central Americans, absolutely anti-American," and that two of them "hate the U.S. from a Hondura-nean viewpoint, i.e., they always see the U.S. in the light of a huge power, which wants to grab up their little country and dominate it; and they go so far as to believe that the U.S. actually foments Central American revolutions in order to have an excuse for landing troops there." The detective concluded that "an official warning given these young Latins, in an official manner, would I believe keep them shut up to a great extent."[62] Detective Arthur M. Allen observed that the town of Tonopah, Nevada, seemed to contain "disaffected groups," including "the Finns, the Irish, and the extreme Socialists of members of the I.W.W." The Finnish community, however, did not pose much of a threat and, observed Allen, was "not regarded as dangerous, only sullen." Those of Irish descent were often "so bitter against England that they oppose any nation which is on friendly terms with it," but fortunately were under the sway of a Pat Mooney, a local figure of patriotic leanings.[63]

Still, not all Justice Department officials viewed an immigrant heritage as inherently subversive. Even Charles De Woody's warnings of alien influence included the caveat that Austro-Hungarian laborers had been largely immune to enemy propaganda. Such resistance, he believed, was "apparently because these workers realized the benefits they enjoyed in this country, the good working conditions which surrounded them, the high wages paid, and the fair and constructive attitude of the Government toward them." De Woody might have added, too, that many immigrants from Austria-Hungary wanted their ethnic homelands liberated from Habsburg rule.[64] Hinton Clabaugh, of the Chicago branch of the Bureau of Investigation, proclaimed that the government could successfully foster immigrant loyalties to America. Speaking at a conference in Chicago in January 1918, he downplayed the espionage threat and emphasized instead the importance of cultivating the allegiance of the foreign-born as "valuable sources of information." Rather than punishment, Clabaugh argued that the "careful handling" of aliens through education could transform them into productive agents of the war effort:

> The spy business is greatly exaggerated. Much of it is just plain bunk. Some of the aliens with whom we come in contact require only careful handling to make them useful to the nation, and it is a fact that some of the most valuable sources of information which we possess are men who have been arrested and shown their error. Why, one man, an engineer on an Austrian vessel which was interned, now working here, after

admitting that, when goaded, he had made unpleasant remarks about the country, has become one of our most valuable agencies in educating his countrymen in loyalty. We go on the theory that you cannot correct evils by putting men in prison, if there is a possibility of their being educated.

Sounding nothing so much like a settlement house worker, Clabaugh claimed that "if the alien were properly educated, at least 80 per cent of the government's troubles with sedition and crime would be eliminated."[65]

Some in the Justice Department seem to have had little doubt about the patriotism of certain immigrant groups. In Nevada, informant Dick Lucich reported to investigator Arthur M. Allen that the Serbs were helping to keep Tonopah's Austrian community in line. Lucich observed no disloyalty among the local Austrian population. Noted Allen, "The reason as it appears to *Lucich*, is that there is a large population of Servians among them and these Servians are keeping so close a watch on the Austrians that they do not dare to say or do anything that will give offense."[66] Likewise, investigator P. P. Mindak, examining a Polish newspaper in Chicago that had supposedly printed items "concerning the mistreatment of German and Austrian subjects," was not worried about the patriotism of the Polish American community. Of the newspaper's parent organization, the Polish National Alliance, he wrote that "the loyalty of this organization cannot be questioned, as they have at all times beene strong American propagandists, and in the Fourth Liberty Loan has subscribed about one half million dollars worth of bonds."[67]

The war years saw a rise in animosity toward African Americans. Many cities in the Northeast and Midwest, as well as the nation's capital, saw a substantial influx of southern blacks—a migration that drew angry reactions from whites who saw the newcomers as potential competitors for jobs. This resentment helps account for the bloody race riots that broke out in East St. Louis, Illinois, in July 1917 and in Chicago and Washington, D.C. two summers later.[68] In the South, whites feared the prospect of blacks serving in the armed forces. As one general noted: "In talking with southern members of Congress, I find a very natural repugnance to the idea [of the draft] due to their own local conditions. It is not that they disbelieve in more or less universal training on principle. But they do not like the idea of looking forward five or six years by which time their entire male negro population will have been trained to arms."[69] Such worries escalated after August 1917, when soldiers from an African American army battalion stationed near Houston, frustrated over the racist attitudes of the local residents and the brutality of the local police, rioted. On the evening of 23 August, a group of soldiers from the battalion ventured into town and shot a number of white residents. The army responded with a court martial that subjected thirteen alleged rioters to the death penalty.[70] The riot sparked an angry reaction in the region. Responding to these fears, the War Department postponed the induction of black draftees, but this failed to soothe white apprehensions, for, as one historian has noted, "Southern members of Congress received numerous letters from white constituents expressing anxiety over the racial inequity (and the danger to 'our sisters and daughters') if the black men were left at home when the white men went off to war."[71]

In this atmosphere of heightened racial tension, some Justice Department employees sought to stifle expressions of racial egalitarianism. In Washington, D.C., Richard Foss, a Greek-born small businessman, was confronted by investigator E. O. Irish about allegations that he had disparaged France and America. In addition, Irish said, Foss had spoken in favor of racial equality: "I accused Mr. <u>Foss</u> os [*sic*] saying that the <u>American</u> white people were no better than the colored people." Believing that anyone who made comments of such a character "was nothing but a yellow dog," Irish threatened Foss with jail time if further such allegations surfaced.[72] Justice Department officials in the South feared that outside influences might undermine the system of Jim Crow. In Arkansas, for example, investigator E. J. Kerwin suspected that the *Chicago Defender*, an outspoken critic of racial bigotry, was serving the Kaiser's cause: "This paper among the negroes beats any German sympathizers and or real Germans to do bad and dangerous work of the propaganda stuff that pleases Germany." Discovering that two blacks might have been trying to sell subscriptions to the *Defender*, Kerwin wanted to know whether "they are paid workers out of Chicago to come into the South especially where the negroes are as thick as at the places indicated by me, and stir up strife in either taking the negroes name and address and sending him the paper for nothing or just soliciting him as a subscriber of the paper."[73] Kerwin wasn't the only investigator in the South to fear outside influences. When Martha Firth, an instructor at Bishop College in Marshall, Texas, criticized racial prejudice in a letter to a friend in Japan, a censor read her mail, and excerpts from her letter were forwarded to the Justice Department in San Antonio. Among the offending comments in the letter: "This old town (Marshall, Texas) is so conservative that it would not be wise for the white teachers to be seen out with the colored ones. Is not that silly?" Firth had also praised the conduct of black soldiers and wrote that in any case, she didn't believe "the 30,000 returning negro soldiers will put up with the snubs of the aristocratic whites." Investigator Lewis H. Henry met with Firth, who stated that she had recently arrived from Nebraska. Henry "was impressed by the total ignorance of subject in the sentiment of the negro race and how to deal with it, and concludes that she came South with the old-time Yankee idea of social equality with the negro." Henry thought that Firth's commentary, though mistaken, lacked "vicious intent."[74]

Departmental officials in the region worried that African Americans, perhaps in conjunction with other "outsider" groups, might become disaffected from the war effort. In Texas, investigator J. B. Rogers called for a crackdown on subversion, stating, "If such disloyalty is allowed to go unpunished, the effect will be very bad in this section especially where there are so many socialists, Germans, and Negroes among who there is now very little respect for the Government."[75]

Thus, the Justice Department tried to curb expressions that might weaken black support for the war. For example, one African American from Texas was reprimanded for having questioned the fairness of the army's mass execution of black soldiers for their alleged participation in the Houston race riot. The investigator, Manuel Sorola, reported allegations that "Henry Canady, said that the negros have done right at Houston, that white folks were to hard with the negro soldiers, they brought them here to San Antonio, keep them in the Guard house, then take them out of there and hang them, that is not right, the negros are not going to stand for it, we have to get a ravenge for that." However, wrote Sorola, the assistant U.S. attorney, Hugh Robertson, "think that the negro said such things through ignorance and what he needs is a good hard talk and warren him." Canady, added Sorola, "was given a good leture and warren" by a Justice Department special agent.[76] On Sunday, 26 August 1917, investigator J. H. Harper led an inquiry into the Reverend Alexander S. Jackson, an African American Baptist minister in Dallas. Harper, working at the offices of the Dallas police that day, learned of alarming allegations about Jackson, who reportedly "was at that time delivering a sermon in which he advocated that the negroes arm themselves and in the event that the Negro Troopers, who commited the outrages of the last few days in Houston were executed, that they proceed to Houston and wipe out that community." Investigator

Harper, accompanied by city detectives Carroll Baird and Albert Dellinger, then traveled to Jackson's church and did not find him making any such comments. Harper then conducted some inquiries and, again with Baird and Dellinger, visited the evening service later that same day as well. The investigators seem to have intended to remain outside the church, but Reverend Jackson, reported Harper, apparently learned of his visitors and "stated that he understood white men were listening to him, and that they were welcome to come in as he was preaching the Gospel." A few of those attending the service approached the investigators "and invited Detective Baird and Employee inside of the church when Mr. Baird plainly told them who we were and our mission." These worshipers, wrote Harper, maintained "that 'Rev. Jackson has too much sense to do that and he is too loyal; that this morning he expressed his regret at the loss of life in Houston, stated that swift punishment should be meted out to those who had committed these murders.'" Having failed to hear anything seditious, Harper did not seem terribly concerned about the loyalty of Jackson, and too, Baird and Dellinger "knew this negro preacher personally, when brought to mind, and gave him a good name." However, Harper was more concerned about T. J. Finch, a white man and a supposed adherent of Socialism, for "he is as much a menace in that negro quarter as any one could be, with his ideas of draft resistance etc., common to his ilk."[77] Harper's comments foreshadowed a belief common in the postwar period—that left-wing radicals threatened the system of racial hierarchy.[78]

During the war, however, southern fears of left-wing subversion had not yet fully materialized, and instead worries focused on the notion that an aggressive Germany might somehow unsettle the tradition of white supremacy. When a black minister, Edward Chambers, stood accused of predicting that a German victory would presage an era of black supremacy, investigator Harper, escorted by a constable, sought to look into the allegations. Chambers was found sleeping in a hut. Harper recalled that he "had intended onoy to talk to him and reprimand him and caution him," but Chambers resisted arrest and dashed away. Chambers was captured, and when questioned said that he'd worked as an itinerant minister and now owned a farm. According to Harper, Chambers possessed "the face of the lowest type of criminal and is nothing more nor less than a brute in a sense." It isn't clear whether or not charges were brought against Chambers following his arrest.[79] The Justice Department's wartime concerns about African Americans marked only the beginning of a long obsession with race. In the postwar era, the department energetically investigated black militants, while J. Edgar Hoover, assuming control of the Bureau of Investigation in 1924, monitored and harassed the civil rights movement in the decades after World War II.

Women were investigated as well, especially as they were expected to make crucial contributions to victory. Governmental and private organizations made concerted efforts to organize women in support of the war effort; to help feed the American forces in France, the U.S. Food Administration called on homemakers to avoid wasting food.[80] President Wilson himself asserted, in April 1917, "Let me suggest . . . that every housewife who practices strict economy puts herself in the ranks of those who serve the nation."[81] Perhaps more importantly, women were supposed to allow their sons to enter the military. "A mother who is not willing to raise her boy to be a soldier," Theodore Roosevelt had declared in 1915, "is not fit for citizenship."[82] As Susan Zeiger has noted, both civilian and military backers of the war believed that women played a vital role in fostering national resolve. General John Pershing, commander of the American Expeditionary Force in France, recognized the value of maternal contributions to soldierly morale when in May 1918 he expressed the following hope: "I wish that every officer and soldier of the AEF would write a letter home on Mother's Day. This is a little thing for each one to do. But these letters will carry back our courage and our affection to the patriotic women whose love and prayers inspire us and cheer us onto victory." For its part, the U.S. Post Office promised to expedite the transport of such correspondence home for the holiday.[83]

Mothers were expected to instill patriotism in their children. In Milwaukee, investigator Paul Kelly paid a call on a Mrs. Mueller, a German immigrant in whose house a picture of the German emperor was displayed. Kelly asked that she take down the image and informed her of the hazards "to herself, to her husband, and to her children in having such a picture of the man who is murdering her relatives and ruining her country." Such an image, he explained, in addition to "poisoning the hearts of her children," left her open to both "persecution by her neighbors, who are mostly Polish," as well as "prosecution in the Federal Court."[84]

Prior to the outbreak of the war, the women's club movement in America had lent its support to the efforts of pacifists. In 1912, the prominent Austrian peace activist Bertha von Suttner had spoken before the General Federation of Women's Clubs convention in San Francisco.

Suttner's talk was followed by a speech by Frances Squire Potter, who asserted that "military warfare deliberately employs murder for its policy."[85] Though women's clubs had generally supported the American war effort, suspicion of the movement as having pacific tendencies may have still lingered, which may explain why the department investigated Lillian Burkhart Goldsmith, an actress and active clubwoman of Los Angeles.[86] After receiving allegations of Goldsmith's disloyalty, special agent Cassius L. Keep sent her a letter asking her to come in for a conference. Goldsmith then consulted federal district court judge Oscar Trippet, whom she knew, about the matter. Judge Trippet, a Wilson appointee, then sought to have the conference take place in his Los Angeles office, but when he called agent Keep on the telephone to this end, Keep, not perceiving that it was a federal judge who was on the line, continued to insist that Goldsmith come to his office instead. After appearing for her appointment at the Justice Department office, Goldsmith was interviewed by Keep. "I do not believe that she intended any of her talks or lectures as pro-German propaganda," wrote Keep, adding, "however, some of the stories she told and statements she made have evidently worked upon the imaginations of the women of Los Angeles women listening to them and have resulted in exciting the minds of her hearers as to the dangers, etc. of men in the army, especially in the aerial division." Keep pointed out to Goldsmith "what effect her lectures were having." According to Keep, Goldsmith acknowledged "that quite a number of women after listening to them had called her stating that she must never deliver this same talk to any of the other clubs." After the meeting, Goldsmith, who protested her treatment in a letter to Judge Trippet, painted a very different picture of her conference. She had arrived on time for her meeting, but then had to wait for more than a half hour. "I was then ushered into an office," she wrote:

> where there were two desks and two gentlemen. I inquired which was Mr. Keep, and I was told to go to the wrong desk. I talked to the man and called him Mr. Keep for five minutes. His manner was very unpleasant, and he was called out of the room, and in leaving he turned and addressed the other gentlemen by name. I then turned and told the <u>real</u> Mr. Keep that I was not surprised that a man would be so discourteous to a lady after knowing he had been discourteous the same morning to Judge Trippet. He replied, "<u>What,</u> Judge Trippet." "Who is Judge Trippet." And I answered "I am referring to the only Judge Trippet I know, the man who was honored by our President, Woodrow

Wilson." He seemed quite taken aback; inquired of a lady present, his secretary, and then discovered that although he had spoken to you over the phone he hadn't realized to <u>whom</u> he had been speaking. He immediately came over to the other end of the room where I was sitting and apologized profusely. I had all my notes of every lecture I have given which I offered to show him, but he refused, saying it was not necessary and they really had no charge against me.[87]

Judge Trippet protested to U.S. attorney Robert O'Connor, and in a later conference between O'Connor and special agent E. M. Blanford, Trippet made clear his displeasure with Keep. "Judge Trippet further stated," recorded Blanford, "that Mr. Keep talked more like a German officer than an American citizen, and that he felt that inasmuch as we are fighting for Democracy and freedom, it should be practised among our officials." Keep wound up receiving a letter from "Chief" (almost certainly A. Bruce Bielaski), who emphasized that there was not much justification for demanding that interviewees come to the office for a conference. "When Judge Trippet called you on the 'phone," wrote Bielaski, "and asked you to come to his office for the purpose of interviewing Mrs. Goldsmith, despite the fact that you did not know who he was, I see little justification for you having stated in positive terms that you would not go to any office to interview Mrs. Goldsmith, and that if she did not call in response to your request, you would send for her. This indicates not only an entirely improper attitude toward the public generally with whom you have to deal, but a very mistaken attitude when it comes to accomplishing results in the way of getting information."[88]

Keep, however, thought it important to continue monitoring Goldsmith. In January 1918 he dispatched Mrs. Lena Smith to observe a presentation by Goldsmith. Smith seemed inclined to think that Goldsmith wished "to give what seems to her a well-rounded performance, rather than to purvey either pro-German or Pacifist propaganda, or to in any wise obstruct the draft." Yet to Smith, Goldsmith, by stirring up maternal instincts, threatened to undermine support for the war: "my deduction is that more women will cling tenaciously to their sons and connive in every possible manner to aid them in evading the draft after listening to 'What the World is Thinking and Feeling,' by <u>Mrs. Goldsmith,</u> than will ever be strengthened by listening to it to give their all in a burst of patriotic enthusiasm." Smith acknowledged that Goldsmith had praised the president, but she also concluded that all in all, "<u>Mrs. Lillian Burkhart Goldsmith's</u> lecture 'What the World is Thinking and

Actress and clubwoman Lillian Burkhart Goldsmith of Los Angeles was called in for questioning regarding a lecture she had delivered concerning the war. (University of Washington Libraries, Special Collections, UW27068)

Feeling' as given by her today is Pacifist propaganda pure and simple and should be dealt with as such."[89]

Goldsmith's upper-class status and political connections afforded her a degree of protection from Justice Department investigators. For that matter, prevailing class and gender expectations played a role in how the department evaluated women. Upper-class women who expressed their dissent in a genteel fashion seemed to pose less of a threat than those from a lower social and economic class. Investigator Donald B. Clark reasoned that the decorousness of Anna May Peabody, a pacifist of Cambridge, Massachusetts, would help insure that she would not directly challenge the Wilson administration. A member of Boston's elite, Peabody had attended classes at Radcliffe College in the 1890s (one of her instructors was the philosopher William James) and had gained some media attention in April 1917 when she was one of a small group of Massachusetts peace activists who, two days before the senate voted for war, called on the state's senior senator, Republican Henry Cabot Lodge, in the Capitol building in Washington, D.C. Peabody implored the staunchly pro-Ally Lodge, "Won't you give it more thought, for the sake of the boys and their mothers and the honor of the country?" A sharp exchange of words between the senator and one of Peabody's fellow delegates, Alexander Bannwart, soon followed, and the two men came to blows. Newspapers around the country covered the brawl. Lodge claimed that Bannwart had hit first, though the *Boston Daily Globe's* front-page story did quote "Mrs A. M. Peabody of Cambridge" as saying that Lodge had thrown the first punch. Clark's reports on Peabody make no mention of the affray, so it is not clear whether he was aware of her role in the matter.[90] When interviewed, Peabody acknowledged her pacific leanings but claimed that she could not perceive any way to act upon them in the current crisis: "She said that her attitude, in the abstract, had always been that war was wrong, but she further said that she did not see that there was anything to do about it at the present time and that she was not doing anything or intending to do anything which in any way would harm her country." Too, Peabody had no kind words for Germany's stance. "After a conversation which lasted for two hours," wrote Clark, "the Agent gained the impression that Mrs. Peabody was an absolutely upright woman with great strength of character, who according to her own words, thoroughly approved of President Wilson's policies, although she felt herself free to criticize the manner of their execution by underlings, who often allowed themselves to do things

in the President's name, which the President disapproved of himself."
Clark nevertheless "warned Mrs. Peabody that this was certainly not the
time to do any discussing which might in any way hinder the prosecution of the war or give comfort to the enemy." Clark concluded, "I do
not think that Mrs. Peabody is a woman that will create any public dis-
turbances; she is a very refined woman."[91]

Conversely, women who lacked gentility or who defied conventional
gender roles appeared all the more subversive. In Philadelphia, when
investigator C. S. Vial questioned a Mrs. Leonard about an accusation
that she had expectorated on the Stars and Stripes, Mrs. Leonard complained of her mistreatment at the hands of others and, according to
Vial, "worked herself into a fury. This woman has an ungovernable
temper and an unbridled tongue." His efforts to test Mrs. Leonard's patriotism only raised further questions: "I then asked her if she were loyal
to America, and she raised her right hand and made oath before God
that she was, and instantly stated that she would return to Germany as
soon as possible." Vial's attempt to converse with the husband yielded
no solution, as "he evidently has no control over her for common report
says she runs him about the house with a butcher knife—the lady looks
the part." The husband's inability to restrain his wife further indicated
her dangerous nature. Noting that Leonard had supposedly stated to
someone else her eagerness to be interned, Vial remarked that "this
woman should be accommodated."[92]

When investigator R. E. Monroe visited a Minerva Hill of Kentucky
to discuss accusations that she had spoken out against the war, matters
quickly spun out of his control: "When I let <u>Mrs. Hill</u> know my business
at her house she immediately called the members of the family out on
the porch in order that they might hear what she had to say and began
a tirade against President <u>Wilson</u> and the Government." Drawing on
scripture, Hill raised the possibility that the recent imposition of daylight
savings time was evidence of Wilson's demonic nature. "She claims to be
a member of the Christian Church and bases her whole argument on
the Bible," Monroe reported, adding that Hill "says that if the president
is the one who ordered the clocks set ahead and back again, he is the
beast spoken of in the Bible because the Bible says that the beast will seek
to change the time." She claimed, wrote Monroe, of having told others
to avoid draft registration, as "she believes that the work of the leaders of
the nation is that of the devil." Deeming Hill "an ignorant woman,"
Monroe feared that "among the ignorant people of the country her

remarks cannot help but have some effect." Hill's approach to matters found an audience among the local population, Monroe suggested, as "She plays heavily upon their superstition." In conclusion, the detective felt that "There is no doubt that in order to save the local situation something must be done to stop this woman's tongue."[93] Another outspoken Kentuckian, Elizabeth Watkins, was convicted of violating the Espionage Act. Allegedly, she had made many seditious statements, such as: "This country would be better off if the Kaiser had it" and "I will not comply with the food regulations and I would like to see the S. of B. come to my house. I would give him the contents of a forty five." U.S. attorney Thomas Slattery sought to justify the charges against Watkins, claiming that she was from an area "inhabited by a large number of people in rather poor circumstances," and that her dissent "was having a very damaging effect upon the morale of the people of that community." Watkins's masculine traits made her even more dangerous. "She is a large, two fisted woman with a voice and ways that are very manish," he claimed, "and it seemed necessary that some action be taken to suppress her, otherwise there would have been serious trouble in her community."[94]

Although some investigators feared that aggressive females could galvanize opposition to the war, at least one investigator expressed his admiration for a woman, who, by dint of necessity, had adopted hard-driven labor. In Portland, Oregon, a detective looking into the life of Maria Fleiss found that her job was to keep railroad cars clean. Fleiss's husband, it appeared, had left her and gone to Brazil, and she was providing for an eleven-year-old son. Observing that Fleiss's "hands are calloused like a hard working man's" and that "her fingernails are worn back of the flesh," the detective favorably contrasted her patriotism with that of women of higher status: "If her statements are true — cleaning cars for American soldiers, maintaining a son and educating him, — a strange comparison when one stops to observe the polished and claw-like finger nails of many females who are born in this country and whose patriotism is loudly acclaimed." Fleiss's regimen of hard work testified as to her loyalty.[95]

The Justice Department also relied on undercover investigations and informants as a means of netting those critics of the war who spoke a foreign language or who exercised discretion about to whom they aired their views. In Illinois, detective P. J. Fergus visited a S. W. Walling, suspected of bad-mouthing war bonds and of general disloyalty. Reported

Fergus, "Got Mr. Walling into a conversation which led him to express his opinions on the Liberty bonds and the United States being at war with Germany." After Walling somewhat cynically suggested that those who purchased war bonds could be more readily manipulated into supporting the war, he was startled to find that he was conversing with an undercover investigator. As Fergus recounted it, Walling "said that the government is anxious to sell bonds to the poorer class because it thinks it can then get the poor to fight more easily than the people who have lots of money. At this point I introduced myself to him. It took him by surprise, and he stood in amazement for at least four minutes. He tried to back out of the statements he had made to me."[96]

Other undercover ploys, however, proved fruitless. In Guthrie, Tennessee, investigator Benjamin H. Littleton interviewed undercover a hotel supervisor suspected of subversive statements. Littleton checked in at the hotel and discussed with the supervisor, an H. C. Hill, "a great deal about the European War." The suspect, wrote Littleton, "didn't know who I was, and he was free to discuss the war." The supervisor stated that as late as earlier that year he had backed Germany but that he currently regarded German leaders as "low down dogs." Others to whom the investigator talked confirmed that the supervisor had been loyal, and Littleton felt that "from my conversation with <u>Mr. Hill</u> I am satisfied that he was merely talking, and did not know what he was talking about, at the time he is alleged to have been pro-German in his remarks."[97] In East St. Louis, Illinois, investigator Louis Loebl talked with a suspect "under cover" in an effort to determine whether or not he posed a danger. The suspect in this case, asserted "that he fully agrees with the policies of our Government to wipe out Germany's autocracy and to establish democracy all over the world."[98] In Kentucky, investigator Leonard Stern's meeting with another suspected disloyalist, Joseph Arbogast, provided little evidence to suggest that the suspect was unpatriotic. Arbogast claimed to be of French heritage and to be a native of Alsace-Lorraine. Stern noted that "This agent talked for awhile with <u>Mr. Arbogast</u> and in a general way regarding the war and at no time, although this agent was under cover, did <u>Mr. Arbogast</u> express any opinion that would lead anyone to believe that he was Pro-German."[99] In Massachusetts, detective William Hill sought to discover the true loyalties of a Lotta Furniss by approaching her undercover. Before meeting with Furniss, Hill spoke with her landlord, who characterized his tenant as a German sympathizer. A few days later, Hill visited Furniss, "on the

pretext that he had been instructed by Mr. Hand, the landlord, to in-
spect the roof and ceiling of her apartment." Furniss, however, seems to
have kept her opinions to herself: "Agent noticed the picture of the Kaiser and Franz Joseph on the wall in her parlor, and remarked, 'Oh, see
who is here,'" wrote Hill, adding, "This failed to draw any reply from
her other than, 'Don't look around.'"[100]

Undercover investigators sometimes visited restaurants in hopes of
turning up leads. Stopping at a Milwaukee restaurant that reportedly
employed disloyalists, detective Charles Bodenbach failed to hear any
criticism of the nation's leadership.[101] In Lynn, Massachusetts, investigator Leonardis Augustus went to a Greek restaurant in his search for
supporters of the Central Powers. Before entering the war on the side of
the Allies in 1917, Greece had been torn between supporters of King
Constantine I and the politician Eleutherios Venizelos. King Constantine, brother-in-law to the German emperor, wanted his country to
remain neutral, while Venizelos wanted Greece to cast its lot with the
Allies. Greek Americans had similarly been divided between partisans
of the king and Venizelos, so Augustus, aware of these divisions, talked
"under cover . . . with a Venizelos man . . . asking him if there were
many Greek Royalists in Lynn."[102]

As the Lynn investigation suggests, undercover investigators also
sought to penetrate immigrant communities, where expressions of opposition to the war might otherwise pass unnoticed by the larger
English-speaking society. Such methods had been anticipated by New
York City's deputy police commissioner, Arthur Woods, who in a 1909
article in *McClure's* argued that undercover operatives were needed in
the fight against foreign-born criminals. Woods worried about the rise
of criminal gangs composed of Italian immigrants whose language was
a shield against outside inquiry. Woods acknowledged that New York
City employed Italian-speaking investigators but said that their duties
had already rendered them unable to function covertly, as "there are so
few of them, and they work so constantly in the Italian colonies, that
their faces are as well known as those of old friends," while the commander of New York City's Italian squad, Joseph Petrosino, was hampered by his fame. Woods argued that if Petrosino's force "could be sup-
plemented by a dozen or twenty men, working always under cover,
never appearing in court or at headquarters, there would be fewer mys-
terious stories in the newspapers, and the jails would be more full of
swarthy, low-browed convicts."[103] In Baltimore in 1918, Harvard College

graduate and Justice Department informant Alex Vonnegut attended a meeting of the Germania Männerchor, which he characterized as a "'hot-bed' of Germanism." The fear of punishment, wrote Vonnegut, discouraged members from speaking out on the topic of the war: "They all frankly acknowledge that if they expressed their sentiments in regard to America's entry into the war they would all be interned." Interestingly enough, the members thought well of Woodrow Wilson. Too, there was some evidence of a long-term trend toward assimilating into American culture. "Several members," he noted, "are surprised that their children although they have been in Germany, and read and write the language are 'violently pro-American' and that they will not try to see the German point of view."[104]

Undercover operations did offer career opportunities for women at a time when police work was an almost exclusively male profession. In Philadelphia, for example, investigator Mrs. F. B. Pond posed as a bookseller in an effort to discover if a certain Miss Stanton was disloyal. Pond approached Stanton, who was staffing a Red Cross stand. Pond announced that she was selling the book *The Emden* and referred to *The Voyage of the Deutschland*. The former text was an account of the 1914 exploits of the German light cruiser *Emden*, as told by an officer who had served aboard her; the latter book, authored by a German sea captain, told of his transatlantic voyage in 1916 from Germany to America and back commanding the cargo submarine *Deutschland*. When Stanton seemed somewhat confused, Pond tried another tack: "I then told her that I was very much surprised to notice that she was selling wool for the Red Cross. When I made this remark, she comprehended my meaning and at once became very indignant." Immediately, Stanton peppered Pond with queries: "She wanted to know who sent me there. . . . She then asked for my name and address. . . . She then endeavored to question me closely as to why I was soliciting orders for these books." Stanton wrote down the title of the book *The Emden*, and Pond judged that "Stanton intended to make a report of the matter to some person or place." After the encounter, Pond wrote that "I might state in conclusion that I am not of the opinion that this woman is pro-German. In fact, I would state that she is very patriotic."[105]

In Portland, Oregon, the department relied on a female informant, known as "Fifty," who conducted investigations and who, working undercover, sometimes arranged social gatherings with women suspected of having German sympathies. A member of the local turnverein (a German social and athletic organization), Fifty twice hosted gatherings of German American women at her home. On 8 January 1918, she welcomed a few women to her house who, by her account, had participated in the German Red Cross movement. (During the period of American neutrality, many Americans had donated to the German Red Cross). She noted that her guests, two of whom she characterized as "extremely pro-German," asserted that local Germans were reluctant to hold gatherings for fear of governmental spying: "These women stated further that the Germans were not having any meetings now; at least, the Germans in their circle were not, for the reason that they and their friends were being kept under very strict surveillance by agents of the Department of Justice, and that by virtue of this strict watch on the part of the government, these people hesitated to attend any meetings, or do anything, that would subject them to censure, or get them into trouble." Indeed, it appears that concerns about department spying had weakened the bonds of community for Portland's Germans. "These ladies further stated," wrote Fifty, "that the Germans of this city were even suspicious of each other; that many of them thought there were spies at every social gathering, and it is absolutely impossible to have a meeting, or go anywhere, without a representative of the Department of Justice ascertaining the facts, and the data in connection therewith. . . . They further stated many of the Germans thought that the Department had dictaphones (detectaphones) in German homes, and other places, where Germans are liable to congregate."[106] Later that month, Fifty asked "various German women to her home in order to be able to ascertain their views, knowing that they would express themselves more freely in a social circle than elsewhere." Her seven guests, "prominent in club life and social activities of Portland, Oregon, and . . . among the leading German families of said city," expressed themselves patriotically. According to Fifty, the guests all sought an American victory and "proposed to do all within their power to conserve food and to aid the United States." Likewise, those present cast a critical eye toward those German Americans who sought to organize: "These women made the statement that the people, if any, who favored German meetings, were neither loyal to the United States, nor Germany, but simply agitators, who were against every kind of constituted authority." One visitor asserted "that it was impossible, even if the Germans so desired, to have meetings without the government knowing it; and furthermore, it is impossible for anyone to say, or do anything, in such meetings without the government knowing what transpired, for the reason that the government has spies everywhere and that it is a fact known to her and others, that the government paid women fifty dollars for each and every report made of disloyalty." On a separate occasion, a German immigrant woman told Fifty that the area's German American community feared the activities of government investigators.[107]

When conducting investigations, Fifty not only noted what suspects told her, but also recorded other behaviors that she thought indicated a person's degree of patriotism. Any sign of indolence, especially during wartime, she believed, indicated poor citizenship. When inquiring into the case of a Brewster Kerr, who reputedly was an unemployed radical of the proper age for military service, Fifty reported "that the neighbors are all indignant over the fact that subject as an able-bodied man and will not work, but leaches upon his aged aunt." Fifty recommended "that this man be severely dealt with."[108] When looking into the supposed pro-Germanism of another Portland resident, she was unable to meet with the occupants of the house but visited a neighbor, who said that the males of that particular household did not seem to be working much. Regarding the suspect's home, Fifty recorded "that these people live in a filthy condition and have the appearance of 'poor white trash'; that there is no evidence of thrift as the yard has grown to weeds instead of a vegetable garden." She concluded that "It might be well for an officer to remind these people that this is the time to work and not loaf."[109] Her interest in what people were doing with their yards reflected a belief that gardening demonstrated dedication to the war effort. Indeed, in April 1917 President Wilson himself had proposed "that every one who creates or cultivates a garden helps, and helps greatly, to solve the problem of the feeding of the nations." Fifty observed that one family had "much space utilized in chicken yard, vegetable and flower garden and fruit trees," while another family possessed "a war garden," and still another owned "a large vegetable garden and many fruit trees." Likewise, Fifty sometimes noted whether the home of a suspect featured signs for the food conservation effort or for the Red Cross. The work of Fifty and other such informants represented the future of the FBI; in the post–World War Two Red scare, the department would rely heavily upon undercover informants as sources of information about subversion.[110]

Investigators could display leniency toward those whose potentially subversive comments seemed to reflect momentary poor judgement, bad temperament, intoxication, or mental deficiencies rather than any real disloyalty. Investigator H. F. Edson visited an allegedly pro-German Californian who admitted that "he had been joshing a cigarmaker in Pacific Grove about Germany coming over here and getting him, but that he did not mean it just that way, as he was always joshing." The suspect vowed that he would "not talk lightly about the war in any of its phases." Edson reasoned that the suspect's comments simply reflected a thoughtless gesture, writing, "I am inclined to think that he is all right at heart but has been inclined to talk without thinking."[111] In Milwaukee, investigator Harry F. Meurer concluded that one suspect, a Henry A. Hovey, who reportedly had upbraided his daughter for having pledged money for war stamps, was more ill-tempered than unpatriotic. Meurer questioned the daughter, who confirmed that her father had chastised her decision to agree to contribute. She explained, however, that her father had not actually criticized the stamps themselves but rather had been afraid that if she were terminated from her position, her stamp obligations would be passed on to him. When interviewed, the father professed his loyalty and said that he had indeed been critical of his daughter's decision, because "she should have consulted him first, as he feared that should she lose her position the pledge would not be met." Meurer thought the whole matter was a family dispute, for though Mr. Hovey had been "peevish and irritable in his home . . . there is no cause for alarm as to his loyalty."[112] Investigators were likewise more willing to forgive dissent that seemed stimulated by alcohol. Investigator L. H. Van Kirk followed up on a report from C. J. Cadwalader that a William Embody had stated that he would rip down the Stars and Stripes and in its place raise the German national banner. Inquiries in Embody's neighborhood turned up no real evidence of disloyalty, but the locals did state that Embody's termination from his job most likely stemmed from his intemperance. Van Kirk visited Embody at home and found that he, at least seemingly, was a patriot. Embody's residence displayed a "faded and weather-worn" Stars and Stripes, a fact that appears to have impressed Van Kirk, who learned that the colors had been there from the American entrance into the war. Embody went so far as to challenge Van Kirk to try to take down the colors decorating his home. Embody repeatedly cried, "For God and Heaven's sake! I cannot understand who could have made such a report about me." (He did, however, speculate that Cadwalader had informed on him.) Van Kirk characterized Embody as harmless but thought it likely that he "drinks somewhat too much and perhaps when intoxicated made some indiscreet remark, although he denied even this."[113] In a similar case in Orange County, California, investigator V. W. Killick was forgiving of a certain Joseph Kiefer, who earlier had received "a thirty days jail sentence for vagrancy and disloyal talk." Under questioning, Kiefer expressed his support for the U.S. government as well as his dislike of Britain and its alliance with America. Kiefer stated that "he knew better than to remark against England at this time, and was not in the habit of doing so, but had been under the influence of liquor when he made the remarks which caused his arrest." Killick decided that a warning would be best: "I spoke kindly to him, advised him to put in some study on the matters in which England had aided the United States and balance up his opinions, to avoid drink and be careful of his speech."[114] In cases where the suspect had mental shortcomings, the department sought to have local residents monitor the situation. Investigator E. H. Waterhouse, for example, found that Anna Choppin, a Portland, Maine, hotel maid who was supposedly the source of subversive statements, was somewhat mentally impaired. In questioning the hotel's housekeeper, Waterhouse "learned that subject, about once a month, had temporary fits of insanity, and at these times is not responsible for what she may say for two or three days." The housekeeper also noted that Choppin wasn't dangerous in the least. Meeting with the maid, Waterhouse "found her in such a condition that she could not be considered thoroughly responsible for what she might say." Waterhouse advised Choppin to avoid making such statements in the future, and both the hotel's manager and housekeeper "agreed to keep watch over subject and endeavor to prevent her from making further remarks of a similar nature as those alleged to have been made by her."[115]

Investigators did not always take accusations of disloyalty at face value, and often concluded that such allegations were unfounded. In Pittsburgh, for example, detective E. B. Speer, after investigation, rejected an allegation from a local Red Cross organization to the effect that a Mrs. Bubacz had expressed hope for a German triumph. Allegedly, Bubacz had solicited the help of the Red Cross to mail a letter to Germany—correspondence that had supposedly contained the words, "The American people are with you heart and soul and hope you will win the war." Bubacz acknowledged to Speer that she had sought the help of the Red Cross but maintained that her letter wasn't seditious. Noted Speer, "She showed Agent a copy of the letter and the sentence objected to by the American Red Cross was a sentence which referred to the people of United States being heart and soul with the Polish in an effort to gain freedom of Poland." In his report, Speer termed the whole affair as rooted in "a misunderstanding."[116] A similar case occurred in Massachusetts, when investigator Joseph Purcell responded to the allegation of Boston schoolteacher Annie H. Pitts regarding a fellow-teacher's student, Elsa Nabor. Asked to play the song *America* before her classmates, Elsa, whom Purcell estimated was around thirteen years old, balked. Although the child reportedly did play the piece to her teacher alone, Pitts attributed Elsa's refusal to play publicly to parental influence. Purcell continued the investigation by going to Elsa's home and interviewing her about the incident. Elsa claimed that her in-class refusal to play "was on account of being bashful and not through any influence received from her parents regarding national airs." Purcell then added, "I spoke to the child's father and mother," who confirmed Elsa's shyness. The parents "explained to me that the child is of a very nervous and retiring nature, and when asked to play the piano before an audience becomes nervous and excited." Purcell concurred that Elsa was indeed "of a nervous type" and believed that the student was most likely "telling the truth regarding this matter." Indeed, wrote the detective, her parents seemed "to be very nice people and not of the pro-German type," and his "investigation of them among the neighbors" resulted in "the best of reports about this family."[117] In Washington state, special agent Charles Petrovitsky, who had earned a law degree at the State University of Iowa and had worked as a lawyer in Seattle, thought that small communities were fertile ground for spurious rumors of disloyalty.[118] After investigating allegations that residents of Auburn were seditious or had made unpatriotic remarks, Petrovitsky wrote that "there is no doubt that some of the people do some talking yet much of this is much misconstrued in small towns where often arguments are started to get some even very good German American angry and state things he would not otherwise think of expressing."[119]

In one case, investigator Roy H. Pickford unearthed testimony that suggested that allegations of disloyalty against a Kansas schoolteacher were rooted in spite. In December 1917, the department received a letter from C. W. Henry, forwarding allegations from students claiming that Sonora Leiss, a teacher, had expressed antiwar sentiments. Investigator Pickford then met with an apologetic Mr. Henry, who "was very sorry that he had made this report and wanted to withdraw same because he had learned since from his daughter and several other little girls who attended this school that Miss Leiss had switched several of these children and the whole thing had been started by these children and their parents and he was satisfied there was no proof in the matter." When questioned by Pickford, Leiss herself asserted that "she had never had anything in her life occur that had hurt her more than this insult" and offered "to have the children sing their patriotic songs and exhibit the flag drills for Agent." Leiss, the detective noted, "denied vehemently every accusation," and, Pickford admitted, "she certainly does not appear to be of the disloyal type." Indeed, he noted that not one of the locals he interviewed put any trust in the accusations against Leiss: "Agent had asked quite a few people around Hudson in regard to Miss Sonora Leiss and none of them accredited any of the remarks that she was suppo[s]ed to have made by her as being true."[120]

Investigators often suspected that malicious motives or personal grudges lay behind accusations of disloyalty, as when investigator Paul J. Kelly decided that allegations against a Milwaukee woman were without foundation. The woman, supposedly a German sympathizer who owned a fortune of eight hundred dollars, had not invested in government loans. Kelly met with the suspect, who said her spouse had abandoned her and that her pay from her factory job amounted to little. Kelly concluded that the original allegation was groundless, "there being no evidence of her being pro-German." The charges of stinginess in regard to Liberty Bonds were likewise false, as the woman "was living in very poor quarters, in fact the slums of the city." Kelly suspected that the charges stemmed from "jealousy or spite."[121] In Chicago, when a man reported his father-in-law as having made anti-American statements and as having ripped apart a U.S. flag, the investigator came to the opinion "that this complaint is probably inspired by some family differences and entirely local in its nature."[122] In Boston, detective F. J. Weyand decided that the person who had written a note against a local resident, Joseph Rodrigues Xigues, was possibly acting on a grudge. After some inquiry, Weyand came to believe "that the person who wrote the letter is perhaps an enemy of <u>Xigues</u> and perhaps not very well acquainted with him, as the writer did not suplly the name correctly and did not give the correct place of his birth."[123] In December 1918, the department received an allegation from a Chicago man accusing a Harvey Hammertree of, among other things, disparaging President Wilson. The man who filed the allegations worked at a factory, so investigator P. P. Mindak met with plant supervisors and was told "that the complainant in this case has had some little trouble with Hammertree regarding certain improper remarks which Hammertree made about complainant's wife." Too, the company's file on Hammertree revealed nothing that would discredit his patriotism, and Mindak judged that "the complainant in this case is seeking to get revenge on Hammertree."[124] In California, investigator George Hartz, looking into allegations of disloyalty against a W. Linderman, reported that "investigation of this matter disclosed the fact that the Informant, JOHN ANDREWS, has had personal differences with LINDERMAN and made up this story for the purpose of getting even with LINDERMAN, as LINDERMAN has a fine reputation in that vicinity."[125] In Wisconsin, another investigator characterized accusations against Albert Zuehlke as "a case of spite work."[126] In El Paso, Texas, an investigator suspected that accusations against J. S. Serrano, "a high type of Spanish-American," grew out of in "some personal grievance."[127] Investigator E. B. Speer reached a similar decision in evaluating an allegation made against Stephen Bacur, an employee of the Westinghouse works in Pennsylvania. According to a Joseph Rostar, Bacur had made defeatist statements, accusations Bacur denied. Speer noted that "Joseph Rostar is a native of the same town in Hungary as Stephen Bacur," and thought that "there is a strong indication that Rostar is venting personal grudge against Bacur."[128] When government authorities are given, as one of their chief responsibilities, the power to punish wartime speech, inevitably some citizens will be tempted to settle scores with their neighbors by denouncing them as disloyal or unpatriotic. To their credit, Justice Department detectives on the whole seemed aware of the possibility that some allegations were fueled by spite, but one can only speculate as to how many reprimands or even prosecutions could trace their origins to a spark of personal malice.

Less than two decades prior to the war, then Princeton history professor Woodrow Wilson eloquently defended the principle of free speech. In October 1899 Wilson told a meeting of educators that dissent had an honorable heritage: "We have seen a good many singular things happen recently. We have been told that it is unpatriotic to criticize public action. Well, if it is, then there is a deep disgrace resting upon the origins of this nation. This nation originated in the sharpest sort of criticism of public policy. We originated, to put it in the vernacular, in a kick, and if it be unpatriotic to kick, why, then, the grown man is unlike the child. We have forgotten the very principle of our origin if we have forgotten how to object, how to resist, how to agitate, how to pull down and build up, even to the extent of revolutionary practices if it be necessary, to readjust matters."[129]

Wilson's Department of Justice engaged in a systematic campaign to stifle those who objected, resisted, or agitated against the government's decision to enter the war in April 1917. For that matter, anyone who expressed any idea that could potentially weaken morale on the home front ran the risk of being rebuked by Justice Department detectives.

3

Policing the Clergy

In 1917 and 1918, Justice Department investigators feared that ministers might use their prestige to sow antiwar sentiments among their congregations. Thus, the department investigated countless clergymen suspected of subversion, and its detectives saw nothing wrong with prying into the private affairs of congregations and confronting those ministers who seemed antagonistic or apathetic toward the war effort. The government deployed undercover investigators to listen in on sermons and to meet with pastors under false pretenses to elicit their genuine opinions about the war.

Clergymen from many different denominations were targeted. A Baptist minister from Vermont, a Mennonite pastor from Ohio, and a Methodist preacher from Texas were all charged with violation of the wartime sedition statues.[1] Several denominations—in particular, the Russellite, Lutheran, and Catholic churches—received a good deal of scrutiny from the department. The Russellites (later known as the Jehovah's Witnesses) were staunchly opposed to fighting in earthly wars, and one of their publications, *The Finished Mystery*, characterized nationalism as chauvinistic and asserted that "under the guise of patriotism, the civil governments of the earth demand of peace-loving men the sacrifice of themselves and their loved ones and the butchery of their fellows, and hail it as a duty demanded by the laws of heaven." The leaders of the sect were convicted of violating the Espionage Act in 1918.[2]

The Lutheran churches came under investigation less for their doctrines than for their ethnicity. Many Lutherans were of German descent, with some churches still holding services in German. During the period of American neutrality, Lutheran publications had sometimes expressed sympathy for the German cause as well as suspicion of the Allies. With the onset of American intervention in the war, patriotic organizations accused the Lutheran churches of failing to back the war with adequate enthusiasm. Indeed, while many Protestant pastors in the larger English-speaking community depicted the war as a Manichean contest between good and evil, some in the Lutheran church, at least in the initial stages of American involvement, took a more temperate view of the matter; one Lutheran publication in the summer of 1917 criticized as un-biblical the notion that the war was a struggle of Christianity versus wickedness. The use of the German language in Lutheran parochial schools was depicted by zealous patriots as prolonging the attachment of students to Germany, and stories spread that church pastors, as part of their initiation, swore allegiance to the kaiser.[3] The army, too, worried about the loyalty of its Lutheran chaplains. One letter from army intelligence to Bureau of Investigation director A. Bruce Bielaski suggested that the Reverend George F. Schmidt, identified as an official of the Lutheran Army and Navy board, "be kept under surveillance," noting that "in common with nearly all members of the Lutheran clergy he is an object of suspicion."[4] Another communication from army intelligence advised that a chaplain be investigated: "This office has received information tending to show that Rev. P. W. Erickson, Lutheran Chaplain at Camp Pike, cannot be fully trusted. He is now at Argyle, Wisconsin, on a leave of absence, and we would appreciate it if his activities and utterances, while at Argyle, could be investigated and this office informed as to the same."[5]

Suspicions surfaced about the loyalty of Catholic clergymen as well. During the period of American neutrality, the Catholic Church had remained divided in its sympathies for the combatant nations. Many nationalities in the American church, including the Poles, Italians, French, and Belgians, had reason to cast their lot with the Allies. At the same time, many German Catholics had sympathized with Germany, while many Irish Catholics resented the British governance of their homeland, a sentiment possibly stoked by London's severe response to the 1916 nationalist uprising in Dublin. Differences of opinion regarding the war also appeared in the Catholic press—with some journals leaning toward the Allies, and, perhaps more commonly, others tilting toward the German cause. Many Catholic publications, however, showed no marked sympathy for either side, and given the divisiveness of the issue, the church hierarchy was generally hesitant about appearing to favor any of the European combatants. With the declaration of war in 1917, however, the American church backed the American war effort. Nonetheless, numerous Catholic clergymen came under the scrutiny of the Justice Department.[6]

Typically, clergymen were investigated on charges of having either questioned the war or of having failed to back openly the war effort. In one case, a Pennsylvania minister, Rev. F. D. Sutton, stood accused of using his Sunday service to criticize a cinematic depiction of German war atrocities and was alleged to have publicly refused a suggestion that he announce in church the upcoming draft registration. When confronted by an investigator, Sutton disputed the charges, asserting that "he is of nearly pure English descent and hates the Germans himself." Sutton defended his earlier pronouncements, asserting that he had stated that American soldiers should be motivated by noble sentiments and not rage. Sutton also maintained that he had indeed announced the upcoming registration but added that he had also declared that he thought such matters should be kept out of the church, for "he believes that the pulpit is not the proper place for such things and that the standing of the church is lowered by getting off of religious subjects." In any case, Sutton promised "that in his next sermon he would correct any impression he had made last Sunday."[7]

A Wisconsin nun was likewise investigated for alleged subversive conduct. In June 1918, special employee Charles Bodenbach visited Sister Marion, a teacher at a Milwaukee parochial school. Sister Marion acknowledged that she had pulled down and ripped up a classroom poster for war bonds and that at the time she had stated that the poster was of little value in its location. But Sister Marion also claimed that the poster had become damaged and dirty prior to her removing it and asserted that she had merely been commenting on the state of the poster and its placement. Sister Marion defended her patriotism, maintaining that she "has always been loyal to this country even in thought." Nevertheless, Bodenbach advised her to be more cautious, while also issuing a warning to Sister Superior Wenzeslaus "that any complaint against any of their number in the future would be thoroughly investigated, and that it would be to the interest of all concerned to consider the import of anything spoken in the schoolroom, as such utterances might be easily misconstrued."[8]

The department showed little tolerance for those clergymen who failed to enthusiastically support the war effort. For example, special employee Irving Best feared that Father Eugene Scheuer, a Catholic priest of Holdingford, Minnesota, was failing to inculcate patriotic sentiments among his congregation. A postmaster whom Best had interviewed asserted that the priest had not contributed to war loans or to the Red Cross, had criticized American involvement in the war, and had blocked the wishes of his flock to raise a flag over the church. Furthermore, the postmaster maintained that the priest had been less than ardent in carrying out the bishop's instructions to hold a patriotic assembly, an allegation that Best summarized as follows: "after Bishop <u>Bush</u> of St. Cloud had held a loyalty meeting a couple of weeks ago, which Father <u>Scheuer</u> contrived not to attend, the Bishop directed Father <u>Scheuer</u> to hold another loyalty meeting after mass on one of the following Sundays. That about 350 or 400 people attended this mass, but because of Father <u>Scheuer's</u> half hearted way in announcing the meeting, and his known reputation for disloyalty, only about 20 persons stayed to the loyalty meeting, which lasted only about three minutes."[9] Best's subsequent interview with Father Scheuer only deepened his concern. According to Best, Scheuer acknowledged that he did not contribute to the Red Cross and stated that he had read accounts of waste in that organization. "He thought also that the Catholic Tribune of Dubuque, Ia., had published that the Red Cross money did not reach the soldiers," reported Best, who also claimed that Scheuer asserted that government-owned hospitals should be funded by tax revenue. Scheuer's questioning of Red Cross efforts and his criticism of government policy only provided further evidence of subversion. Since Scheuer "is absolutely disloyal and is using every effort to dampen the work in favor of the government among his congregation," Best concluded that measures "should be taken at once to remove him from his position of influence among the German farmers at Holdingford."[10]

When a Mennonite clergyman in Missouri admitted to investigator Sydney W. Dillingham "that he had never told anyone not to buy bonds but had said he could not personally consistently buy bonds as they were an instrument of war and his faith would not allow him to take part in war," Dillingham told the minister "to have a number of his members, pastors, deacons and himself m[e]et agent at 10 a.m. at Sheriff's office" the following day. In the subsequent conference, Dillingham told the Mennonites "that the Government would not allow them to talk against the sale of Liberty Bonds, Baby Bonds, or Thrift Stamps." The Mennonites, perhaps nudged by Dillingham, were willing to contribute to the Red Cross: "Through the efforts of Agent," recorded Dillingham, "the Mennonites signed a contract with a committee of three appointed by agent as follows, R. M. Levesay, H. A. Young and Samuel Daniels that they will deposit in the First National bank . . . $500.00 on or before the 10th of each month to the credit of the Red Cross."[11]

Likewise, a Southern Baptist minister of El Campo, Texas, Rev. W. M. Joslin, was grilled over his failure to direct his church's resources in support of the war effort. In the course of his inquiry into the matter, investigator W. N. Zinn questioned a Mrs. Hiddleston, the secretary of the local Red Cross organization. According to Hiddleston, Rev. Joslin, while not traitorous, had discouraged his congregation from attending a festival for the Red Cross because part of the activities had included dancing. Hiddleston also suggested that Joslin had been less than cooperative in organizing work projects: "Joslyn, in conversation with Mrs. Hiddleston, stated that he had had the women of his congregation refuse to take part in the work as an organization because he believed church work was first and that he would not allow them to give up their Ladies Aid Evening to the Red Cross." When questioned, Joslin asserted that while he approved of the Red Cross, he did not approve of dancing. Noted Zinn: "Subject stated that he believed in Red Cross work and supported it as an individual and from the pulpit, but that he was opposed to dancing and when the members of the Red Cross wished to hold a dance in connection with the Fourth of July celebration he opposed it and kept his congregation from attending as he could not countenance their support of a celebration which had a dance connected with it."[12] Zinn also queried Joslin about his congregation's work record: "Regarding the failure of the Baptist women to organize a workers circle as done by other denominations at El Campo, subject admitted that he would not let them give up their church evening to Red Cross work because he believed church work was first, but when asked why they had not adopted another evening or shifted their church evening if necessary, stated that the ladies had been unable to decide on any particular evening and that they did as much work as individuals as they would otherwise have done."[13]

In his report, Zinn characterized Joslin "as being merely a religious fanatic," and mentioned that he had given the minister a patriotic nudge: "Employee interviewed him at length and suggested that it cast some reflection on his church at El Campo that it was the only one not organized for Red Cross work, which fact had apparently not heretofore occurred to subject." Joslin, though "loyal to this country," seemed "to be more interested in his local church work than in work connected with the entire country."[14] For detective Zinn, passive loyalty to the war effort was inadequate.

Even those who subscribed to a pacifist theology were expected to make at least a token contribution to the war effort. In North Carolina, for example, investigator Denver H. Graham enlisted the help of community notables in his effort to silence W. S. Bradley, a Russellite whose opinions were reportedly having a dangerous effect.[15] Graham arranged a meeting between Bradley and local citizens, including Mayor R. G. Shackel, lawyer A. Paul Kitchin, and several businessmen, including an N. B. Josy and a C. Vaughan. Bradley showed up at the meeting, scheduled at eight in the evening, and proclaimed "that it was his belief and the act of God that we should not fight our fellow men." When Graham asked Bradley whether he had invested in any war loans, he responded that no, he hadn't, as buying bonds was participating in the war effort. When Graham inquired whether Bradley "would be willing to purchase just one 25¢ Thrift stamp to show his loyalty to the United States," Bradley turned him down. Other entreaties were to little avail: "When Mr. N. B. Josy, Capitalist interrupted and asked Bradley would he be willing to buy from $100.00 to $500.00 in Liberty Bonds if he would loan him the money on very easy terms," his offer was rejected. Bradley even acknowledged that he had—unsuccessfully—tried to keep his son from joining the army. Graham discussed the matter privately with committee members Kitchin and Vaughan, who thought that Bradley wasn't going to change his mind anytime soon, and who "suggested that some action or other be taken for this was certainly going to spread amongst the other members and conditions would be bad in the next Bond or Stamp Drive." As Bradley was proving impervious to community influence, Graham fell back on the threat of legal action. Graham returned to Bradley, and "censored his remarks," telling him "that his case would be taken up with the Officials of this Department with the recommendation that he be prosecuted for his disloyal remarks etc. etc."[16]

In its effort to curb what it regarded as the disloyalty of particular Catholic priests, the Justice Department sometimes sought the cooperation of especially patriotic elements within the church. When special agent Ralph Izard inquired into the activities of Father J. Pop of Aurora,

Illinois, he eventually ended up appealing to the diocesan bishop for assistance. Izard's investigation was sparked by an "anonymous complaint that this Priest is insisting on his people continuing their allegiance to the old country thus preventing them from becoming citizens of the U.S." From a local banker, Izard learned that Pop conducted banking transactions for members of his congregation. From further investigation, the agent "learned that he tolerates no organizations not under his immediate control and supervision; that the young men in the church organized a kind of social club and the Father gradually broke it up by refusing to allow them to use the hall and putting every possible obstacle in their way." Izard then called on the minister, and, following a "somewhat difficult" conference, the agent decided that although the priest was "a Romanian by birth" (Romania having joined the Allies in 1916), he still posed a public danger. Izard wrote that Pop's "sympathies are entirely with the Central Powers on account of having spent all his life practically in Hungary; that he does advise his Austro-Hungarian members to retain their allegiance to the old country; probably, however, more for the purpose of keeping them in such ignorance as will guarantee a continuance of their subjection to him which is absolute, than from any desire to develope antagonism to the United States."[17] The priest was keeping the melting pot from coming to a full boil, as it were. In suggesting that Pop was hindering the assimilation of immigrants and that he held an iron grip over his congregation, Izard was echoing some of the time-worn themes of anti-Catholic nativism.[18] Interestingly, however, Izard's solution to these difficulties was to draw on Father Pop's supervisor for assistance: "I have suggested to Bishop Muldoon who was about to visit Aurora that he caution Father Popp to be very careful and am sure that this will be done as Bishop Muldoon is full of loyalty and ready to insist on an equal amount on the part of the priests under his control."[19]

An agent looking into charges of disloyalty against another Illinois priest, Father Peter Kluck of Rock Island, sought a similar solution. Special agent William Roat's interview with Father Kluck disclosed that the priest harbored some sympathy for the enemy: "I called on the Rev. Kluck and conversed with him about his attitude. He informed me that he was American born and that he was with this country but he had certain ideas about the cause of th war and that he could not help but feel for the Germans as he had many relatives in the war and that he was a Cousin of the <u>Great General</u> Kluck of the German Army." As in other cases, support for war-related activities served as a useful measure of a minister's patriotism: "I asked him if he had ever made any speeches in any of the Patriotic activities at Rock Island and he replied 'No' that he staid very close to home. . . . I asked him if he did not think advisable to associate with the citizens and come out publicly and declare himself by making Patriotic Speeches and assisting the cause when ever he could. To this he replied. That he always staid at home etc."[20] Kluck mentioned his relationships with a newspaper publisher and with Rev. James Koppes, a priest from Lincoln, Illinois, both of whose loyalty seemed suspect to Roat: "Seems queer that he should be so well acquainted with these two men as both were considered very pro-German at the out set of the war." Given the potential danger posed by Kluck, Roat felt that he would have to appeal to a higher authority: "In view of the unquestioned loyalty of the Bishop, this case is respectfully referred to the Right Reverend Edwin M. Dunne, Bishop of the Peoria Dicese for such Action as he may deem fit."[21]

In dealing with a Massachusetts priest of supposedly lukewarm patriotism, special agent James F. Terry turned to Bishop Thomas S. Beaven of the Springfield diocese. A previous investigation had reported that a Father Martin Murphy of Great Barrington had failed to provide moral support to those of his congregation who were going off to fight overseas and had not boosted war bonds. While it did not appear that Father Murphy was actually a German sympathizer, the preliminary report concluded "he is of the old school of catholic clergy, rigid, critical, inclined to be parochial minded and with the natural animosity and prejudices against England."[22] Subsequently, Terry sought out Bishop Beaven at his home in Springfield. He was impressed with Beaven's Americanism, as "the Bishop's residence gave evidence in the nature of the national banner being displayed upon the door, windows." The bishop was not unsympathetic to Terry's concerns about Murphy, and "stated that the subject was a typical Irishman." However, Beaven also asserted that Murphy was not a German sympathizer. Terry "stated to the Bishop that the subject appeared to have his church void of roll of honor, necessary prayers for the soldiers and sailors and service flag, all of which were very conspicuous in other churches of the dioces[e]." Beaven told Terry that "the matter would be given his attention and he felt certain that in his own good way he could approach subject and obtain the desired result, namely a satisfaction to his parishioners that he was not-pro-German."[23]

It does appear that the church took action in the case of Karl Ostenkoetter, an Illinois priest who, in addition to allegedly questioning the war, had occasionally dressed as a woman. The investigation of Ostenkoetter began thanks to detective Ward Thompson's vigilance; Thompson recalled that he had been in Freeport, "standing in the lobby of the Senate Hotel, about 10:00 P.M.," when "a person enetered said hotel dressed fully in woman's attire, and registered as 'Helen Wieners, Rockford, Ill.' The actions and conduct of this person caused me to become suspicious and I procee[d]ed to the room occupied by said person and after experiencing some difficulty I succeeded in securing admission to the room and discovered that said person was a man."[24] The man in this case was Karl Ostenkoetter, whose home church was in Shannon, Illinois. Thompson reported that Ostenkoetter was a German alien who, it seemed, had authored "disloyal" items on the topic of the war and the war effort; the priest was detained in a local jail. Shortly thereafter, investigator J. C. Drautzburg traveled to Shannon, where he "learned that subject is very strongly pro-German and his talks to his congregation are strongly pro-German," and where, searching the priest's residence, he discovered "a complete outfit of ladies wearing apparel." The following day, Ostenkoetter acknowledged to Drautzburg that a few years earlier he had tried to start a theatrical career impersonating women. Drautzburg concluded that while Ostenkoetter was not engaged in espionage, he was "very strong against the war on account of his parents and brothers being in Germany." Indeed, the detective noted that "the welfare of his parents and brothers is constantly preying on his mind." Drautzburg thought that the "mentally unbalanced" priest "should be sent to a sanitarium or be interned." The following day, the department contacted Peter J. Muldoon, bishop of the Rockford diocese, inquiring "if he would take charge of Rev. K. Ostenkoetter and send him to a Sanitarium." Shortly thereafter, a priest notified the department that Ostenkoetter had been dispatched to an Oshkosh, Wisconsin, hospital run by the Alexian Brothers, a Catholic order.[25] Had the Justice Department viewed Ostenkoetter simply as a vocally antiwar German alien, it's likely that he would have faced some kind of routine punishment, either prosecution or, more likely, internment; it's also likely that by crossing a gender boundary, Ostenkoetter insured that both the church—to avoid unfavorable publicity—and the Justice Department—to avoid unnecessarily embarrassing the church—would want his removal from the public eye to be discreet.

The Justice Department used undercover informers to keep it apprised of the activities and sentiments of religious organizations. Investigator Leonidas Augoustos, sitting in on a Russellite presentation in Massachusetts, feigned a sincere interest in the doctrines of the movement. To the speaker who had just delivered the presentation, recounted Augoustos, "I said, 'Tell me, I am sorry I dont know much about the subject but I would like to have it explained to me and attend the future meetings.' He said, 'We are trying to discover the truth about religeon and the Government is after us and they arrested seven of our brothers in New York just because we are preaching the truth.' I said, 'That is too bad, you people are against the war are you not, I believe your religeon does not allow it's members to fight.' He said, 'Absolutely, we dont believe in war, We are trying to make an honest living by reading the Bible and saving many others who are the victims of Capitalism.'" Augoustos added "I told them that I would try to attend other meetings because I was very much interested."[26]

One of the Justice Department's most prolific informants was Werner Hanni, whose reports of his investigations of midwestern ministers provide perhaps the best understanding of the methods and ideology of the government informer. Hanni, who could converse in German as well as English, had been born in Berne, Switzerland, in 1892, had migrated to the United States in 1913, and had joined the Justice Department in 1916. Hanni's supervisor was Marshal Eberstein, agent in charge in Omaha, and many of Eberstein's reports contain narratives from Hanni.[27] Several times, Hanni reported on church services he had attended, as in the summer of 1917 when he recounted his experience at a service in Crete, Nebraska: "I attended the morning sermon of the Rev. Schrein held in the German language. He was preaching purely out of the Bible and he had no political remarks in his sermon. He also had the sermon well prepared and I entered the church as a perfect stranger and I could tell that he had no other sermon prepared. . . . Schrein appears to be a good man."[28] That same summer, Hanni recorded his observations of another Nebraska pastor: "Batzle preaches in English and the members of the church as well as he are Americans. . . . The pulpit is covered with the Stars and Stripes and the bible laying thereon. . . . Batzle is a young man and I do not believe that he ever said anything anti-American before his congregation. They are not Germans and they wouldn't stand for anything anti-American."[29] Later, in the spring of 1918, Hanni recounted yet another church service: "I attended

Ehgel's church for the German Lutherans last Sunday a week ago. The preaching was in English and no political remarks were made. Ehgel is German and I am told that he was born in this country. . . . I can say nothing against him and he is shrewd enough to keep within the law."[30]

On other occasions, Hanni tried to befriend a suspect minister and through casual conversation determine his attitude toward the war. In 1917 Hanni reported the views of Father Anton Link, a Catholic priest of Sidney, Nebraska: "[Link] is a man in the 30s and his church is composed of Germans, [I]rish and Americans. He preaches in English and gave a patriotic sermon a week ago today. . . . He gave me a warning to keep my mouth shut and told me not to tell anyone that I was not an American citizen. He had no bad words for America but hopes that America will gets things settled before her army gets over to the front. I went to see him telling him that I wanted to buy land that Father Lombardi in Blue Hill had told me that he would lend a Catholic a helping hand. Well I was a good Catholic and Father Link helped me in every way possible."[31] Hanni concluded that the patriotic tendencies of the congregation would help check any possible disloyalty on Link's part: "I believe that Linck is O K for more than half of his church here would not stand anti Americanism."[32] On one occasion, Hanni may have tried to entrap a pastor into making seditious comments:

> I met Rev. Kloeckner at his home and had a conversation with him. Kloeckner was willing to help me out and called several farmers on the telephone to find work for me on a farm with a German farmer. . . . [he] noticed that I was wearing a "Iron Cross" ring and he says "take that off, this country is at war with Germany and it is against the law. We Germans have to be careful now and have to obey the law. You better take that ring off or else you will get in trouble." I told Kloeckner that there is nothing wrong with the ring and that the money I paid for the ring went to the German Red Cross but of course the Americans now say that the money so collected was being used for German propaganda. To this Koeckner said the words "Oh yes." I could not get anything further out of him and really do not believe that the man is a rank pro-German.[33]

Hanni believed that cultural pluralism threatened national unity. In January 1918, Hanni, working undercover, met with Rev. H. Athrop of South Dakota for several hours, afterward reporting that the minister thought that the United States had entered the war for financial reasons. Pastor Athrop's taste in literature was likewise suspect, for "he has German books, written by Proffessors of the Minnesota Lutheran synode, dealing with the teaching of Luther and in these books, there are remarks that are absolutely not fit to be brought to the American people while this country is in war with England against Germany." Those such as Athrop endangered American society because they kept the next generation from assimilating. Athrop, wrote Hanni, "has a little girl that cannot speak english but speaks good german."[34]

Hanni didn't see anything wrong with breaking and entering a suspect's residence. Seeking information on a Reverend Huebner, Hanni went to the pastor's church, at Emerald, Nebraska, but finding him absent, "then made sure that nobody could see me and tried to enter the house, knowing that the preacher is an alien enemy." Apparently having trouble gaining entrance ("the door's, however were all locked and the windows also and screens on each window, which were fastened from the inside"), Hanni set off on foot to town. A passing motorist (who turned out to be Huebner) offered a ride to Hanni, who repaid him by reporting the pastor as disloyal. As evidence, Hanni offered the following: "We talked about the war, and <u>Huebner</u> says, 'we Germans, especially if we are not American citizens have to be very careful now. The U.S.A. government cannot expect from us alien enemies to be loyal to America nor can the German government expect from the Americans that are in Germany expect to be loyal to Germany.' This statement means the same as [if] he would say 'as an alien enemy I am not loyal to the U.S. Government, I am loyal to Austria.'"[35]

Sometimes, Hanni's attendance at sermons resulted in unpleasant consequences for the preacher. After listening to a pastor in Lincoln, Nebraska, Hanni reported the following: "I kept my promise to Rev. Matenzer today and attended his sermon which was held in the German language. Again Matenzer discussed the present crisis and through his words had the women crying and had the men silent and attentive. Remarkable is how he stirred up the people in his church with the following remarks out of his sermon. 'The administration has forced the law of universal military service. Soon your sons will have to go to Europe to be used by the French and English as cannon fodder against Germany. Your sons will have to take the places of the black hordes from Africa and the Indians from India occupied for France and England.'" Hanni talked briefly to the minister, "but didnt ask him whether he is a citizen or not. It would have drawn suspicion after such a sermon."[36] Hanni's report probably explains why the U.S. attorney for

Nebraska, Thomas Allen, called Rev. Matenzer in for a discussion later that month in which "Mr Allen convinced Rev Matzner that it would be far better to forego any more attacks on the Government."[37]

Hanni's investigations appear to have contributed to the internment of two unnaturalized German-born immigrant ministers, William Krauleidis of Nebraska and Paul Hempel of South Dakota. Before calling on Rev. Krauleidis, Hanni conducted some background inquiries. He visited a Mrs. Grassmeier, who maintained that the minister was a German sympathizer who had been in contact with Johann Bernstorff (the former German ambassador to the United States) and that Krauleidis had stated that he had transmitted funds to Germany. Hanni then called on Krauleidis, seeking to win the minister's sympathy ("After telling him all my misfortunes . . ."). Hanni reported that Krauleidis was an enemy alien who kept a firearm (under federal regulations, enemy aliens were barred from possessing such weapons). Furthermore, Hanni wrote, Krauleidis had "told me if some of those crazy Americans came around his house again like they did when they raised the flag on the church, that he was going to shoot."[38] In response to a query from U.S. attorney Thomas Allen about Krauleidis, the Justice Department in Washington advised that if the minister had a gun, he should be arrested.[39]

Krauleidis was arrested by a deputy U.S. marshal and taken to Grand Island, Nebraska.[40] In response, members of his church filed a petition of protest with the Justice Department. Acknowledging that Krauleidis owned a gun, the petitioners asserted that the pastor had been the target of recent harassment and had expressed concern about his personal safety. Allegations that the minister had used his church to spread propaganda were wrong, as "services in our church are and have always been confined to things spiritual and to an interpretation of the scripture, and political matters are never discussed."[41] The petition had little effect on Thomas Allen, who, in a letter to the attorney general, asserted "everyone who signed his petition is a member of his church and presumably in sympathy with his views." Allen noted that special agent Marshal Eberstein felt that internment was appropriate in this case, writing, "it is Mr. Eberstein's idea that an example should be made of this man's conduct for the effect it will have on the large number of other German Lutheran ministers in the state who have been exceedingly pro German since war was declared." Allen himself recommended internment for similar reasons: "I believe it will have a salutary effect on the large German Lutheran population in this state." Krauleidis was not released from his internment until after the conclusion of the war.[42]

After some inquiry, Hanni characterized the Reverend Paul Hempel of South Dakota as a threat to the American political fabric. "I knocked at the door of Rev. Hempel's residence Monday evening," recounted Hanni, "after having made a three mile walk, and asked to get a cup of hot coffee. Mrs Hempel invited me in and I had a good supper." Hanni claimed that while visiting he learned that pastor Hempel was spreading disloyalty among the faithful: "Hempel admitts that he is anti-American and he is giving the people of his congregation false news and brands the American newspaper reports as lies. . . . He is mis-informing the people, makes the people turn against the U.S. Government and praises everything from and made in Germany." Hanni forecast that Hempel's disloyalty could have lasting repercussions: "Hempel has four children all of them born in America. How shall they become Americans? They go to the German school, learn and hear nothing else but pro-Germanism."[43] Reverend Hempel was subsequently interned in January 1918.[44] For Hanni, cultural assimilation was a necessary component of patriotism.

Hanni also played a key role in securing an indictment against William Windolph, a Catholic priest in Creighton, Nebraska. Masquerading as a salesman for a newspaper, Hanni visited Windolph. The two men then fell into a conversation about the war, and Hanni reported the priest as saying that: "The american government is rotten and the officers from the president down are not honest." Windolph, wrote Hanni, thought that the American people as a whole lacked integrity and believed that the war effort was crippled by greed and graft—notions that were all the more dangerous, given the priest's tremendous influence: "Father Windolph is a powerful man in this town and he has succeeded in making many of the Irish people of his church disloyal." Hanni's allegations were included in an indictment charging Father Windolph with violation of the Espionage Act.[45]

Hanni himself worried that others in the Justice Department were insufficiently zealous in pursuing disloyalty. In November 1918 Hanni traveled to Minnesota to follow a lead on a "suspected Pro-German." Stopping by the St. Paul office on 8 November, he conferred with the local agent in charge, T. E. Campbell. The conversation that transpired was apparently so upsetting to Hanni that he felt impelled to write a letter describing the encounter to John F. McAuley, agent in charge at Sioux Falls, South Dakota. Hanni reported that Campbell regarded him as something of an interloper: "I informed him that I am an under-cover man and working out of the Omaha Division and at present was sent to South Dakota to work out of that office investigating Pro-German matters and suspected Violations of the Espionage act. Mr. Campbell to this replied, well you tell your damn Agent in Charge in Sioux Falls to keep his men in his own field and to not come and interfere in my territory."

Campbell further said that pursuing the particular case that Hanni was investigating was almost certainly a waste of time: "Mr. Campbell then stated that there are people from all over the world coming to Rochester and you are on a wild goose chase. . . . We get piles of such reports like you have there and we don't investigate we simply write back and ask for evidence if they fail to give any we are through with the case. 99% of these reports coming in of suspected German spies and Pro-German activities there is nothing to it, there are no German spies in this part of the country and even if there were, I can give a German spy work in this office and he cant harm the Government in no way. All we got out here is Pro-German propaganda but that does not harm."

Campbell added that inquiries into visa applicants could be handled with a minimum of effort: "The Visa-Investigations we dont investigate by sending an Agent to the places, the girl here in the office is doing all that over the telephone and that is sufficient." Hanni took issue with Campbell's approach: "I don't agree with Mr. Campbell in how things ought to be worked." In Hanni's view, national security could be achieved only through intensive policing: "In regard to Visa-Investigations I am convinced that this is a matter that should be toroghly investigated, it is a matter vital to the Nation and failure of proper investigation may result disasterous to the United States. History shows that in no country have the natives been the ruin of a nation, they were foreigners in all cases. Pro-German reports also ought to be investigated as I think and know that Propaganda is as dangerous as a Spy!" Whether or not Hanni was accurately representing Campbell's perspective is open to question. It is easy to believe that Campbell, presumably inundated with unverifiable reports of subversion, had adopted a skeptical attitude toward such allegations, but it is also possible that Hanni, having incurred the anger of an agent in charge, was seeking to protect himself by depicting Campbell as complacent about German disloyalty. Hanni's letter also reveals his insecurities as an immigrant who was not accorded the white-skin privilege to which he felt entitled. He complained that "All this talk on side of Mr. Campbell was spoken in a tun something like a man would talk to a convict or cattle and believe me he was talking in earnest and I did not care to remain there any longer. I considered myself a white man and I would like to be talked to like man talk to man!"[46] Hanni, of course, could prove his faith in America by informing on supposedly disloyal immigrants.

In a similar episode the following spring, Hanni alleged that another higher-ranking Justice Department official had perhaps lacked wholehearted devotion to the task of rooting out subversion. In April 1919, Hanni, worried about the possibility of being laid off, sought assistance from his previous superior, Marshal Eberstein, now the police chief of Omaha. In a letter to Eberstein, Hanni complained that James H. Daly, the current agent in charge in Omaha, had been looking for a reason to push Hanni out of the department. Furthermore, Hanni appeared to suggest that Daly had had little interest in rooting out wartime disloyalty in the Catholic church: "Mr. Daly has no good reasons to act towards me as he does. The only reasons he has are, FOR I FAILED TO SHIELD THE CATHOLIC ELEMENT THAT HAS BEEN PRO-GERMAN DURING THE WAR and for the letter I wrote to Mr. McAuley about my conversation with Mr. Campbell St. Paul." Daly, wrote Hanni, "believes in 'my church first and then my country.' I am strongly inclined to believe that he even pledged to the catholic element of Nebraska and to Mr. Campbell to use all his power to get me out of the service."[47]

Hanni's distrust of Catholicism may have been rooted in his immigrant background—his native canton, Berne, was majority Protestant, and animosity toward the Catholic church was common in nineteenth-century Switzerland. More specifically, Hanni's fear that Daly was placing his religious loyalties above his national allegiances may have been a reflection of the political experience of Switzerland, where in the nineteenth century the civil authorities had sought to exert more influence on and limit the power of the Catholic church. Such efforts, dubbed the *Kulturkampf* (or struggle for civilization), roused the ire of many Swiss Catholics, and the resulting conflict, lasting from around 1870 into the first half of the 1880s, was especially heated in the canton of Berne. Perhaps Hanni saw himself as a participant in an American *Kulturkampf* and thought that his efforts to corral clergymen—especially Catholic ones—was contributing to the proper ascendancy of governmental over religious authority.[48]

In Maryland, investigator Alex Vonnegut went undercover to find out more about Julius Hofmann, the German-born pastor of Zion Lutheran Church in Baltimore. A member of the National German-American Alliance, Hofmann had tried to assist Germany during the period of

American neutrality, at one point authorizing the use of a church building by the German-Austrian Red Cross Aid Society.[49] In 1918 Vonnegut, working undercover, sought to sound out the pastor's views on the
war. That August, Vonnegut ran into the minister in a tavern, where the
two talked at length (they had met previously). In his report, Vonnegut
described a pastor who admired autocratic leaders and vigorous, manly
governments. Hofmann, he wrote, "believes in Monarchy and he himself is a Monarch." Hofmann's esteem for forceful chief executives even
extended to former president Theodore Roosevelt, for the pastor "sees
in T. R. the ideal man, the big Super-Man, the student of Nietsche who
should be the next President because he incorporates all that is ideal in
Monarchy." To draw out the minister, Vonnegut alluded to the Indian
writer Rabindranath Tagore's critique of potent national governments.
Acknowledging that such a stance had its merits, Hofmann asserted
"that man does not live in the spirit only, and that so long as man was
the brute that he always has been he must see to it that his Nation is
strong and Powerful." Later that night, Vonnegut and a mutual doctor
acquaintance accompanied Hofmann to his residence. In his report,
the detective praised the pastor's taste in interior decoration ("his home
is not a pretentious one, but very comfortably and beautifully furnished.
The man has a fine sense of the beautiful. No nick-nacks, nor Mid-
Victorian suggestions,"), but did note that "a large picture of Bismark
and Beethoven are the most conspicuous things on the walls." Characterizing the pastor as a "Jekyel & Hyde" figure, Vonnegut promised to
maintain contact with Hofmann, a "diabilically clever" man who held
"undisputed sway over his large congregation," and expressed his confidence that Hofmann is in "touch with the German agents in this
country."[50]

However, a subsequent visit with the Hofmann family turned up
little that was actionable. Vonnegut noted that while Hofmann's wife appeared to think that Germany's invasion of Belgium was legitimate, his
"daughter (about 17 years) seems to waste no love on Germany." The
pastor himself "had nothing but most outspoken praise for the President, whom he regards as the AUTOCRAT OF AUTOCRATS. That he 'is'
an autocrat pleases him immensely because he believes in AUTOCRACY.
Over and over again he mumbled smilingly to himself that Wilson is extremely clever." Such a position would, of course, have helped to inoculate the pastor against charges of disloyalty.[51]

The APL, too, participated in an undercover inquiry, taking a leading role in investigating Rev. Albert Theodore Beussel, a German immigrant pastor of a Lutheran church in Bristol, Connecticut. In this particular case, it does appear that the pastor had some degree of sympathy for his native land. In 1914 Beussel had been visiting Germany, and in late July departed to return to America. While his ship was at sea, the European war had broken out, and after he had arrived back in Connecticut, the *Hartford Courant* devoted an article to his voyage home and to his observations about the conflict. "The entire tone of the pastor," noted the *Courant*, "was one of resignation to the war, mingled with an intense feeling for his country in its fight." Whatever his feelings for the land of his birth, pastor Beussel had become a naturalized American in October 1916 and, by his own later admission, cast a ballot for Republican Charles Evans Hughes in the presidential election the following month.[52]

It was due to the APL's efforts that Beussel was convicted of violating of the amended Espionage Act in July 1918. At Beussel's trial, three witnesses played key roles for the prosecution: Leonore Murphy, Marie Kerr, and (probably to a lesser extent) her husband William Kerr. Marie and William Kerr had lived in the same building as the pastor, and the pastor and Marie had become acquainted, while Leonore Murphy, described in the press as "a young woman of striking appearance," was a paid informant for the APL. On 23 May 1918, pastor Beussel, Marie Kerr, and Leonore Murphy had dined together at the Heublein Hotel restaurant in Hartford. At the subsequent trial, Kerr and Murphy both testified that at this dinner, the pastor had asserted that American servicemen lacked loyalty and had mercenary tendencies. Four days after the dinner at the Heublein, on the 27th, Beussel was invited over to the Kerrs', where he met with Leonore Murphy, as well as with Marie and William Kerr. At the trial, Ms. Murphy recalled that on this latter occasion Beussel had derided the Allied military leadership and had objected to the efforts of the Red Cross, while Mrs. Kerr remembered that the pastor had praised the German nation and had described the American entrance into the conflict as unwarranted. Mr. Kerr alleged that the pastor had been dismissive of the Red Cross.[53]

Both the gatherings of the 23rd and 27th appear to have been arranged in advance by the APL with the intention of gathering information on the pastor. APL official Major Clarence Woodruff, testifying at the trial, took responsibility for the investigation into the pastor.

According to the *Hartford Courant* reporter covering the proceedings, Major Woodruff "said that he had heard rumors of Buessel's alleged disloyalty, and had arranged to have Miss Murphy pose as Mrs. Kerr's guest in order that she might investigate the case."[54] On the witness stand, Beussel stated that he had become intoxicated at the Heublein Hotel restaurant, and as a result couldn't recall what had happened or what he had said; he further testified that he had consumed four glasses of wine at the party at the Kerrs' and that he lacked more than a few memories of that night as well.[55] In his summation, the defense attorney argued that his client had been entrapped by the American Protective League, by Marie Kerr, and by Leonore Murphy. Asserting that at one point Murphy had prepared a drink for the pastor, the attorney acidly observed that "when a man can drink an old fashioned whiskey cocktail, on an empty stomach, and mixed by someone who wants to get him, he must be a man of some experience."[56] The jury returned a verdict of guilty, and the judge, declaring pastor Beussel to be a "counterfeit citizen," sentenced him to ten years in the federal prison in Atlanta, Georgia.[57]

Werner Hanni continued his work for the Bureau of Investigation after the war. In 1919 he became a special employee, in 1921 he was appointed to the position of special agent, and in 1923 he became the special agent in charge of the bureau office in Sioux Falls, South Dakota. He eventually served as special agent in charge in Minneapolis, in St. Paul, and in Omaha, retiring from the FBI in 1954 at the age of sixty-one.[58] Alex Vonnegut seems to have had second thoughts about the usefulness of his wartime service. The novelist Kurt Vonnegut recalled that his Uncle Alex "told me one time that he had been an American spy in Baltimore during the First World War, befriending German-Americans there. His assignment was to detect enemy agents. He detected nothing, for there was nothing to detect."[59]

Following the armistice in November 1918, the Justice Department's leadership gradually lost interest in prosecuting opponents of the war, although investigations continued. In Texas, Justice Department special agent V. L. Snyder inquired into allegations that a Methodist minister, the Reverend John Pluenneke of Seguin, was disloyal. After interviewing a number of local residents who asserted that Pluenneke favored the German cause and had been a source of pro-German statements, Snyder called on Rev. Pluenneke and conducted the following interrogation: "Agent went to the home of subject and asked subject why he thought we should hang our heads in shame on the day that peace was signed. He said that his reasons for stating this was that on account that we had no business to enter this horrible war. Agent also asked subject why he made the statement that we did not enter this war until it touched our pocketbook. He could not give any satisfactory explanation why he made this statement, only he believed that our politicians who were at the head of our Government were controlled by money power." The agent engaged the minister in a discussion of the morality of German military methods, asking "if he did not think Germany had conducted the war in a barbarous way, especially in their introducing poisonous gas on unprotected soldiers and also in regard to their unrestricted submarine warfare on unarmed merchant and passenger ships."[60]

Three days later, on orders from U.S. attorney Hugh Robertson, Pluenneke was arrested for violation of the amended Espionage Act.[61] Subsequently, the church stewards asked Pluenneke to step down from his job as pastor. On 14 December 1918, Robertson wrote the attorney general asking if Pluenneke's case should be taken before a grand jury. Although the war had been over for more than a month, Robertson was still concerned about the authority Pluenneke might exert over the townspeople. "Seguin," he wrote, "is what might be described as a German community. Pluenneke, by reason of his being pastor of perhaps the largest church there, exercises considerable influence." John Lord O'Brian replied with a letter recommending against further pursuing legal action, "as, in view of the armistice, it is difficult to make the facts fit into the intents and purposes against which the Espionage Act is directed." O'Brian added, "The Department does not absolutely object to your going ahead if that be your preference, but all in all deems it not a case for further prosecution."[62] Unfortunately, O'Brian's letter, dated 26 December, proved immaterial, for on 16 December 1918, Rev. Pluenneke had killed himself.[63]

The Justice Department's badgering of supposedly disloyal clergymen violated First Amendment guarantees of speech and of religious freedom. Many investigators believed that churches should serve as auxiliaries to the government, while some detectives viewed immigrants as a potential threat to national unity. The nativist fears of Werner Hanni were echoed by some Justice Department officials over the potential disloyalty of Lutheran congregations of German descent.

These wartime inquiries were an outgrowth of longstanding fears that the Catholics' loyalty to the pope compromised their allegiance to America. Special agent Ralph Izard's worry that Father Pop of Aurora,

Illinois, sought to hinder the assimilation of his congregation, echoed, in diluted form, the charges made by the Know-Nothings of the mid-nineteenth century. However, the willingness of investigators to turn to the Catholic hierarchy for help indicates that some investigators viewed disloyal priests as renegades that could be corralled with the assistance of Church leadership. From the perspective of these detectives, the supposed disloyalty of some Catholic clergy was rooted in ethnic bonds rather than fealty to the Vatican.

The pressures exerted by the Justice Department pushed churches toward a policy of assimilation. The Catholic Church's attitude to Americanization, for example, changed a great deal during and after the First World War. Before the war, the clergy generally viewed assimilation as a natural consequence of immigration but did not believe that concerted efforts were necessary to accelerate the process. However, during and after the war there was an increased attempt by the Catholic hierarchy and organizations to foster assimilation of the immigrant.[64] Similarly, the years after the war saw a fairly quick abandonment of the German language in the Missouri Synod of the Lutheran Church.[65] To a large extent, the pressure for churches to assimilate culturally came from local or state governments or from patriotic organizations. But the Justice Department's investigations of ministers certainly contributed to this pressure for cultural homogenization.

4

⮿

Policing the Left

During the First World War, the Justice Department went to war against American radicalism. Before 1917, the chief repressors of left-wing movements had been local governments and the private sector. Local law-enforcement agencies had long harassed radicals and labor organizers, while employers had hired private security firms to investigate and undermine unions. But with the advent of war in 1917, the responsibility of containing the Left shifted to some extent from local authorities and private detective agencies to the federal government.

Outspoken Socialist opposition to American intervention in the conflict brought down the wrath of federal prosecutors and investigators on the party. The department was also hostile to some of organized labor's demands during the war and bore a special animus toward the radical union the Industrial Workers of the World (IWW). The department's prosecutions of Socialist Party and IWW members have received a good deal of coverage from historians, but in addition to these very public activities, the Justice Department waged a covert campaign of intimidation against Socialists and radical labor activists that helped undermine two of the bastions of the prewar Left.

Although, as a whole the department remained hostile toward Socialists and radicals, the reports filed by investigators reveal a diversity of opinions in the department in regards to radicalism. Some detectives believed that any criticism of the nation's political and economic system, by undermining support for the government, deserved censure. Yet other investigators were tolerant of the Left, some detectives believing that the expression of Socialist ideas did not necessarily threaten the war effort, and with some prosecutors and investigators expressing sympathy to the cause of organized labor. The reports of various Justice Department investigators also reveal that its animosity toward the Left was bound up with long-standing fears that immigrants were subversive. The federalization of this nativism paved the way for the department's postwar efforts, under Attorney General A. Mitchell Palmer, to deport radical immigrants.

Since its founding in 1901, the American Socialist Party had enjoyed substantial success in attracting adherents and in building an organization. Socialists were elected mayor of cities across the country, from Butte, Montana, to Minneapolis, Minnesota, to Star City, West Virginia.[1] Oklahoma was in the vanguard of the movement; in 1914 Sooner voters elected more than 160 Socialist candidates to positions in local or county government, while the party's candidate for governor won more than a fifth of the statewide vote.[2] Milwaukee in 1910 and New York City in 1914 and 1916 had sent Socialists to the U.S. House of Representatives. In 1912 the party's candidate for president, Eugene V. Debs of Indiana, won roughly 6 percent of the national vote.[3]

From 1914 to 1917 American Socialists were steadfast in their opposition to military involvement in the European crisis, and focused their efforts on keeping America from getting drawn in to the conflict. As the likelihood of American intervention increased in early 1917, the party scheduled an emergency convention in St. Louis. Before the conferees had even had a chance to meet, however, Congress had already acceded to Wilson's call for a declaration of war against Germany. Undeterred, the Socialist convention drew up a platform harshly critical of the decision for war.[4] American intervention in the conflict, it declared, was not on behalf of democratic government but "was instigated by the predatory capitalists in the United States who boast of the enormous profit of $7,000,000,000 from the manufacture and sale of munitions and war supplies and from the exportation of American foodstuffs and other necessaries."[5]

The St. Louis platform appealed to many Americans who were reluctant to go to war, and elections over the course of 1917 suggest that a substantial number of voters, many of whom otherwise did not consider themselves Socialist, cast their ballots for the party as a protest against the war and its accompanying intolerance. In numerous local contests, the Socialist vote rocketed upward. In 1916 the Socialists of

Dayton, Ohio, had won 6.5 percent of the vote, but in 1917 that percentage shot to 44 percent, while in Rockford, Illinois, the Socialist vote more than quadrupled, from 7 to 29.8 percent. In Eureka, Utah, the Socialist percentage of the ballots cast increased from 6.9 to 36.4 percent.[6] The 1917 New York City mayoral race likewise demonstrated the breadth of the party's appeal. The Socialist candidate, Morris Hillquit, eschewed the opportunity to buy war loans and attacked the wartime suppression of dissent. Incumbent mayor John P. Mitchel, running as an independent, depicted himself as the patriotic candidate in the race and his campaign (as did some of the city's newspapers) attacked Hillquit as disloyal. Tammany Hall's nominee, John Hylan, received the enthusiastic support of the isolationist press baron William Randolph Hearst, a fact that likewise opened Hylan up to charges of disloyalty. Nonetheless, on election day, the supposedly treasonous Hillquit garnered more than a fifth of the ballots cast, the allegedly disloyal Hylan sailed to victory, and the nationalistic Mitchel went down to defeat.[7]

Over the course of 1917 the Justice Department indicted many Socialists, and the success of the party at the polls only strengthened the desire of prosecutors to target Socialists and like-minded people. Indeed, the spring and summer of 1918 saw charges filed against several Socialist leaders.[8] In March 1918 prosecutors announced that they had indicted former congressman Victor Berger of Wisconsin (as well as four other Socialists) on Espionage Act charges. The indictments were made public less than two weeks before a special election to fill a U.S. Senate seat in which Berger was the Socialist candidate. Prosecutors indicted him again shortly before the November elections, in which Berger was running for the House of Representatives.[9]

While the Justice Department put leading Socialists on trial, it was simply not possible to do the same to all of their followers. Thus, prosecutions were reinforced by a campaign, much less publicly evident, of intimidation against citizens of a Socialistic bent. In Syracuse, New York, investigator James C. Tormey and assistant U.S. attorney Frank J. Cregg jointly issued a warning to an Otto Nachant, believed to have expressed "radical statements" and to have derided Woodrow Wilson. Tormey reported that Nachant "was later brought to the Court House when Mr. Cregg and myself questioned him and gave him some fatherly advice which will have the desired effect." Under questioning, Nachant confessed something of an adherence to Socialism and to having called the president "a son of a b—."[10] A passenger on a Milwaukee streetcar who challenged the legality of U.S. involvement in the war and who suggested that Wilson had entered the war on behalf of Allied nations and capital was overheard by investigator John E. Ferris, who told him to appear for a meeting two days later. At this later conference, Ferris "outlined the system that the German Government has employed to embarrass the U.S. government through the spread of socialism in this country."[11] In September 1918, Robert Gilmore, an employee at an East Liverpool, Ohio, pottery and a suspected adherent of left-wing ideas, was charged in Cleveland with having violated the Espionage Act. The Justice Department, however, apparently concluded that Gilmore was not mentally sound and quickly allowed him to return home. The special agent handling the matter seems to have thought it unlikely that the case would come to trial. He concluded his report not only by admonishing and advising the suspect but also by securing an agreement from Gilmore to report back to him regularly in hopes of helping him "reform" his ways:

> Subject was released . . . and was taken to the Penn. R.R., where ticket was purchased by Subject for East Liverpool in presence of Agent. Subject was cautioned by Agent that he should give up his Socialist tendencies; not to associate with any Socialists whatever or men or like ideas; to give up his position at the pottery and work on his farm . . . which has enough potatoes, corn, etc. to demand Subject's attention. Subject admitted to Agent that he had been the tool of the Socialist Party in East Liverpool and that they had used him as a means of furthering their propaganda, etc., and that he saw the error of his ways. . . . Subject agreed to write Agent at least once a month and keep Agent informed regarding his health, occupation, etc. It was clearly stated to Subject that this Department is as desirous of making good citizens of persons who have been in error and wish to reform their ways, as the Department is desirous of apprehending the enemies of this country. Case closed.

In Philadelphia, investigator Todd Daniel interviewed a man suspected of disloyal speech and found him to be "a Socialist." The man "denied, emphatically, having said, 'To Hell with the President, he ought to be done away with.'" Daniel, though "inclined to believe that he perhaps never made this statement," issued a remonstrance: "I admonished the defendant that he should not be free in his conversation at the present time in enunciating revolutionary principles as he would find himself without the law and in jail before he knew it."[12]

Ironically, if department officials had shown more acceptance of Socialists (or at least had recognized that Socialists were not devotees of the kaiser) the foreign policy objectives of the Wilson administration would have been better served. Indeed, in late 1917 and early 1918, some Socialists gradually came to appreciate aspects of the president's approach to world affairs. Wilson's Fourteen Points speech of January 1918, with its call for a just and equitable postwar settlement, won sympathetic reviews from many on the Left, including Morris Hillquit and Eugene Debs. Events in Russia, too, had caused many party members to reconsider their opposition to the war. Socialists celebrated the triumph of the Bolshevik revolution in November 1917; the German resumption of offensive operations against the new Soviet regime the following February demonstrated that Germany's imperial ambitions in eastern Europe stood in the way of peace.[13]

Some investigators seem to have realized that Socialists were not necessarily supporters of the German cause. In examining allegations of German sympathies against a Herman Hanemann of New Jersey, investigator John S. Read found that Hanemann, an adherent of Socialism, also was "an admirer of <u>Liebkneckt</u> [*sic*] and a hater of the Kaiser and Junkerthum in general." Hanemann admitted to having been sympathetic to Germany in the period of American neutrality, and said that he now wished that Germany would lose. Noting that the original allegation was somewhat vague in nature ("with nothing specific to back it up") and that Hanemann had financially contributed to the war effort, Read decided "this man was evidently loyal enough."[14] In covering a Carnegie Hall gathering by the Friends of the Russian Revolution, investigator Joseph F. Kropidlowski observed that one orator's presentation "was loyal throughout as far as this Government was concerned, it being directed more against capitalism than anything else."[15]

In Butte, Montana, investigator E. W. Byrn Jr., thinking that those who advocated domestic reform did not necessarily embrace the nation's foreign foes, discounted a report to the effect that an Edward Ladendorff was engaged in espionage and had expressed himself disloyally. Ladendorff was indeed "a radical Socialist" who "has indulged in a good deal of talk both before and since this country entered the war" reported Byrn, who added that "the talk being aimed not so much in favor of any of this Country's enemies as it was opposed to the existing order of things and in favor of a Socialist commune." Thus, concluded Byrn, "From personal knowledge of this man's activities, I do not feel that he is a particular menace at this time, or that he is in any way connected with the German Government or the German propaganda."[16] Byrn's tolerance for Socialism may have been explained in part by his distrust of corporations. He believed, for example, that Congresswoman Jeannette Rankin, a progressive Republican, was a target of the state's mining firms. Rankin, Byrn observed, was having a hard time obtaining venues for her appearances on behalf of war bonds. The U.S. attorney for Montana, Burton K. Wheeler, himself a progressive and thinking the matter worthy of inquiry, set up and attended a conference between Byrn and Rankin, where Rankin asserted that her efforts to boost war bonds by making public appearances across the state had encountered numerous roadblocks, including resistance from war bond organization officials. After the interview, Byrn concluded that the "whole chain of events impresses me as a political effort to discredit Miss Rankin for the reason that she has seen fit to antagonize the large copper companies of this State who have heretofore, controlled most of the politics in the State and are now making a desperate effort to maintain that control."[17]

Other investigators were not tolerant of socialism. Even voting for a Socialist candidate could lead to censure. In Menomonie, Wisconsin, Willard N. Parker investigated a Martin Krogstad, an interim postal employee, on allegations of having spoken out against the war. During questioning, Krogstad presented himself as a moderate Socialist, as he "disclaimed any belief in anarchy, and emphasized the fact that his Socialism meant only government ownership of government utilities." Believing that Krogstad had cast his ballot in support of Socialist Victor Berger, Parker characterized the postal worker's views as beyond the pale: "in the judgment of Agent, no man can vote for Berger, as subject did, and be considered a loyal citizen." Parker recommended to the postmaster that Krogstad be fired, and "gave subject, Krogstad, to understand that his conduct in the future would be watched with care by the United States government."[18]

Even those Socialists who rejoiced over the downfall of Germany's militaristic regime in November 1918 could run afoul of the Justice Department. In Missouri, investigator Fred Dunn examined the case of a Walter Brown, who had displayed a red flag before his shop to celebrate the end of the war. When interviewed, Brown acknowledged having been a member of the Socialist movement and noted that the red banner reflected the collapse of the German monarch and the advent of socialism in Germany. Indeed, the results of Dunn's inquiry suggested that

Brown had been celebrating the role played by the German Left in the collapse of the kaiser's regime. A local retailer asserted that on the day of the armistice, Brown, in purchasing some red fabric, had declared, "We beat the American Boys to it just a little." The retailer "stated Sub-ject [Brown] referred to the fact that the Germans had surrendered to the Socialist party." A deputy night marshal testified that Brown, after being warned that a display of the red banner might cause problems, had responded, "No I won't do it, they won't cause any trouble when they understood it,—That's the flag the Germans surrendered under." Dunn also interviewed two locals who testified that Brown had stated on Armistice Day, "Every time I see the Stars and Stripes, my bowels want to move, and I've got to go now." Dunn concluded that Brown's "inter-est centers in the Socialist Party and the Red Flag, and values these more than our Country and our flag."[19] Thus, in the eyes of Dunn, what Brown himself thought of the war was of secondary significance; more importantly, he rejected patriotism in favor of Socialism. In short, Brown's public rejoicing over the defeat of Germany was for the wrong reasons, and the assistant U.S. attorney concluded that Brown merited prosecution under the amended Espionage Act. The attorney general's response to the prosecutor's request to pursue the case revealed a some-what greater tolerance for Socialism. Thomas Watt Gregory, while con-tending that Brown's denigration of the flag was illegal ("remarks about stars and stripes if shown by clear and credible proof would constitute violation that clause amended section relating to bringing flag into dis-repute etc."), added that "your observations concerning Socialists and red flag irrelevant."[20] Had the department as a whole shown more tol-erance toward Socialists, many in the party might have been willing to support Wilson, or at the least, temper their criticism of his foreign pol-icy. Indeed, the department's continued prosecutions and harassment alienated many on the Left who otherwise might have come around to supporting the war effort.

As with other groups, investigators went undercover to solicit the opinions of suspected leftists regarding the war. In San Francisco, inves-tigator S. J. Adams called on a Henry Gross, a shoemaker, hoping to test allegations that Gross was disloyal. Adams visited Gross's shop (the two men were acquainted with one another), and, striking up a conversation, "started to talk to him casually and finally drifted on to the subject of the War." Although Gross's "inclinations seemed to be towards favoring the United States Government and during the conversations he stated that he hoped that Uncle Sam would win this war," Adams was convinced that this was something of a facade: "I am sure that he is a radical So-cilaist and is simply keeping back from expressing himself in general or in the open for fear that he may get into trouble."[21]

In addition, the department monitored speeches and rallies that es-poused general left causes. Journalist Lincoln Steffens came under ob-servation, with investigators monitoring talks he gave in Chicago on events in Russia.[22] Informant Henry J. Lenon attended a Pittsburgh rally in support of labor activist Thomas Mooney, who was then facing the death penalty for his alleged role in the 1916 bombing of a Prepar-edness Day march in San Francisco. The mere presence of Justice De-partment investigators, along with representatives of other law enforce-ment agencies, probably encouraged orators to moderate their rhetoric. An investigator who observed a similar pro-Mooney rally on the Boston Common suggested that the presence of law enforcement had a stifling effect: "according to informants in the bandstand, close to the speakers, the discovery of the presence of several men from this office, caused a change in the program and a curtailing of some of the subject matter which was to be included in the speeches."[23]

Anarchists, too, received the hostile attention of the department. In Paterson, New Jersey, investigator E. T. Drew was eager to find some-thing on local anarchist Firmino Gallo. Gallo had migrated to America from Italy more than a quarter century earlier. He ran a bookshop and frequented the local anarchist society, where his son, William, was a gui-tarist in the society's band. William later recalled his father as "a very quiet type" who "never sought publicity."[24] To Drew, however, "Gallo was the leader of a dangerous anarchistic group in Paterson" and "pos-sibly the 'brains' of the more recent propoganda."[25] Drew had Gallo charged with violation of the amended Espionage Act for allegedly hav-ing distributed literature excoriating the war and discouraging draft registration. In his report to the department, Drew characterized Gallo as "a dirty, sneaking cowardly Italian" who was ideologically poisoning the community: "Many young Italians . . . have become adherents of the No God-No Government anarchistic adicts through the reading matter which they have secured in his store."[26] The case went to trial in Newark; the jury could not agree on a verdict, and the case was dropped.[27]

During the First World War, the Justice Department tried to cripple the Industrial Workers of the World—the most prominent radical union in the country. Since its founding in 1905, the IWW had borne the reputation of being dangerously subversive. Calling on workers to struggle against their exploitation by employers, the IWW deemed nationalism and religion as blinders that kept workers from recognizing the brutality of capitalism. But none of these ideas constituted a violation of federal law, and before 1917, despite entreaties from employers and others, the Justice Department had not taken legal action against the union.[28] The response of some in the union to the congressional declaration of war in 1917 further heightened suspicion of the IWW. Many Wobblies remained unconvinced of the need for intervention in Europe, and the journal *Solidarity* advised that "All members of the I.W.W. who have been drafted should mark their claims for exemption, 'I.W.W.; opposed to war.'" However, the IWW does not appear to have engaged in widespread draft resistance. Although some members of the IWW refused military duty, "roughly 95 per cent of the eligible Wobblies registered with their draft boards, and most of those served when called," according to historian Melvyn Dubofsky, although he adds that "some apparently entered the service in the hope that they could foment anti-militarism from within."[29] At the same time, the department came under intense pressure from business interests to curb the union. Wobbly successes in instigating strikes in the western mining industry (in particular Montana and Arizona) and in the Pacific northwest logging industry helped generate gusts of protest from employers and politicians in those parts of the country.[30]

For his part, Thomas Watt Gregory ordered that investigations of the union be made a priority, and on 5 September 1917, Justice Department investigators, aided by local law enforcement agencies, raided Wobbly offices throughout the nation. Before the year was out, 165 members of the union would be indicted in federal court in Chicago.[31] The department's battle against the IWW, however, did not turn into a crusade against labor in general, in large part because the other leading union, the American Federation of Labor (AFL), openly supported the war effort. The British-born AFL chief Samuel Gompers had begun to favor the Allies during the period of American neutrality and in 1917 helped swing the leadership of his union into a firm commitment to assist the war effort. Too, the AFL's more moderate stance on labor issues in general, plus its budding alliance with the Democratic Party, made it less vulnerable to persecution during the war. For his part, John Lord O'Brian recognized Gompers's commitment to help win the war, and in the spring of 1917, publicly credited the AFL chief with having played a role in foiling a German-backed conspiracy to subsidize labor unrest in the United States. Before joining the department as assistant to the attorney general for war work in October 1917, O'Brian had been one of team of prosecutors who had charged German naval officer Franz Rintelen and others with having tried to block the shipment of munitions to the Allies during the period of American neutrality. The government maintained that Rintelen had sought to accomplish this goal by promoting worker discontent. At Rintelen's trial in May 1917, however, O'Brian declared that Gompers had helped to check the German's efforts to influence American workers.[32]

In any case, whatever the sentiments of the administration and of the top leadership of the Justice Department, the local offices of the department enjoyed a good deal of discretion in handling labor matters. When investigator John Dillon met with an Andy Shirlich, a union official who supposedly had been stoking unrest among Pennsylvania mineworkers, he learned of the difficulties mining families faced. The miners, Dillon wrote, lived in company housing, which, according to Shirlich, was unfitted for the harsh elements of wintertime. Dillon reported that mining families also had difficulty getting access to water: "They have only two wells for the entire colony and these are considerable distance from the homes, which makes it a hardship on the women folks to have to haul their own water for cooking and drinking purposes." By Shirlich's account, a group representing the mineworkers had simply asked for some amelioration of the housing situation and for the creation of new wells. "Agent spent considerable time with Shirlich," wrote Dillon, "and is of the opinion that this man is not engaged in any propaganda and is further of the opinion that the demands of these people are justified and will suggest, through the U.S. Attorney, that the Coal Company be advised to take steps to improve the living conditions for these people."[33]

Other detectives strove to maintain a neutral stance, as when two investigators in Connecticut refused to become involved in a potential labor dispute. When officials from two companies contacted the Justice Department, asserting that workers were contemplating a strike, the detectives responded by telling the businessmen that the department's hands were tied in the matter. As one of the investigators noted in his report, "as this was purely a buisness proposition, we could not take any action." Still, the two investigators advised the companies to keep the department apprised in the future of any improper actions by unnaturalized immigrants from enemy countries.[34] Indeed, efforts by employers to enlist federal help in smothering unions bred resentment in some quarters of the department. When a representative of the Panhandle Lumber Company in Idaho approached investigator F. A. Watt, complaining that operations at Panhandle had been shut down by the IWW, Watt "explained to him that the Government had nothing to do with strikes in local lumber mills and that no Federal Law had been made which could give him any relief." Watt bristled at the suggestion that the Justice Department should be called on support timber owners: "As a matter of fact, Agent is a little bit disgusted with the attitude of the lumber men of the Panhandle district; they seem to consider that because the United States is in the market for timber to build ships, that all they have to do is to simply close down their mills when a strike is talked about and let things rest until the Government wants the lumber, but just how they expect the Government to remedy conditions then, is more than Agent can comprehend."[35]

However, while some in the department were sympathetic toward the cause of labor (or were at least resistant to the entreaties of management), others believed that workers' loyalty to their union could come at the expense of patriotism. A Mobile, Alabama, shipyard worker, C. W. Vink, who supposedly had shown an unfriendly attitude toward a war bond march, was interviewed by investigator G. C. Outlaw. "From his manner of talking, and his general appearance and attitude," concluded the detective, "I would say that Vink is not a desirable citizen." To Outlaw, Vink's "whole tone in regard to the union shows that he holds the Union above every thing, even a mandate of the Government." Lacking a specific legal justification for driving Vink from his job, Outlaw decided to monitor him, "and at the first opportunity will remove him from the ship yards, when it can be done in such a manner as will not cause friction with the Union."[36]

Investigator E. J. Kerwin's inquiry into the activities of labor activists among rice workers near Stuttgart, Arkansas, demonstrated a similar hostility to organized labor. On 25 September 1917, Kerwin, on receiving a telephone report from Stuttgart's mayor that the IWW was causing problems, requested permission from his supervisor to visit the town. Before Kerwin received authorization, however, vigilantes struck. At about one o'clock on the morning of 26 September, four men who were in the town jail for union activities were abducted by a mob and were lashed, tarred, and feathered. Arriving in Stuttgart later that day,

Kerwin was told that a B. F. Sullivan had suggested that vigilantism would lead to retaliatory violence. According to one man Kerwin spoke with, Sullivan had stated the following on the morning of the 26th (a few hours after the labor organizers had been abducted): "<u>Just let them start their damn mobs around here; you know what we done to them in the West; there will soon be a bigger mob than that around here and get some of them. These god damn rice growers around here won't pay over 50 cents a day if they can get men to work for that.</u>" Words such as Sullivan's, Kerwin concluded, demanded a response: "something ought to be done with <u>B. F. Sullivan</u> at Stuttgart. He is one of these loud mouth agitators who do the harm; and while what he says is bad enough yet I do not believe he has courage enough himself to do anything, but with hundreds of laborers coming in there every day and the rice harvest a week off <u>Sullivan</u> will unwittingly or otherwise cause serious trouble by having others do in deed what he says by word of mouth."[37]

Some in the department tried to contain or halt strikes. When a possible work stoppage apparently loomed at a Philadelphia sugar plant, investigator J. F. McDevitt interviewed a number of workers and "explained to them the necessity of sugar production to the successful prosecution of the War." Although the workers proved to be "an ignorant, sullen lot" who "could hardly speak a word of English," McDevitt thought that his intervention "may have settled matters temporarily."[38]

Investigators used a variety of methods to discourage strikes. When workers struck at a Pennsylvania mine, investigator John Dillon, accompanied by another investigator, met with a union official, Paul Slimick, who "was advised to exert his influence to call this strike off." According to Dillon, the strikers were merely asking for a pay hike—and this had already been agreed to by the mine managers "and the officials of the Union of Washington, D.C.," and was merely awaiting the imprimatur of national fuel administrator Harry Garfield. The fact that Slimick had yet to sign up for conscription may have allowed Dillon some leverage over the union official: "In the interview with Slimick, it developed that although he is of registration age, he had failed to register. He was therefore directed to appear at Agent's office at 10:00 A.M. to-morrow. He stated that in the meantime he would do all he could to cause the strikers to return to their work."[39]

Investigators William Buchanan and E. D. Strickland likewise worked to curb labor activism among Buffalo's workforce, advising a

Ladislaus Suntakowski, suspected of creating discord at a factory, "that we were going to keep him under strict surveillance and that if he made the least move that seemed to be in any way hostile to the interests of this country or designed to stir up labor troubles, we would have him dealt with by law." For his part, Suntakowski "solelmly agreed that he would conduct himself very properly in the future."[40] Buchanan and Strickland tried to end a strike at the American Radiator plant in September 1917. The two investigators, accompanied by an Arthur Barkey, met with some of the workers on strike and tried to convince them to come back to their jobs. "After much discussion," recorded Strickland, "we almost persuaded them to return to work but they finally decid[e]d to appoint a committee and to await a decision regarding hours and wages." The investigators suggested to the strikers "the fact that it was their patriotic d[u]ty not to do anything to interfere in the progress of the Government work."[41] In the meantime, the department sought to end the strike using indirect means. On the following day, Buchanan conferred with tavern owners, appealing to them for help. The owners "agreed to get together tonight and intercede with some of the core makers to get them to go back to work," observed Buchanan, who added, "I had convinced them that it was to their interest to do this, as if any trouble of any kind occurred, their places might be closed."[42] Shortly thereafter, investigator Strickland asked a Catholic cleric for his assistance: "I endeavored to secure Co-operation of the priest in an appeal to the men on patriotic grounds." The apparently unreceptive priest recalled that his efforts to intercede in an earlier strike at another firm had been accompanied by rumors that the firm had given him thousands of dollars. The priest, recorded Strickland, "tells me that the men are so steeped in socialism that they pay almost no attention to the church."[43]

When it came to labor unions, the Justice Department reserved its greatest enmity for the IWW. Fearing that distribution of the radical journal *Liberator* might foment dissatisfaction among the servicemen and workers in the area of Newport News, Virginia, one detective observed that "There have recently been strikes and walkouts amongst the lumbers and ship yard workers here and it can readily be seen that the promulgation of I. W. W. or Bolshiviki theories in this vicinity at this time would be of the utmost detriment and danger to the government."[44] In 1917, federal prosecutors in Chicago secured an indictment charging 165 members of the IWW with hindering the prosecution of the war, with stirring up rebellious sentiments within the armed services, and with fomenting opposition to the draft. In addition, the indictment claimed that the defendants' strike activities had infringed upon the legal prerogatives of employers. (An additional count, that the defendants had tried to cheat employers, was tossed out by Kenesaw Mountain Landis, the presiding judge). At the trial the following year, prosecutors tried to prove that the IWW was an outlaw union, with a history of violence and sabotage, and was strongly opposed to the war effort. By depicting the organization as a whole as illegal, the prosecutors hoped that the jury would conclude that all remaining 101 defendants deserved punishment (a large number of those originally charged had had their cases dismissed). The strategy of proving guilt by membership succeeded, for in August 1918, all defendants were found guilty on all counts. Fifteen of the defendants were sentenced to stays of twenty years behind bars, and dozens of others received shorter sentences.[45] Other federal mass IWW trials followed. One group of Wobblies were convicted in December 1918 in Wichita, Kansas. In December 1918, forty-six Wobblies were put on trial in Sacramento, California, and were declared guilty by a jury in January. A band of Wobblies in Nebraska was arrested in November 1917 and indicted the following month, but never went to trial and had their case dismissed in April 1919.[46]

Other IWW members, besides those who were defendants in these mass trials, faced harassment from Justice Department investigators. In Buffalo, investigator William Buchanan interrogated Jack Murphy, a suspected Wobbly. Murphy protested that he had joined the IWW as a means of keeping his employment, "and as soon as he found out what the I. W. W. organization was, he immediately quit and would have nothing to do with them." Murphy's wife backed up her husband's explanation, and Buchanan, believing the suspect was being forthright, let him go. Murphy "promised to inform this office in regard to any persons belonging to the I.W.W."[47]

Informal methods of intimidation were especially useful for those department employees who, for whatever reason, were unable to secure a prosecution against a suspected Wobbly. Indeed, there seems to have been some difference of opinion in the department as to what was necessary to bring charges against a member of the IWW. The prosecutors conducting the trial in Chicago relied heavily on the principle of guilt by membership, but elsewhere, some prosecutors and detectives in the field appear to have held themselves to a stricter legal standard.

In Wyoming, for example, the U.S. attorney's office refused to try two Wobblies on federal charges. In Casper, the local police had notified investigator W. B. Holliday that they had detained two men on suspicion of being IWW activists. Allegedly, the men had been conversing about matters of the union, and one of them had posted an IWW sign. Unsure that the pair had done anything illegal, Holliday suspected that a larger labor conspiracy was afoot. "I do not know that these two men have violated any law," he wrote, "but rather consider that they are a menace to the community, and are being used by some more capable men." Holliday told the local authorities to retain both men in custody, justifying this detention on the notion that by distributing IWW materials they "are aiding the enemy by attempting to create bad conditions here at home among our working men."[48] However, assistant U.S. attorney David Howell advised Holliday that membership in the IWW was not illegal and expressed doubt that the men had engaged in sedition. "The mere fact of being an I.W.W. or distributing that propanda," suggested Howell, "is not in its self a crime unless the propaganda is seditious in its nature, that is opposing the draft or tending to cause mutiny or disloyalty in the forces of the United States." Holliday subsequently asked that the suspects be freed from jail, but complained that the lack of an appropriate statute in such cases "invites the people to take the law into their own hands."[49]

The legality of the IWW's activities, at least in the minds of some in the department, meant that investigators hostile to the IWW, in lieu of forwarding the case to the U.S. attorney, would have to resort to more creative forms of intimidation or punishment. In Montana, investigator Charles L. Tyman decided not to pursue legal action against a Finnish immigrant Wobbly, especially given that there was no conclusive proof that the suspect had actually disseminated IWW materials. Unable to find a reason for bringing charges against the suspect, Tyman encouraged him "to believe that he would be deported." In questioning another suspect, a Finn named Charles Hill, Tyman likewise worked to foster in Hill the notion "that he would be deported to Finland and denied the privilege of ever coming to the United States again." In response to this threat, Hill "promised that he would have nothing more to do with the I.W.W.'s."[50]

In Utah, investigator E. O. Reading sought to have Con Silva, an alleged agitator and an ex-employee of the Ogden Packing and Provision Plant, conscripted into the military. Plant president James Pingree had complained to Reading that Silva, whose allegiance he believed lay with Germany, was stirring up worker discontent. He feared that Silva, who had been fired, was contemplating sabotage. Reading later met with plant workers who claimed that Silva had circulated Wobbly materials, while a private detective hired by the company told Reading that Silva had expressed a desire to murder a plant employee.[51] Plant president Pingree met with Reading a second time, and, reported Reading, demanded that Silva be punished: "he [Pingree] could not understand why such men as Con Silva were permitted to run at large inciting trouble and unrest among employees, and stopping the production of food stuffs, and threatening the lives of men who were working in perfect harmony with the Government." Reading replied that Silva's citizenship status and the dearth of proof that he had broken the law meant that the Justice Department's hands were tied: "Agent explained to Mr. Pingree that he would do all he could in the matter but, owing to the fact that Con Silva was a citizen, it took sufficient evidence to show that he had violated a federal law in order to make an arrest and to prosecute him and so far Agent did not have that evidence. Also Agent explained that the Government did not interfere with organized labor unless they violated some law."[52] Although arrest was out of the question, at least for the moment, Reading still had one card left to play. In an earlier interview with Silva, Reading had found that the suspect was divorced and that Silva's two children stayed with Silva's parents. After his second meeting with the insistent Pingree, Reading checked Silva's draft registration file; as it turned out, Silva's status as the father of two youngsters meant that it was unlikely that he would be drafted. Reading seems to have thought that if he could show that Silva's children were less dependent on their father for support, Silva in turn would be rendered more eligible for the draft. Reading visited a Mr. Haywood, the chair of the draft board, and recommended that Silva be inducted into the armed forces. Reading recounted that he "informed Mr. Haywood that Con Silva's children were living with Con's father and mother and Agent suggested that it might be a good thing for the Local Board to re-classify Con Silva and put him in the Army." The draft board chief replied that "he would take up the matter. By doing so the ends of Justice would be met."[53] In short, if the courts were unavailable, investigators sometimes concocted their own means of administering justice.

The department also tried to infiltrate the IWW with informants. Such efforts followed in the footsteps of private security firms; in the nineteenth and early twentieth centuries, employees of the Pinkerton National Detective Agency, masquerading as union members, reported the activities of labor organizations to employers.[54] In the Southwest, informant S. Guzman presented reports to the Justice Department concerning Wobbly internal affairs. Posing as a Fernando Aguilar, he attended a meeting of IWW members in 1917 and was elected the group's financial officer, a position Guzman termed as "honorary." Guzman boasted that "matters of every description go through my hands," such as "correspondence, their plots, matters of membership, the location of respective members, and in fact everything."[55] Attending an underground IWW gathering in Arizona the following year, Guzman reported that plans were afoot for a brief, daylong strike in support of imprisoned labor activist Thomas Mooney.[56]

Nativism and antiradicalism had been mutually reinforcing sentiments almost since the founding of the republic. In 1798 the Federalist Party, fearing the influence of French and Irish immigrant radicals, passed the Alien and Sedition Acts, while in the antebellum era, apologists for slavery resented the German forty-eighters' advocacy of Free-Soil doctrines. To varying extents, various left-wing movements of the late nineteenth and early twentieth century America—Socialism, labor activism, and anarchism—had been viewed by native-born Americans as European importations corrosive of American traditions of individual liberty.[57] True to this tradition, the Justice Department's anticommunism was laced with a thick streak of nativism. After an inquiry into conditions in the town of Lawrence, Massachusetts, investigator Norman L. Gifford asserted "that the population of the mill cities consists largely of Lithuanians and Germans; that many of them have pro-German sympathies and socialistic tendencies, the same individuals very often combining both these sentiments."[58] Reporting on matters in Clifton, Arizona, investigator Claude McCaleb blamed a great deal of the local radicalism on those of Mexican origins: "They have had a strike there, and dissatisfaction is due to the fact that Mexican agitators keep the situation in a turmoil. There is no doubt but that the foreigners (Mexicans) are committing offences against the US laws in that field every day. Of course, it will be very hard to prove, but they are encouraging open rebellion and a lot of silly things of that kind—and the ignorant Mexicans are easily influenced."[59]

One of the most vehemently nativist employees in the entire department, an L. S. Perkins, feared that left-wing immigrants, especially Jews, were weakening the fabric of American society. "The Russian Jews," he complained, "with their ultra-Socialists and anarchists, and the Galicians and Ruthenians and Little Russians and Italians with their anarchistic and I.W.W. plotters, are never idle."[60] Filing his reports from New York City, Perkins warned that America was endangered by Communist infiltrators: "This is an enemy element that is daily growing in strength and aggressiveness, and it must be suppressed in some way, or made less dangerous, or this country will suffer to some extent the fate of Russia. Not alone Russians, but Finns, Italians, Irish and even some Japanese are lining up together, but the Russian Jew is the preponderating element here."[61]

Perkins didn't draw much of a distinction between various factions on the Left; in his mind, conservative Socialists worked hand in hand with Communists. Referring to New York, Perkins wrote that possibly "more than 100,000 Bolsheviki (mostly Russian Jews, headed by Morris Hillquit) are located in this City." The revolutionary legions, he thought, drew followers from a hodgepodge of different causes: "Socialists, single taxers, birth controllers, pacifists, conscientious objectors to draft, Sinn Fein Irishmen, and the whole nondescript army of the discontented, are lining up more or less distinctly with these imported agitators from Russia, and behind it all is the sinister hand of Germany."[62]

Perkins's characterization of Jews as radical subversives represented an increasingly prominent aspect of American anti-Semitism, one whose roots stretched as far away as Czarist Russia. Perkins himself recalled that his fears of Communism had been stimulated by Russian immigrant Boris Brasol: "My attention was first called in November, 1917, by Lieut. Boris Brazol [*sic*], formerly of the Russian Army, and now of the United States War Trade Board, to the impending danger of a great Bolshevik movement in the United States, and his words are being verified by the impudent boldness of the Russian population and their allied agitators."[63] Brasol, a former Russian prosecutor and army officer, had arrived in the United States in 1916 carrying out war-related tasks for the Czarist government, but had abandoned his duties with the advent of the Bolshevik revolution in November of the following year. Embarking on a crusade on behalf of the toppled monarchy and seeking to portray communism as a Jewish conspiracy, Brasol proffered *The Protocols of the Elders of Zion* to U.S. army intelligence. The *Protocols*, a forgery invented by the Czarist regime shortly before the turn of the century, claimed to be the secret program of revolution and machination by which Jews planned to seize control of the world. After the war, Brasol anonymously published the *Protocols* in the United States as part of a larger book in which he claimed that the Bolshevik revolution was part of the international Jewish agenda. The Justice Department's Perkins was not the only American who welcomed Brasol's views: the Russian immigrant also lent his help to Henry Ford as the car magnate's newspaper, the *Dearborn Independent,* churned out articles in the 1920s alleging the existence of Jewish plots to weaken America.[64]

The nativism of some in the Justice Department was mirrored in other branches of the federal government. In February 1917 and October 1918, Congress enacted laws facilitating the deportation of alien radicals. The former act allowed for the eviction of aliens who proselytized in favor of various subversive notions, such as anarchism, while the latter act went so far as to allow the expulsion of unnaturalized immigrants who were members of groups that espoused revolution. The 1918 law, passed with the support of the Justice Department, laid the legal groundwork for the postwar efforts of A. Mitchell Palmer to round up and deport radical aliens.[65]

The Justice Department's campaign against the Left had a number of repercussions. The Socialist Party, suffering from the department's harassment and prosecutions, collapsed in the postwar era. However, the Socialist Party probably would have split apart anyway, even without Justice Department persecution. Many of Socialism's most talented spokesmen had left the party to support to the war effort, and the party's opposition to the war had crimped its efforts at outreach to other Progressive organizations.[66] Perhaps most importantly, the triumph of the Bolsheviks in Russia put tremendous strains on the party, with radical and conservative wings of the party hotly disagreeing over how to respond to the revolution. The radical wing believed that the American Left should try to emulate the Bolsheviks and should prepare for a revolution here in the United States. The position of the radicals was bolstered by a recent influx of immigrants into the party who hoped that the Russian experience could be duplicated in America. In contrast, conservative Socialists argued that the party should maintain the course it had sailed since 1901 and should agitate for change within the political system. The dispute tore apart the Socialist movement, and in 1919 radicals left the party en masse to form the Communist and Communist

Labor parties. The Socialist Party never recovered from this split, and aside from a brief revival during the Great Depression, ceased to be a significant actor on the national stage.[67]

The Justice Department dealt a severe blow to the IWW. The arrests, prosecutions, and prison terms knocked the union's leadership out of commission, while legal costs drained funds that could have otherwise been spent to organize workers.[68] The Harding administration's offer of amnesty to IWW prisoners in the summer of 1923 sowed disagreement within the union as well. Some of the imprisoned Wobblies were offered clemency as long as they first consented to obey the law and to not promote tendencies of others to violate the law. This gift of conditional clemency proved to be an apple of discord within the IWW, as acceptance of the terms could be seen as a tacit acknowledgment that one had indeed engaged in criminal activities; those who consented to the government's terms were viewed by other Wobblies as having sold out. In any case, all remaining Wobbly prisoners were freed from prison by the end of 1923, whether they had promised to obey the law or not.[69]

The federal assault came at a particularly bad time for the union, as the postwar years brought about a number of changes that made it more difficult for the IWW to organize among its traditional constituencies. The timber-harvesting and copper-mining companies, as a result of their wartime experience, had begun offering their workers a slightly better deal, introducing mildly kinder employment policies that, as intended, limited the appeal of unionism. Political changes, too, threatened the union, as some IWW members switched allegiance to the newborn Communist parties.[70] Surprisingly enough, despite the wartime persecution, for a few years after the war the IWW continued to organize successfully agricultural and oilfield workers in the nation's midsection. But in the 1920s, technological changes sounded the death knell for these last Wobbly strongholds. On the Great Plains, mechanical combines replaced the teams of field hands that had brought in the harvest. At the same time, the increasing prevalence of the automobile made it more difficult to organize agricultural workers; it had been easier to locate and proselytize potential converts when the majority of workers had been riding the rails rather than driving cars. By reducing the number of workers needed to build new lines, new methods of constructing oil pipelines devastated the oil workers union.[71] Perhaps the union could have adapted to these changing conditions by developing new tactics or by finding new industries to organize, but the Justice Department's prosecutions meant that for several critical years, the IWW would be short on money and that many experienced Wobblies would be behind bars.

For its part, the department continued its struggle against radicalism in the postwar years. J. Edgar Hoover, having joined the Justice Department in 1917, became chief of the bureau's anti-radical division in the summer of 1919 and played a leading role in organizing the roundups of alleged alien radicals, which began that November. Hoover enthusiastically dedicated himself to the task of expelling immigrant subversives. The violations of civil liberties that accompanied these raids provoked much criticism of attorney general A. Mitchell Palmer, but even after Palmer's departure, the Bureau of Investigation continued to monitor and harass radicals. In 1922, for example, the department organized a roundup of Communist Party members meeting secretly in Michigan and assisted in a subsequent prosecution of the suspects for violating a state antiradical law. In 1924, after revelations of graft in the Justice Department and the Bureau of Investigation, President Coolidge appointed Columbia Law School chief Harlan Fiske Stone as attorney general. The new attorney general issued a proclamation asserting that the bureau would inquire after only criminal activities, an order that temporarily curbed some of the bureau's excesses. However, Stone's appointment of Hoover to head the Bureau of Investigation, first as acting director and then as full director, assured that the bureau would remain hostile to radicalism for a long time to come.[72]

5

Policing Wisconsin

As the nation stood on the brink of war in early April 1917, a referendum took place in Sheboygan, a city in eastern Wisconsin of more than 26,000 where, according to the 1910 census, 17 percent of the residents were German immigrants and where an additional 25 percent had been born in America to German parents. Ballots asking the question "Shall our country enter the European War?" were circulated around the city, including to churches. When municipal judge Otto Bassuener, Justice of the Peace Adam Trester, and lawyer Fred Vollrath tallied the responses on 3 April 1917, the count was 4,112 opposed to entering the war to 17 in favor. Indeed, of all the states in the union, Wisconsin may have been the one most reluctant to enter the First World War. The day after the referendum, eighty-two members of the U.S. Senate voted to declare war Germany, and on 6 April, 373 members of the House followed suit. One of the six senators and nine of the fifty House members voting against war were from Wisconsin. Of the state's eleven-member House delegation, only two representatives cast their votes in favor of war.[1] As subsequent months would show, the antiwar sentiment represented by these votes did not disappear when the United States entered the war, but rather continued to simmer. The Justice Department conducted a sweeping campaign to silence dissent in Wisconsin. Targets of its inquiries ranged from the Socialist Party of Milwaukee to the Catholic bishop of the Superior diocese; those receiving admonitions included pastors as well as a student at the University of Wisconsin. Indeed, for a time, the Justice Department assumed an important role in the state's political culture, in the process becoming enmeshed in local journalistic and ethnic rivalries. The department's activities themselves became an issue in the political campaigns of 1918 and helped to shape the outcome of that election.

Wisconsin's reluctance to enter the war stemmed from a number of factors, not the least of which was a tendency among some residents toward pacifism. For example, the board governing state education had for some time been encouraging schools to use antiwar materials in the classroom. In March 1914, the *Educational News Bulletin* of the office of the state superintendent of public instruction had advised the state's educators that "the schools can do no greater service to humanity than to help bring about international conditions which shall practically eliminate war as the means of settling international controversies."[2] The *Wisconsin Memorial Day Annual,* a pamphlet distributed by the state office of public instruction, provided a variety of pacifist materials for use in conjunction with Peace Day, which fell on May eighteenth. The 1915 *Annual* included an essay written from the standpoint of a personified "War," which began, "I was conceived in passion, hatred, envy, and greed, born in the morning of antiquity, and have a genealogy whose every page drips with the red blood of murdered innocence," as well as a passage from Tennyson's poem "Locksley Hall," which forecast an eventually peaceful planet: "Till the war-drum throbb'd no longer, and the battle-flags were furl'd / In the Parliament of man, the Federation of the world."[3] To observe Peace Day in 1915, Madison High School sponsored a talk by Richard Lloyd Jones, editor of the city's *Wisconsin State Journal.* Denouncing military conflict as "the greatest breeder of poverty," Jones expressed his hope for the establishment of a tribunal for settling disputes between countries.[4] One of Jones's fellow Madisonians, Julia Grace Wales, an instructor at the University of Wisconsin, had earlier formulated a proposal for laying the groundwork for ending the European war. Her plan, known as "Continuous Mediation Without Armistice," called for the creation of an international panel representing neutral countries that would arbitrate between the belligerent nations. Her idea won the endorsement of both houses of the state legislature, as well as the backing of nationally prominent pacifists Jane Addams and David Starr Jordan.[5]

There was also an ethnic aspect to the state's hesitation to go to war. As of 1910, 27 percent of Wisconsin residents were either German born or of exclusively German-born parentage—a higher percentage than any other state. More than 40 percent of those living in the state's most populous county, Milwaukee, were of German nativity or had two German-born parents.[6] In August 1914, thousands attended a Milwaukee rally to demonstrate their sentiments in regards to the war. "This gathering of Americans of German, Austrian, and Hungarian descent," explained one speaker, "is an expression of our sympathies for Germany in the war that has been forced upon her for her existence."[7] Perhaps the most sizable display of sympathy for the Central Powers came in the spring 1916 charity bazaar in Milwaukee to benefit German and Austro-Hungarian victims of the war. Those wishing to underwrite war relief efforts could purchase all kinds of goods or could buy nails that in turn would be pounded into an oversized mockup of an iron cross. Apparently referring to the latter fund-raising method, Leo Stern, chair of the Wisconsin branch of the German-American Alliance, declared that "today we shall hear the strokes of the hammer which shall tell our fighting brethren across the sea that we who are of German or Austro-Hungarian stock are ready too for sacrifices in order to help those who are offering up their life or their health in the defense of their homes."[8] Among the thousands of visitors to the festival were such personages as Republican governor Emanuel Philipp (who praised the fair as "a work of charity and love of humanity") and the Catholic archbishop of Milwaukee, Sebastian Messmer.[9]

Some daily newspapers in Milwaukee, such as the *Free Press* and the German-language *Germania-Herold,* favored Germany. In the eyes of the *Free Press,* England was "perfidious Albion," while the German kaiser "has been first and always an instrument of peace and progress."[10] As the *Lusitania* was sailing on her final voyage in May 1915, the *Germania-Herold* asserted that the British liner carried munitions and was a legitimate target for German U-boats.[11] Two days after a German submarine had sunk the liner off the coast of Ireland, the *Free Press* laid blame for the tragedy at the feet of the ships owners' and Britain's rulers, who were guilty "of stocking this passenger boat with war materials and thus contemptuously inviting the fate which has overtaken it."[12]

Contributing to the pacific strains in the state was the Socialist Party. Socialist activity in the state was centered in Milwaukee, and as early as 1904 the party had won seats on the city's aldermanic council.[13] Nineteen-ten had been a banner year for the party, with victories for its mayoral candidate, Emil Seidel, and its nominee for Congress, Victor Berger. Both candidates lost their bids for reelection two years later, but in 1916 Daniel Hoan won the mayoralty, a position he would hold for the following twenty-four years. The party's success was partly due to its close ties to the local labor unions and to its effective use of publicity. A "bundle brigade" could quickly and methodically distribute 100,000 pieces of campaign literature in neighborhoods around the city. The party's daily newspaper, the *Milwaukee Leader*, boasted a circulation of more than 37,000 and played a vital role in rallying public support.[14]

The Milwaukee party was to some extent a German American organization and could trace its lineage back to the German reform and radical movements that had appeared in the city since the middle of the nineteenth century. In elections for city offices, the party depended heavily on support from German wards.[15] Still, the Socialists succeeded in attracting both leaders and followers across ethnic boundaries. One key party administrator, Elizabeth Thomas, was of New York nativity and of Quaker heritage. The journalist and poet Carl Sandburg, whose parents were Swedish immigrants, had served as a party organizer before becoming secretary to Mayor Seidel. Daniel Hoan, who was of Irish, German, and English descent, had in his 1916 mayoral victory won majorities in predominantly Polish neighborhoods on the city's south side.[16]

Shepherding the party's rise to prominence was the Austrian-born Victor Berger, who had migrated to America as a teenager. Converting to Socialism, Berger became a crucial organizer and publicist (he founded and edited the *Leader*) for the local party. Berger was not enamored of armies in general. Victor's wife, Milwaukee native Meta Schlichting, maintained that her husband's departure from Austria-Hungary in the 1870s had been motivated by a wish to avoid conscription. In 1895 Victor Berger argued that "all progressive people are opposed to all militarism as far as military display is concerned," adding the current martial establishment was "simply a uniformed rank of Pinkertons kept by the state for the benefit of the capitalists."[17]

American Socialists, as were most of their countrymen, were distressed over the onset of war in Europe. The party's revulsion toward the war was partly the result of the fact that Socialist doctrine had declared that wars were the result of capitalist competition. Berger's *Leader*, however, downplayed economics as a cause of the war. An editorial of 7 August 1914 blamed the outbreak of the fighting on "the surviving relics of feudalism—by czarism and kaiserism," while subsequent editorials described how animosities between nations and ethnicities contributed to the onset of the war. Capitalistic rivalry did explain the entrance of Britain into the conflict, for England wished to wipe out Germany, "its most dangerous competitor in the world's market." Germany came in for its share of criticism—dominated as it was the "Yunker class," a privileged aristocracy. "The mere existence of a caste of that type," opined the *Leader*, "is a standing menace to the peace of Europe because Yunkerdom is the personification of German militarism." All things considered, however, the *Leader* preferred a German victory over a Russian one. "And in case that the czar and his allies should win, humanity would have to endure for some generations barbaric czarism in Europe as a ruling influence—an influence," it claimed, "which in every respect is much worse and a greater menace to progress than German cesarism."[18]

Socialist and pro-German sympathies overlapped, to some extent. Berger's opposition to the war may have also stemmed in part from an admiration for things German. Victor had attended the massive 1916 war relief bazaar, where his wife, Meta, was working. But his approbation did not extend to the German monarchy, a fact that rankled some. In August 1914 the *Free Press* lacerated Berger "for the under-current of malice which attends his utterances their palpable purpose to arouse prejudice against the German emperor, the defender of western civilization."[19]

Even during the period of neutrality, the Milwaukee party faced divisions over the war. Algie M. Simons, as a member of the editorial staff of the *Leader*, increasingly felt that the city's Socialists were too sympathetic to Germany. As early as August 1914, Berger noted in a letter to his wife that "I have my dire troubles and tribulations with Simons who now openly admits that he hates everything German and tries to sneak in some venemous head-lines." In an effort to counter Simons's sympathies, Berger brought Ernest Untermann, a native of Germany, on board the *Leader* in an editorial capacity. Berger's efforts, however, at maintaining an equilibrium proved unsuccessful. In April 1916 Untermann quit, alleging that Berger had complained that his text was too pro-German. Simons left his post at the *Leader* the same year, denouncing the party as alienated from America and as lacking in principle. "Intellectually and politically," he charged in the pages of the *New Republic*, "the mind of the party is in Europe." The Socialist media was largely "un-American" in nature and the party, Simons suggested, inclined toward Germany.[20]

A final factor contributing to the state's antiwar tendency was its strong progressive movement. While some progressives, such as Theodore Roosevelt, favored expanding the armed forces, others in the movement were wary of such calls. Fearing that the nation's defense contractors were pushing military expenditures as a way of boosting profits, the state's most prominent progressive, Republican senator Robert La Follette, proposed in 1915 that the nation's weapons factories be put under government ownership. Such a move, he thought, would remove "from private interest all incentive to increase army and navy appropriation bills."[21] The following year, he advocated legislation that would allow for a national referendum on whether the nation should enter a war. From a legal standpoint, such a referendum could not compel a particular course of action by Congress, La Follette admitted, but it still would let the government know where the people stood.[22]

Still, many in the state favored strengthening the armed forces. As early as 1914, the conservative Republican *Milwaukee Sentinel* advocated expanding the military and was later joined in its call by the *Milwaukee Journal*.[23] In May 1916, the University of Wisconsin saw the creation of a special student unit of the National Security League, a patriotic organization devoted to military readiness.[24] But the preparedness movement had its critics as well. The following June, the rules committee of the Milwaukee School Board turned down a proposal to release to military recruiters the identities and addresses of high school alumni aged nineteen or older. Board members opposing the proposal included Elizabeth Thomas and board president Meta Berger, both Socialists, as well as Elizabeth Kander, a leader of the settlement house movement in Milwaukee. Noting that the meeting witnessed "a heated debate over the question of patriotism," the *Sentinel* observed that Meta Berger had referred to "this wave of patriotic—no, I will not call it patriotic, but rather military, hysteria sweeping over the country."[25]

The debate over foreign policy revealed the depth of partisan and ethnic divisions in the state. The Democratic-leaning *Milwaukee Journal*, having endorsed Wilson in 1912 and strenuously backed him for reelection, went to great lengths to highlight criticism of the president's diplomacy by German American or pro-German sources.[26] "The *Free Press* has steadily abused the administration and upheld every act of Germany in the controversies of that country with the United States," the *Journal* declared in February 1916, adding that its rival "has hesitated at nothing in its warfare on America."[27] In June the *Journal* identified the *Free Press* as part of a "movement to foment disloyalty among American citizens."[28] As the presidential race heated up that fall, the *Journal* ran news articles examining the attempts of German American organizations to rally support for Republican presidential nominee Charles Evans Hughes. Such efforts, argued the *Journal,* represented an attempt by a foreign bloc to interfere in American politics and foreign policy.[29]

In conflating criticism of the president with disloyalty, the *Journal* drew on the help of recent hire and Harvard College graduate Frank Perry Olds, who translated materials from German-language newspapers.[30] Deeply wary of German influence in America, Olds claimed in the September 1916 *Atlantic Monthly* that German sympathizers were trying to manipulate American foreign policy for the benefit of Germany. In particular, he asserted, the German American media were denouncing Wilson while taking a much less unfavorable view of Hughes.[31] As if to substantiate Olds's assertion, in mid-October the *Journal* offered a sampling, translated from the German, of editorial commentary from the *Germania-Herold*. These extracts, the *Journal* claimed, would demonstrate the *Herold*'s efforts "to consolidate the political strength of German-Americans to influence the country's foreign policies in favor of Germany." Among the translations that the *Journal* provided was an excerpt from a March 1916 editorial, which had stated that Wilson "is ready to let the country be dragged into the bloody vortex of war only that a few 'idiots' and 'arch-traitors' may be given the thrilling sensation of traveling on an armed merchant vessel under protection of the stars and stripes." The *Journal* sought to couple such criticism of Wilson with German American political assertiveness. Another editorial translated by the *Journal* argued that "in the interests of America, therefore, we must seek to bring into office as many fellow citizens of German descent as possible. In the interests of America, therefore, we shall have always to choose on principle among equally worthy candidates the candidate of German descent." The *Germania-Herold,* lamented the *Journal,* "has used every endeavor to make sympathy with Germany the determining favor in electing a government for America."[32] Later that month, the *Journal* printed translations of passages critical of Wilson that had appeared in the German-language weekly *Excelsior*. Although Wilson lost the state to Hughes in November, the *Journal* took solace in the fact that "the city of Milwaukee, the home of The Germania-Herold, The Free Press and Excelsior, all organs of disloyalty, the headquarters of Mr. Leo Stern and the German-American alliance of Wisconsin and of several allied organizations just as alien in purpose—has given President Wilson a significant plurality—6,000 votes."[33]

After Germany's declaration of unrestricted submarine warfare in January 1917, and following the subsequent exposure of the Zimmermann telegram, some in the state asserted that war was a potentially legitimate response. Addressing a mass rally in Madison at the end of March, Guy Goff, former federal prosecutor for the eastern district of Wisconsin, stated that Germany's conduct demanded strong recourse. "Shall American citizens go and come as they please on the free seas of the world," he asked, "or shall they be murdered and drowned with no chance for their lives?" *Wisconsin State Journal* editor Richard Lloyd Jones, who in 1915 had cautioned about the dangers of war, now told those assembled that "democracy can never be safe anywhere on earth so long as the kaiser's kind is anywhere allowed to reign." The sympathies of the audience seemed clear; one reporter noted that "the whole crowd leaped to their feet at the tribute to France, waving flags and shouting."[34]

Other Wisconsinites, however, continued to press for peace. In February, the State Federation of Labor, in a petition to government officials, advocated cutting off commerce with European countries, claiming that such a move would reduce the chances that America would get entangled in the conflict. In the same month, a meeting of the Milwaukee Emergency Peace Committee endorsed the notion of a national referendum on the question of whether to go to war. Speakers at the meeting saw little need for a military solution to the diplomatic crisis. "Militarists and commercialists," maintained Mrs. Alan Roberts, "are working to force this country into war," while Meta Berger declared that "We must do our share in educating diplomats and statesmen to the belief that international disputes can be settled without wholesale murder."[35] A February antiwar meeting featuring prominent Socialists drew a crowd of four thousand and endorsed a proposal to cut off trade with Europe. Speakers included Mayor Daniel Hoan, who stated that "war is not only hell, as Sherman said, but damnation as well," and Victor Berger, who forecast that the war could curtail civil liberties. Asserting that recent rioting over food in New York City had been blamed on German influence, Berger sarcastically suggested, "Watch out, Comrade Schmidt, some night at 11 o'clock when you are going home from a game of schafskopf that Pinkerton detectives don't get you as a 'German agent'!"[36] In March 1917, as war approached, the Socialist Party's nominees for the Milwaukee school board issued a platform censuring "the teaching of militarism in our public schools."[37] Later that month, the school board's rules committee approved a proposal to authorize a navy recruiter to give talks in high schools—but not without protest from some board members. "The boys of high school age are very impressionable," noted Elizabeth Thomas, while her fellow board member Elizabeth Kander reflected, "If only the ultimate object were not to kill people, I would be very glad to have our boys join the navy or learn all about it."[38]

To some extent, members of the Milwaukee party assisted the war effort. Soon after the congressional declaration of war, Mayor Hoan helped found the local Council of Defense, and as head of the council's bureau of food control worked to ensure that the city's residents had an adequate diet.[39] But the Socialist Party remained staunchly opposed to the war. In June 1917, the *Leader,* discounting the Wilson administration's explanation of why America needed to enter the conflict, instead implied that the nation had gone to war in part to protect powerful economic interests and warned that "under the guise of fighting for democracy in Central Europe, our plutocracy and its government in Washington is now establishing an absolute autocracy in our country."[40] When Berger ran for the U.S. Senate in a special election in 1918 (sitting Senator Paul Husting had died as a result of a hunting mishap), he ran on a platform that maintained that "the American people did not want and do not want this war. They were plunged into this abyss by the treachery of the ruling class of the country."[41] Later that month, the local party denounced the increasing influence of martial notions and practices in the classroom, criticizing "the poisoning of the mind of the pupil with imperialism and militarism" as well as "the drilling of the youth to act like puppets."[42]

Criticism of the war was not limited to the Socialists. Robert La Follette belittled the official justifications for entering the conflict. Before a receptive audience at a meeting of the Nonpartisan League in St. Paul, Minnesota, on 20 September 1917, the senator, a progressive Republican, appeared to mock the notion that America had been the victim of German maritime aggression. "I don't mean to say that we hadn't suffered grievances," he stated, adding, "We had—at the hands of Germany. *Serious* grievances! We had cause for complaint. They had interfered with the right of American citizens to travel upon the high seas—on ships loaded with munitions for Great Britain." President Wilson, he asserted, had been aware that the *Lusitania* held war materials and should have kept her from leaving port. La Follette suggested that the effort to uphold freedom of the seas would come at a tremendous and unjustifiable cost: "that the *comparatively* small privilege of the right of an American citizen to ride on a *munitions loaded ship flying a foreign flag* is too small to involve this government in *the loss of millions and millions of lives*!!"[43]

The senator's comments ignited a firestorm of criticism around the country. Contributing to the vehemence of the reaction, which included demands for his ejection from the Senate, was the fact that the Associated Press ran an incorrect—and somewhat more controversial—version of his remarks, asserting that the La Follette had said, "We had no grievance against Germany."[44] At the height of the furor, on 6 October 1917, La Follette addressed the Senate on the question of freedom of speech in wartime. Citing a news report that a Texas judge had expressed his hope for La Follette's execution, the Wisconsin senator observed that "it is not alone Members of Congress that the war party in this country has sought to intimidate." Rather, Americans themselves were the subject of an effort to smother opposition to the war:

> The mandate seems to have gone forth to the sovereign people of this country that they must be silent. . . . To-day and for weeks past honest and law-abiding citizens of this country are being terrorized and out-raged in their rights by those sworn to uphold the laws and protect the rights of the people. I have in my possession numerous affidavits estab-lishing the fact that people are being unlawfully arrested, thrown into jail, held incommunicado for days, only to be eventually discharged without ever having been taken into court, because they have commit-ted no crime. Private residences are being invaded, loyal citizens of un-doubted integrity and probity arrested, cross-examined, and the most sacred constitutional rights guaranteed to every American citizen are being violated. It appears to be the purpose of those conducting this campaign to throw the country into a state of terror, to coerce public opinion, to stifle criticism, and suppress discussion of the great issues in-volved in this war.[45]

Democratic senator Joseph Robinson of Arkansas delivered a stinging rebuttal. Observing that La Follette "has characterized as diabolical the acts of the executive department of this Government in making inves-tigations of those who were suspected of being disloyal to this coun-try," Robinson expressed his confidence that most of those subjected to such inquiries were guilty of something. Occasionally, perhaps "unnec-essary investigations have been made," he claimed, and added, "but I suspect that if the Senator from Wisconsin would produce his evidence here, it would be found that those who made the affidavits to which he

has referred in his condemnation of his Government are German sympathizers, and some of them German spies." Americans, he declared,
had a simple choice between fealty to the German Emperor or loyalty
to President Wilson, and now that Congress had decided the issue,
Americans had no option but to support the war.[46] Closer to home, the
Milwaukee Journal lumped La Follette with unpatriotic elements and
derided his concern for civil liberties: "If The Journal had 1,000,000
tongues, it would take them all to tell the outrages committed by the
German Government against the United States and the harm done
America by propagandist newspapers, treasonable individuals, and such
lackloyal citizens as Senator La Follette. All their talk about free speech
is pretty, but disloyally so. When a man is trying to burn one's house or
murder one's children, men cannot talk about free speech."[47]

Indeed, Justice Department detectives were systematically trying to
silence critics of the war throughout the state.[48] In April 1918, investigator Charles Bodenbach told a Milwaukee man "in very severe language
that any further remarks by him derogatory to this Government would
result in immediate action being taken against him" and later that year
advised a resident of Beaver Dam "that if he allowed himself to utter
another word derogatory to our army or navy, or cast any reflections in
any way upon the allied successes in Europe, he would be immediately
taken into custody and prosecuted by this department."[49] Even a fairly
innocuous criticism of aspects of the war effort merited reproof. A bank
employee who allegedly had audibly demonstrated a lack of enthusiasm
for the federal savings stamps program was interviewed by a detective,
who in his report characterized him as "a Slacker" and noted that he
had "admonished subject for his attitude."[50] All in all, during the period
from April 1917 through November 1918, at least thirty-one individuals
received verbal warnings or admonitions from the department. (I am
counting as one the collective warning delivered to workers of the Phoenix Knitting Company in Milwaukee, where an investigator "interrogated all the employees" and "cautioned them in severe terms to make
no further disloyal remarks.")[51] Undoubtedly Justice Department records contain many more such admonitions.[52]

Of the thirty-one recipients of warnings, nine were pastors.[53] The
department recognized the importance of clergymen as community
leaders and their potential to either rally or discourage support for the
war. One pastor was encouraged "to do his utmost in his status of an
American citizen, to foster loyalty to this country among the members

of his church."[54] Remaining neutral on the war was not sufficient. When the Reverend George Scheible of Markesan "emphatically insisted that he has not uttered one word in disparagement of the Liberty Loan, neither has he voiced his favor of it," the investigator "condemned his attitude of indifference, by his own admission" and "discussed with him at length the duties of an American citizen in this national crisis but came to the conclusion that it is useless to seek his patriotic co-operation, governed as he is, by the fear of his German congregation."[55]

The media received special attention as well. Recognizing the power of the press, the department conducted numerous investigations of newspapers. In some cases, these inquiries were fairly short-lived and were in response to a particular item that had surfaced in the pages of a newspaper. For example, the *Racine Correspondent,* a German-language weekly, had repeatedly run an English advertisement for *Cassell's New German Dictionary* that asserted that "every patriotic German will feel in duty bound to further and encourage a knowledge of the language of the Fatherland." Investigator Charles L. Harris then visited the *Correspondent* proprietor and editor Henry Bonn, asking "why he continued to run such an advertisement at this time." Bonn replied that he had had the plate for the ad since 1915 and that the actual content of the ad had since slipped his mind. Bonn "stated that he was very sorry that there was anything objectionable about it."[56] When the *Chippewa Herald* printed an item suggesting that sickness had been prevalent in army camps and that soldiers were receiving toxic injections, investigator Willard N. Parker thought that it looked as though the *Herald* was attempting to undermine efforts to inoculate local residents during an outbreak of smallpox. Parker called on the editor of the paper, and "cautioned him against any further allusions to the anti-vaccination matter which would discredit or discourage enlistment in the army."[57] The *Racine Times-Call* received a visit from the Justice Department after running a letter which claimed that a local man had been conscripted despite his illness and that "his wife and children are left behind to starve for all anyone seems to care." When investigator John E. Burke met *Times-Call* editor (and future governor) Walter Goodland, Goodland asserted that he had been out of town when the offending item was printed, and he acknowledged its potentially harmful consequences. "Upon reading the article," noted Burke, "Goodland stated that he realized that its effect might be to give encouragement to those who sought to impede the government in its raising of an army and stated that in the future he

Willard N. Parker, a prominent Wisconsin educator, went to work for the Justice Department as an investigator during the war. This photograph was published in 1900, when Parker was serving as Wisconsin State Teachers' Association president and as assistant state superintendent of the state Department of Education. (courtesy of University of Wisconsin Archives)

would see to it that no such article would appear in his paper." In any case, Goodland almost certainly never had any intention of undermining the war effort, as he had earlier served as secretary of the Wisconsin Loyalty Legion, a patriotic organization.[58]

Loyalty investigations were collaborative enterprises, requiring information from local people or organizations. Thus, investigators often consulted with postmasters, who provided their assessments of the patriotism of a particular individual or of the degree of support for the war among the local residents.[59] In one case, a postal official forwarded to the Justice Department the contents of a letter. As the official described it, an "unsealed" letter, lacking an adequately specific destination, was opened by a postal worker and was found to contain a personal message to a local resident not to comply with the draft.[60] Postal officials assisted in other ways. On occasion, postmasters escorted detectives as they conducted their inquiries, and in one case, arranged for car transportation.[61] When investigator Lewis E. Sawyer visited Waukesha, the postmaster offered to summon local notables for a conference about the state of patriotic sentiment. When Sawyer consented, the postmaster telephoned Waukesha's police chief and a county council of defense official, who then showed up at the postmaster's office. During the subsequent meeting, Sawyer learned that it seemed "that in the rural districts about Waukesha more or less pro-Germanism is in evidence." Both the police chief and the council of defense official promised to take the initiative in checking "disloyalty."[62] Investigator Julius Rosin sought to enlist postal officials as auxiliary chasteners of the department. He concluded his report of a conversation with an assistant postmaster by noting, "I instructed him that all cases of seditious talking be handled by the postmaster and only aggravated cases should be reported to this office."[63] Rosin seems to have arrived at similar understandings with other postmasters as well.[64]

In ferreting out disloyalty, investigators also conferred with local officials, including representatives of law enforcement agencies and county councils of defense.[65] Educators, too, offered their insights. The Milwaukee superintendent of schools, Milton Potter, expressed interest in assisting the Justice Department in the case of an allegedly antiwar schoolteacher. The source of the accusations in this case was a Miss Schmitt, who, noted the investigating detective, J. E. Ferris, was "acting upon the suggestion of her father, Peter Schmitt." Ferris observed that "Miss Schmitt . . . informed the writer that said Henry B Fleischer, instructor of manual training at the Center Street School . . . had been very active in distributing the speeches of <u>La Follette</u> in connection with his obstructive propaganda against war." Miss Schmitt additionally "stated that said Fleischer was violently socialistic and had been actively engaged in spreading pro-German propaganda." Ferris took up the matter with Potter, who in turn said "that he would call upon teachers in the Center Street School, and the principal, whom he knew to be loyal to this government, with a view of verifying the allegations of said Peter Schmitt and his daughter, and that if said allegations could be verified proper action would be taken."[66]

A dean at the University of Wisconsin in Madison, Scott Goodnight, was also eager to help root out disloyalty on campus. The university as a whole had demonstrated its stance on wartime dissent when more than four hundred of its faculty endorsed a round robin censuring Senator La Follette's "unwise and disloyal utterances giving aid and comfort to the enemy."[67] When Socialist Adolph Germer came to speak at Madison's Turner Hall in March 1918, he was confronted by a crowd of university students, who, after his lecture was finished, insisted that he pledge loyalty to the government. Dean Goodnight lent his support to the student inquisitors. According to the *Capital Times,* he demanded of Germer, "You claim to be a loyal citizen, will you swear to support the government of the United States till the war is won?" Germer complied.[68] The university also helped guide the Justice Department's more discreet investigation of a student organization known as the Wisconsin Forum. Founded in 1916 to promote intellectual discourse on campus, the forum had in the following year sponsored talks by, among others, the Socialist Max Eastman and Professor John Dewey.[69]

In February 1918, Professor Victor Lenher advised the Justice Department that the forum tended toward Socialism. According to the Justice Department report, the professor also asserted that forum member Doris Berger (whose father was Milwaukee Socialist Victor Berger) was apparently able to tap into an inexhaustible supply of financial resources.[70] The inquiry into the matter received a boost in March, when the army informed the department that an imprisoned conscientious objector had received a letter from Jessica Colvin, a member of the forum. "What difference does it make," Colvin had written, "whether your action has any sound effect or not on a society which is stupid enough to punish men who have ideas for which they're willing to suffer?" Investigator Willard N. Parker turned to Dean Scott Goodnight,

JESSICA B. COLVIN . . . . . *Evansville, Ill.*
LETTERS AND SCIENCE
Delta Gamma.
Thesis—Dostorvsky's Influence on English Novelists.

Jessica Colvin, a student at the University of Wisconsin at Madison, was interrogated by Justice Department investigator Willard N. Parker. (courtesy of University of Wisconsin Archives)

who provided information about the forum's leadership and who identified four members, including Colvin, as being worthy of further inquiry. Subsequently, Colvin was summoned to appear before Parker, who asked her if she were a Socialist, or if she had "ever expressed any pro-German views." Colvin acknowledged that in her letter to an imprisoned draft resister she had said "that I had sympathy for those who stand up according to their own conscience," a stance that was outrageous to Parker. "Supposing that we all," he asked, "that you and I and everybody, extended sympathy to those who refuse to respond to the law of our country when it said that men between ages of twenty-one and thirty-one must register for war service, that we may fight this battle for our country's salvation and for the world's salvation, where would the laws of this country be; where would we be in this war." When Colvin argued that she was indeed a backer of the war, asserting that she had bought bonds and that some of her relatives, including her brother, were "in the war," Parker responded, "For family's sake, for brother's sake, for blood's sake, how dare you lift your little finger to do anything which will interfere with the success of our army."[71]

The Justice Department also worked with local prosecutors to bring disorderly conduct charges against those who openly expressed themselves unpatriotically. In a December 1917 letter to a county prosecutor, investigator Ralph Izard wrote that "we have successfully prosecuted, with the assistance of the county prosecutors, a great many cases with fines of $100 and from sixty to ninety days in jail, where it may be reasonably charged that the utterances of the defendant were calculated to incite riot or disorder." The blame for violence resulting from the expression of controversial remarks fell on the speaker, and Izard demarcated as illegal a broader set of rhetorical offences than did the Espionage Act of 1917. "We consider, and I think with reason," added Izard, "that a man who, when we are at war, openly boasts of his allegiance to Germany or hopes for the success of the central powers, or abuses the President of this country or the Congress or any of the high Federal Officers of the Government, is undoubtedly guilty of disorderly conduct, inasmuch as it is clear that such statements made publicly, are likely to incite riot and disorder." Izard's criminalization of the criticism of federal officials was reminiscent of the Sedition Act of 1798 and anticipated the Sedition Act of 1918.[72] Investigator W. E. Cox brought a man suspected of making antidraft and antiwar comments before a local court. "Not believing that further evidence could be gathered and that these statements were made due to the influence of Victor Bergerism and Lafollettism," recorded Cox, "Employe' took subject before Justice of the Peace, Hazeltine, where a plea of guilty was entered and a fine of $50 and costs passed by the Court and was paid."[73] In Milwaukee, investigator Charles Bodenbach collected testimony from two witnesses claiming that a Frank Schmidt had damned war bonds and the Red Cross. Bodenbach and the two witnesses testified at Schmidt's trial for disorderly conduct. Convicted, Schmidt faced a choice of a fine or a prison term.[74]

The Justice Department's reliance on local courts came to annoy one local official. On the day Schmidt's case (as well as the case of another man alleged to have made disloyal remarks), came before the court, the Milwaukee city assistant attorney protested. "I am getting tired of having the government officials come into this court and prosecute the makers of seditious remarks under the city warrant for disorderly conduct," he declared, stating that he would inquire of Thomas Watt Gregory "as to why seditious remarks cases are not prosecuted in the federal courts."[75]

At the same time, the department sought to insure the success of the federal prosecutions that did take place by gathering information on prospective jurors. Such background checks could have allowed prosecutors to pick jurymen who likely would have been unsympathetic to defendants charged with violation of the Espionage Act or with other war-related offenses, such as draft evasion. In a letter, Ralph Izard provided investigator William Steiner with the names of nine men, and directed him to "investigate these men as to their loyalty and whether Socialists. This information must be gathered for use of U.S. Attorney in the examination of these men before they are chosen as Jurors."[76] Detective

Charles L. Harris conducted a similar inquiry "under cover in regard to the loyalty and character" of Racine resident and potential jurors William Harvey Jr. and H. E. Rehwald. Harvey, Harris found, had a superb reputation, and "has been an enthusiastic and energetic supporter in patriotic movements." Harris added, "Politics republican." H. E. Rehwald was an "old resident of Racine" whose "wife is very active in Red Cross and patriotic work." Unable to determine Rehwald's partisan allegiances, if any, Harris was "reasonably certain that he is not a socialist."[77]

These investigations were a collaborative process, requiring the assistance of concerned citizens, local officials, or other federal agencies. The Justice Department depended on people to come forth and identify dissenters. In some cases, accusers may very well have had ulterior motivations for making charges of disloyalty. Some allegations seem to have been rooted in ethnic or journalistic rivalries, while at other times, employers sought to use the department to quash labor militancy. Detectives sometimes, indeed, worried that they were being drawn into battles that had little to do with questions of allegiance to the war effort.

In one instance, tensions between ethnic groups within the Catholic Church likely fueled a loyalty investigation of Bishop Joseph M. Koudelka of the diocese of Superior. The inquiry began after Father Philip Gordon told the department that Bishop Koudelka had asserted that a German defeat would signal the demise of the Catholic Church in America. Koudelka, a native of Bohemia, had served as bishop of the Superior diocese since 1913.[78] The Justice Department subsequently interviewed a number of priests, some of whom claimed that the bishop lacked patriotic fervor or was actually pro-German. The Reverend S. A. Iciek, for example, contended that while Koudelka was not engaged in anti-American propaganda, he was definitely sympathetic to Germany, while the Reverend Walter Kalandyk suggested that the bishop was subtly undermining the war effort.[79] Father Peter Rice complained that his campaign of patriotic lectures had more or less been halted by Bishop Koudelka.[80] Father Joseph Arts claimed to have been a victim of a conspiracy involving Koudelka and certain clergymen. Arts had been giving patriotic presentations condemning German atrocities, but pro-German priests, Arts charged, had met with Koudelka and decided on Arts's ouster from the diocese; subsequently, the bishop's secretary had sent Arts a notice informing him that he should leave the diocese.[81] Father Patrick O'Mahoney, while acknowledging that Koudelka had

Bishop Joseph M. Koudelka of the Superior, Wisconsin, diocese was questioned by Justice Department investigator Willard N. Parker. (Cleveland Press Collection, Cleveland State University Library)

not been actively trying spread his pro-German views, maintained that the bishop was not in sympathy with the American cause. O'Mahoney alleged that at the start of the war in Europe, Koudelka had been in Austria, meeting with members of the government there, and that after returning home he had expressed his affinity for Austria and Germany. Koudelka was especially a problem, maintained O'Mahoney, because many priests were loyal to him. There was a fundamental division, he maintained, between the Irish and German clergy: "The Irish and German priests in the diocese had little to do with each other, principally, according to Father O'Mahoney, for the well known reason that the latter were pro-German in their sympathies relative to the war and opposed to the course taken by the United States, whereas the former are patriotic American citizens and resentful of the attitute the latter have taken." Koudelka appeared to have something of a following among the Germanophone priests, and O'Mahoney "seemed to be of the opinion that this section of the country would gain considerably from the removal of the bishop to some other section of the country, and from a general overhauling of the clergy in the diocese."[82]

Ethnic tensions do seem to have contributed to some of the animosity toward Koudelka. Two of his critics, Peter Rice and Patrick O'Mahoney, were Irish immigrants, while others belonged to ethnic groups who might have reason to be wary of anyone whose sympathies might lie with the Central Powers. Joseph Arts had migrated from Belgium, and two other critics were of Polish descent—Walter Kalandyk was a native of Poland, while S. A. Iciek was the son of Polish immigrants.[83] But it also appears that this ethnic rivalry may have helped save the bishop from more severe actions by the Justice Department.

In the summer of 1918, Justice Department officials had grown concerned over Bishop Koudelka's attitudes. In a memorandum to John Lord O'Brian, Justice Department attorney John Hanna suggested the possibility of internment: "In case he [Koudelka] is an alien enemy I am inclined to think he should be interned, unless he is removed from his present position in which he can do so much to quench the growing enthusiasm of Slavic peoples, for the American cause." Later that month, Hanna sounded a bit more optimistic, noting that the bishop had "delivered a patriotic sermon" and as of late had endorsed the efforts of the Red Cross. Hanna stated that although this likely only reflected a greater caution on the part of Koudelka, there was a chance that the bishop's Bohemian roots were affecting his attitude toward the

Central Powers. "Since he is a Czech," wrote Hanna, "it is possible, if unlikely, that he has now some genuine doubt about the righteousness of the German and Austrian position."[84]

On 17 July 1918, investigator Irving Best, accompanied by another detective, visited Koudelka and authenticated that he was indeed an American citizen. In September 1918, investigator Willard N. Parker met with Bishop Koudelka in Superior. Parker realized that attitudes about the European conflict were just one source of division in the diocese, noting in his report that while Bishop Koudelka had sided with the "wets," Father Rice had taken the opposite position on alcohol issues. Parker tried to start the meeting on a conciliatory note: "In opening the discussion, Agent took the ground that he had called for a conference with Bishop Koudelka for the purpose of promoting patriotism among the people of his parish in the diocese." Parker then began to inquire into the bishop's attitudes about the war. It appears that Koudelka may have tried to defend his patriotism by offering the agent materials he had written indicating his support for the war; much of Parker's report of his interview quoted from or summarized these items. Parker, for example, quoted extensively from a letter to the governor of Wisconsin in which Bishop Koudelka had asserted his loyalty and had noted his support to the Czechoslovakian nationalist movement. Parker, after asserting his own impartiality ("Agent will say that not being of the Catholic faith himself he has no prejudices in this matter"), decided "that Bishop Koudelka is not guilty of disloyalty." Parker reported that the bishop might have held some kind of sympathetic attitude toward "some of the institutions of Germany" before American entry into the war. Still, continued Parker, as "it hardly seems probable that a man of his intelligence and wisdom would put himself in a position of disloyalty to this country," the affair "should be attributed to differences of opinion founded upon nationality rather than upon a question of patriotism." Antipathies between Irish and Germans in the diocese had existed for years, Parker stated, "and when the United States declared war on April 6, 1917, the Irish priests took the occasion to attempt to win in the controversy by declaring Bishop Koudelka disloyal." Parker recommended that "It would therefore seem that this Department should not in any way whatsoever mix in the fight involved between the nationalities of the Priests of the Diocese of Superior."[85]

Likewise, when the department conducted an inquiry into the *Capital Times* of Madison, it feared that it would become entangled in a journalistic competition. The city's progressive *Wisconsin State Journal*, edited by Richard Lloyd Jones, had become a fervent supporter of the war and a harsh critic of Senator La Follette. "The thing we cannot understand about Senator La Follette," railed the *State Journal* in August 1917, "is that his every attitude is one of criticism of the American spirit somewhere, anywhere while at the same time the things he says lend aid and comfort to the sympathizers with the enemy if not to the enemy itself." The editorial further suggested the potential of pecuniary ties between La Follette and German sympathizers. Should Senator La Follette hope to run for president "upon a pro-German platform," the *State Journal* claimed, his scheme "will of course have to be financed by pro-German and booze money."[86] That year, *State Journal* administrator William T. Evjue, unhappy about his employer's hostility toward Senator La Follette, quit his job and helped start a new newspaper, the Madison *Capital Times*, which was closely allied with La Follette's supporters.[87] For its part, the *State Journal* sought to raise questions about the patriotism of its infant competitor, and a week before the *Times*'s debut in December 1917 featured an article by Samuel Hopkins Adams, who alleged—with some justification—tight links between La Follette and the *Capital Times*. More explosive, however, was Adams's claim that the new newspaper had sought financing from German sympathizers in Wisconsin. The pitch used by the sales force attempting to attract investors in the new paper ran as follows, claimed Adams: "The Germans aren't getting a fair show here. All the papers are abusing them. . . . Our paper will be on the level with its news and editorials. It will be a real American paper, not a pro-British one." Adams further mentioned an allegation that financial support for the new paper "is supposed to have come from Milwaukee Germans."[88] A *State Journal* editorial two days later sought, obliquely, to inflame the suspicions raised by Adams: "The way the Prussian propaganda conducts itself now is thru long-distance, subterranean financial channels to the subsidized press that declares its loyalty but does not dare come out and hit Germany for her championship of Prussianism and hit the men in Congress who have declared that the Germany of despotism has been patient with the democracy of America." An informed reader would have recognized the reference to La Follette (the senator had declared in April 1917 that "Germany has been patient with us") and might also have recognized the implication that any newspaper uncritical of La Follette might have some kind of German funding.[89]

As early as October 1917, the rumor that German sympathizers were subsidizing the new Madison newspaper had reached the Justice Department, and in early November investigator George R. Mayo was instructed to examine the sources of funding for the as-yet-to-be published newspaper. The letter directing Mayo to conduct an investigation cited an allegation even more inflammatory than the one that would be purveyed by Adams. "Certain citizens of Wisconsin," it stated, "believe that it [the new paper] is being financed with money of the German Government."[90] Mayo submitted several updates, at one point observing that "the only advertisements the newspaper carries are those of German and Norwegian merchants; most of whom are considered Pro-German."[91] Mayo compiled detailed reports on the funding sources for the *Times,* even going so far as to prepare to enlist the help of a secretarial assistant in Robert M. LaFollette's law office. "I have been able to make a very satisfactory arrangement with the stenographer in charge in the offices of Senator LaFollette and Albert Rogers, who practise law under the firm name of LaFollette & Rogers," wrote Mayo, adding, "anything going through this office of a suspicious nature will be reported to me."[92] Mayo also met with the *Capital Times* editor William T. Evjue and had the opportunity to examine financial records of the paper. In his memoirs, Evjue recalled that Mayo, after perusing the records, declared that "I am ready to state here that I found nothing to substantiate the charges that came from Madison to the Department of Justice."[93]

In his report, Mayo advised his superiors that the charges against the paper's loyalty were overblown. To be certain, he noted, the paper had sometimes featured "editorials that might be construed as intended to array labor against capital," and on occasion had "seemed to give undue prominence to telegrams mentioning German successes." However, Mayo believed that rumors that the *Capital Times* was financed by German sympathizers were simply wrong: "My investigation shows that there is no truth in any of these reports; that they originated chiefly from the established newspapers, who did not want a competitor in the field, and these reports were carried and exaggerated by the ancient political opponents of Senator La Follette's." In particular, Mayo identified the editor of the *Wisconsin State Journal* as a source of much of the notion that the *Capital Times* was disloyal. Referring to the financial supporters of the *Capital Times,* Mayo asserted that "at the most, their disloyalty consists entirely of faith in Senator La Follette, though many of them are outspoken in denouncing his attitude on the war." The presumably exasperated Mayo, whose inquiry had lasted months, concluded that "the whole matter seems to be an effort of interested parties to use the Department of Justice to put a competitor out of business, with no excuse other than because they are Senator La Follette's old friends and supporters, they must all be disloyal citizens."[94] After Mayo's visit, Evjue appealed to the attorney general to provide a report as to what the investigation had found. Subsequently, the Justice Department sent a letter to the *Capital Times* noting that "no information has come into the possession of this Department which would warrant it in taking any action of any character against your company." The *Times* reproduced the letter on its front page, and the whole experience seems to have informed its postwar denunciation of the national security bureaucracy. "When a system is introduced whereby without any complaint being filed personal mail is opened, telegrams read, bank books examined, the press censored, public meetings denied and dispersed; . . . there is bound to be doubts raised about our boasted democracy," the paper charged in December 1918:

> Especially it is distasteful to self-respecting Americans to have their ordinary privacies spied upon and cheap tattling invited. When thousands upon thousands of green men are taken into the government secret service, anxious to win their spurs as government sleuths there is sure to be some unjust accusations and when to this more thousands upon thousands are invited to volunteer as tale bearers the wheels of justice are likely to become clogged. At such times petty and discredited politicians, cheap and snoopy lawyers without practice and gossiping neighbors come to the front.[95]

I have found no evidence that the Justice Department's inquiry into the *Capital Times* was directly aided by the *State Journal*. A similar department inquiry into the activities of the *Milwaukee Free Press* was, however, assisted by the *Milwaukee Journal*. Before the declaration of war in 1917, the *Free Press* had been openly sympathetic to the German cause, a stance that had brought it into conflict with the *Journal*. As early as February 1916 the *Journal* was privately suggesting the possibility that the *Free Press* was financed, at least indirectly, by Germany. That month, a department investigator met with Henry C. Campbell, assistant editor of the *Journal*, who asserted that the *Free Press*'s treasurer had allegedly been receiving funds from foreign sources. The investigator wrote that "Mr. Campbell's information was as follows. . . . that it has been brought to the attention of the Journal management that <u>Gustave Trostel,</u> a millionaire tanner and violent pro-German, who is the Treasurer of the Free Press . . . has been footing the bills for the Free Press; that he in turn is reported to be supplied with money from abroad, presumably from Germany; that Mr. Campbell or no other member of the Journal management has proof of this receipt of money from Germany but that it is confidently believed, not only by the Journal management but by many other people in Milwaukee."[96] The department's investigation of the paper continued into 1918. Interviews with people formerly connected with the paper failed to uncover any clear link with the German government. For example, Gilbert Seaman, a former *Free Press* official, had little love for his former employer. Seaman, previously president of the company that owned the newspaper, had departed from the *Free Press* in 1916 and would later explain his decision publicly by saying that "I could have no connection with a paper, which, in my opinion, was not loyal." In his March 1917 interview with the Justice Department, Seaman asserted that he had been very involved with the *Free Press* until March 1916, around which point he became alienated from the newspaper's leadership. Seaman conceded that "he knew very little of what was going on" at the newspaper since then. He asserted that the German ambassador had not helped to purchase the paper when it had been sold in 1915 and had not assisted the paper before March 1916. Although Seaman was unaware of whether or not the newspaper had been supplied with money from Germany after March 1916, he "does not take any stock in the rumor which has become current in Milwaukee that the paper has been financed or is being subsidized by the German government."[97]

The *Journal* continued to supply information about the *Free Press*. In March 1917, assistant editor Campbell tipped off the department to an impending conference of those owning shares in the *Free Press* corporation and provided a written account, purportedly authored by a *Free Press* official, portraying some of those affiliated with the newspaper as being discontented.[98] In January 1918, George Mayo, then in the midst of his *Capital Times* inquiry, prepared for an investigation of the *Free Press*. Mayo conferred with officials of the Free Press Corporation, "who offered me access to all books, records, letters, papers, and the bank accounts of the company." An executive with the paper, Theodore Kronshage, described by Mayo as "a big, blustering, bullying kind of a man," then appeared and made clear that he did not want the paper to cooperate. Kronshage, a prominent lawyer, soon relented, agreeing to release the material, noted Mayo, as long as the attorney general affirmed "that any information I obtained would be strictly confidential." The Justice Department in Washington soon afterwards sent Kronshage a letter promising discretion in the matter.[99] To judge from the file on the *Free Press*, it appears that the investigation soon petered out. In any case, the *Free Press* printed its last issue in December 1918 and merged with the *Wisconsin News*.[100] The nationalistic crusade that the *Journal* had carried on in its pages earned it a Pulitzer Prize for journalism in 1919, with the awards committee commending the newspaper "for its strong and courageous campaign for Americanism in a constituency where foreign elements made such a policy hazardous from a business point of view."[101]

Some Wisconsin employers saw the Justice Department as a tool for curbing labor unions. When Madison butchers went on strike in 1918, a local meat shop owner complained to investigator Willard N. Parker that an Anton Artner had ruthlessly intimidated those workers who wanted to return to their jobs. Parker then met with the chief of the Madison Federation of Labor, Joseph Brown. In Parker's estimation, Brown was no radical but rather a sensible advocate of labor's cause: "a conservative man, who is doing a great work for union labor in this city." Defending the actions of the butchers, Brown asserted that the strikers had eschewed violence. After his discussion with Brown, Parker decided that the department would intervene only if "violence is threatened or a demand is made by one side for an investigation. When this happens all parties concerned on both sides will be brought into a conference, but this outlook seems to be that the entire affair will be settled without any further action by this Department."[102]

In another labor case, however, the Justice Department response seems to have tilted in favor of management. In late August 1918 investigator Frank Wolfgram recorded that "E. A. Oliver, Pres. of the Milwaukee Patent Leather Co, reported to this office that there was a strike on at his place; that several of the leaders of this strike were German alien enemies." After meeting with Oliver and with some strikers, Wolfgram concluded "that there was nothing more than a demand for wages." In his report, Wolfgram took no position on the legitimacy of the workers' claims, but he apparently wanted to end the strike, presumably because the factory produced "leather for trench shoes for the United States government." He conferred with the strikers, "who," he noted, "after having conditions explained to them, returned to work and expressed a willingness to go back to work and take the matter up with wage board if they considered they were not receiving sufficient money."[103]

In the case of a potential labor dispute in Marinette, however, detective A. A. Viall sided quite openly with management and sought to disrupt union activities. In early June 1918, Richard Hoskins, an official from the Marinette and Menominee Paper Company advised Viall that some kind of work stoppage might be brewing. Presumably as a way of encouraging federal intervention in the matter, Hoskins mentioned that there had been some problems with the quality of the paper product his company was supposed to supply to the Rock Island Arsenal.[104] Viall quickly visited the plant, and in the company of Hoskins questioned three employees—Albert Tetzlaff, William Williston, and N. P. Gaffney—"with regard to their knowledge of the impending strike and with a view of ascertaining if possible whether they were members of the I.W.W." Over the course of the meeting, Hoskins secured the departure of Williston and Gaffney from his employ, and at some point, either during or, more likely, after the meeting, Tetzlaff too was fired. Viall believed that since the company was under contract to the federal government, and that since, in his opinion, the workers were treated well and paid adequately, the workers' right to agitate should be sharply circumscribed. Viall told Tetzlaff, Williston, and Gaffney "that any attempt to interfere with the completion of a Government contract would result disastrously for those implicated, and that the question of Unionism had no part in it; that the working conditions at the plant in question were very good, and from their own admissions they had received four raises in wages within the past year, and in addition had been granted a bonus on their last year's wages." Another perspective on Viall's talk came from his interrogation subjects, who later provided statements as to what had transpired. By Williston's account, included in the investigative file, Viall was deeply hostile to organized labor: "Mr. Viall then said, do you know what you are, you are a pro-German to which I said no, sir, I am not pro-german. He said, you are an agitator. Aint you been agitating around the mill asking [men] to join the Union? I said, yes, at noon and when off duty. He then said, didn't you tell men in the mill if they didn't join the union they couldn't work there? Answer. No sir, never. . . . He said, dont you know you are killing your son in France? I said No sir. He said, dont you know this is war time, that we want to keep the wheels going, not to be agitating, making trouble." Mr. Gaffney recounted that Viall "wanted to know why and educated man like me wanted to be president of a Pulp Workers' Union, he also warned me as to what the penalty was for striking on a job which had Government contracts." And Tetzlaff maintained that Viall, after asking some questions, had escorted him to jail, where "he called the Jail Keeper and turned the key on me." Tetzlaff asserted that he had been imprisoned for several hours.[105]

Viall's actions may have temporarily put a damper on labor militancy (several weeks later, he reported that Hoskins had "stated that labor conditions were quiet") but may have raised the eyebrows of his superiors. At some point that summer, the U.S. attorney for the Eastern District of Wisconsin, H. A. Sawyer, came into possession of the three workers' accounts of their treatment by Viall, while a "supplementary report" by Viall from early August struck a defensive tone. Viall acknowledged that Tetzlaff had been held at the jail (something he hadn't mentioned in his earlier report) but maintained that this stay had been "solely for the purpose of making Tetzlaff realize, if possible, that it was better to give civil answers and treat the situation with less flippancy." Viall sought to make clear that he hadn't been trying to disrupt labor activity: "There was absolutely no intention of detaining this man simply because he was interested in the union." [106]

In short, a number of citizens in the state, for a variety of reasons, sought to enlist the Justice Department as an ally. To some extent, these appeals in at least some cases were probably rooted in genuine concerns that particular individuals or organizations were acting against the national interest or were breaking the law. But some detectives came to believe that other motives were likely fueling some of these accusations of disloyalty.

Almost certainly, the most wide-ranging and thorough single investigation in Wisconsin focused on Victor Berger, the chieftain of the Socialist Party of Milwaukee. Investigators reviewed copies of his publications, and the *Journal's* Frank Perry Olds provided translated material from the *Vorwaerts*, a German-language journal published by the *Leader's* parent Social Democratic Publishing Company.[107] The department also talked to people who had some kind of connection with the party or with the *Milwaukee Leader*. The *Leader's* editor for sports, Thomas Andrews, did not claim to have intimate knowledge of the management of the newspaper but did volunteer "his opinion that Victor L. Berger has entire charge and is boss of the Milwaukee Leader." Andrews added "that he had informed Berger that some of his writings were rather radical."[108] Louis Borchardt and Clarence Anderson, previously employed at the *Leader* as administrators, offered their insights as to how the paper was run.[109] A former editor, Osmore Smith, maintained that during the period of American neutrality, the *Leader*'s proprietor had "called him into his office and informed him that he wanted German victories played up and Allied victories down," while another former editor offered a similar story of Berger wishing to soft-pedal Germany's setbacks.[110]

In its search for information, the department was able to draw on divisions within Socialist ranks—in particular, among former Berger associates who now supported the war. Algie M. Simons, after his departure from the *Leader*, had taken to publicly bashing Socialists as allies of Germany and had enlisted in the Wisconsin Loyalty Legion, an organization dedicated to invigorating support for the war effort. His wife, the Socialist May Wood Simons, shared her husband's nationalist sentiment and assumed a leading role in the Milwaukee County Council of Defense's Americanization Committee.[111] To the Justice Department, Algie Simons provided a copy of a report he had drafted, which asserted that during the period of American neutrality, the *Leader* had taken up the German cause. Holding forth the possibility that the *Leader* had been receiving financial support from Germany, the report called on Berger to disclose the sources of revenue for his newspaper.[112] It also appears that the Justice Department drew on the writer Carl Sandburg, who formerly had served as an organizer for the party in Wisconsin and had been an associate of Berger's. Sandburg, however, had since had moved to Chicago and later became a supporter of the war effort. A report from the summer of 1918 noted that a "Carl Sanburg," interviewed in Chicago, asserted "that he has known Victor Berger" for some time and characterized the Milwaukee Socialist as a German sympathizer and as self-centered to boot.[113]

On one occasion, detective John E. Ferris shadowed Berger as the latter traveled from Milwaukee to Sheboygan and back. Presumably thinking it important to record anything that might indicate where Berger's loyalties lay, Ferris discerned that Berger, in talking with his fellow Socialists on the rail journey returning to Milwaukee, "manifested a demeanor of considerable pride when he stated 'The Bavarians were the shock troops of the German Army.'"[114]

In addition, the department worked with Milwaukee school superintendent Milton Potter to see if Socialist members of the school board had violated the law. Potter was a devoted nationalist who had helped organize the massive patriotic parade in the summer of 1916 in Milwaukee.[115] In November 1917, a convention of the Wisconsin Teachers'

Association passed resolutions expressing "our confidence in our chosen commander-in-chief, President Woodrow Wilson," while lamenting "that Senator Robert M. LaFollette fails us in this, the greatest of all, crises"—resolutions that enjoyed the support of the association's president Milton Potter.[116] Socialists Meta Berger and Elizabeth Thomas, on the other hand, voted against measures that would have more fully incorporated the school system into the network of home front activities. In October 1917, for example, Potter and the Socialists disagreed on the issue of whether or not schools should be involved in the distribution of loyalty petitions for teachers and students to sign. The petitions, issued by the Wisconsin Loyalty Legion, a patriotic organization, vowed support for the war effort; Berger and Thomas thought that the schools should not purvey such pledges, and Thomas explained that students who eschewed affixing their signatures "may be in disfavor with their teachers and stigmatized as traitors by their fellow pupils." Superintendent Potter disagreed and, according to the *Leader,* declared, "I have signed that petition, and if I had my way every man, woman and child would sign it."[117] Potter and the Socialists clashed at a school board meeting the following year as well, when Elizabeth Thomas offered a resolution stating "that individual children shall not be solicited or urged to contribute to funds or to purchase tickets or stamps." Thomas wanted to guard the dignity of those students who could ill-afford to donate money. "She said that in many cases," noted one press account of the meeting, "the children too poor to contribute to funds had been subjected to embarrassment and that in some cases children had stolen money so that they would not be singled out in their classes as 'slackers.'" Such a resolution might have also hindered the ability of instructors to raise funds for war-related efforts in the classroom, which may explain why the meeting took a turbulent turn. "A discussion between [Socialist school board] Director Stern and Supt. Potter," reported the *Leader,* "as to whether one should be ashamed of poverty brought forth the following statement from Potter, which was shouted out angrily: 'Any one who is ashamed of poverty is not fit to be an American citizen.'"[118] A *Leader* editorial pointed out the resolution's relationship to the war effort. "When a man can hardly buy coal and food and shoes for his children," it insisted, "they ought not to be expected to furnish cigars and candy for our soldiers."[119]

Socialist resistance to efforts to enlist student support for the war effort probably explain why superintendent Potter told detective Frank

Wolfgram in August that Meta Berger and Elizabeth Thomas were not backing the government. Potter, wrote Wolfgram, "is fully convinced that subjects are working together and opposing every move they make which might be an aid to the government or likewise." Potter confessed, however, that he could not suggest anyone who might provide more details about Berger and Thomas.[120] Meeting with Wolfgram less than a month later, Potter "stated that <u>Miss Hall</u> . . . was a former friend of <u>Mrs. Berger;</u> that she had since broken relations and that Miss Hall might be able to give some valuable information." When interviewed, Hall, expressing her belief that Meta Berger was a German sympathizer, provided another lead, noting that a Mrs. B. W. Harrington regularly went to the conferences of the school board. Wolfgram paid a visit to Mrs. Harrington, discovering "that she had notes of most every meeting that she had attended." Wolfgram added, "these notes were gone over carefully in an attempt to refresh[en?] Mrs. Harrington's memory as to specific remarks or actions."[121] Nothing seems to have resulted from these inquiries.

The Bergers realized that they were under scrutiny. In July 1917, Victor wrote Meta, "I want *you* to be careful, what you are saying to strangers. . . . I don't want them to arrest you. I have troubles enough as it is. Moreover, I don't want them to make use of your expression as *additional* prove of my 'disloyalty.'" That November he likewise implored his daughter Doris, "Do *not* talk *about the war* to anybody—not even to your best friends." Writing to her daughters in March 1919, Meta advised, "be sure to destroy my letters. Don't leave them about for curious eyes to see. And there are many such, believe me. Not only curious eyes, but willing spies." A later note to her children included the injunction "destroy this letter."[122]

The federal government's actions against the Socialists went beyond surveillance to disrupting the affairs of Berger's organization and targeting him for prosecution. In 1917, the post office decided that the *Leader* would no longer be considered second-class matter and the following year stopped delivering first-class correspondence to the paper. In March 1918, the Justice Department disclosed that it had earlier prepared indictments against Berger on Espionage Act charges; further indictments followed that October. Berger went on trial that December, along with other prominent party members, and was convicted in January 1919.[123]

The Socialists mounted a spirited counterattack to these investigations and harassment. Socialists successfully blocked an effort to pass a city ordinance outlawing seditious expression. The alderman sponsoring the proposal, under which violators would have been subjected to a penalty of up to $250, claimed that he was acting on behalf of Justice Department agent Ralph Izard. A Socialist alderman first tried to amend the proposal with a proviso asserting that the law could not "be used to punish a citizen for freely expressing his opinion on any matter." The bill was passed by the city council without the amendment but was vetoed by the mayor (also a Socialist), Daniel Hoan, who declared, "the idea that people can not criticize an administration whether city, state or national, is one borrowed from the archives of either the kaiser or the czar."[124]

The *Milwaukee Leader* played a crucial role in the Socialist Party's battle against government harassment by highlighting reports of investigators abusing their authority in their search for disloyalty. For example, in February 1918, the paper gave prominent coverage to Martha Huettlin's experience with an investigator from the American Protective League, a volunteer auxiliary of the Justice Department. That month, the department initiated an inquiry of Huettlin after receiving allegations relating to her, including the charge that disloyal statements had been made in or about her boardinghouse. Summoned downtown to the Federal Building, Huettlin met with and was questioned by Harry King, an APL investigator. In an affidavit, Huettlin claimed that King "began to interview me in a rough, bullying manner," and that he "pointed to an 'iron cross ring' I was wearing on my finger which had been given to me because I had made a donation to the Austro-German bazaar for the wounded, held in Milwaukee in the spring of 1916. He asked me why I was wearing it. He then grasped the ring, which was still on my finger, and with great violence pulled at it until it was torn from my finger. In my fright and pain I cried out. He took the ring. I was then on the point of hysterics, as I remember." Shortly thereafter, Huettlin passed out and, after reviving, went by ambulance to a hospital. A reporter for the *Leader*, receiving permission from Mrs. Huettlin to secure her ring, met with King, who made it clear that he was not going to return the piece of jewelry. The reporter alleged that during the ensuing colloquy King inquired of him if he were a native of America and declared, "You are one of these fresh young men, aren't you? Do you know that I can have you clapped in prison? I've dealt with your kind before."[125]

The *Leader* featured the story, as well as a photograph of the widow Huettlin, on its front page with the headline, Woman Removed to Hospital from Federal Bldg. Charges Violence Used by U.S. Sleuth. The *Leader* printed her affidavit of her experience and noted that Huettlin, who it portrayed as "rather frail looking," had filed a protest with special agent in charge Ralph Izard.[126] Izard subsequently said that he would conduct an inquiry, soon afterward asserting that "no one attached to this office would be guilty of treating any woman brutally." In support of his claim, Izard provided notarized statements from King and from another witness to the encounter, both of whom claimed that that Huettlin had pulled off her ring herself.[127]

The *Leader*, in turn, assailed the "miserable whitewash" provided by "Mr. Ralph Izard, 'special agent in charge of the Bureau of Investigation,' which is the high sounding title of the 'spy department,'" and claimed that "intimidation, bullying, and personal abuse of so-called 'alien enemies' by the so-called 'secret service agents,' has become an established practice in the Federal building." The *Leader* took pains to point out that it had no sympathy with the implicit message of such nationalistic jewelry, whatever its origin. "The German 'Iron Cross,' the English 'Victoria Cross,' the French 'Croix le Guerre'—all look alike to us," opined the *Leader*, adding, "to us they are emblematic of crucifying the common d—fool for the benefit of some king or plutocrat." However, "to abuse and man-handle a man or a woman for wearing such a cross is not only brutal, it is also idiotic."[128]

The *Leader* continued to criticize what it termed the federal government's lack of respect for individual freedoms. Later that month Justice Department detective W. E. Cox interviewed Milwaukee restaurateur and Socialist aldermanic candidate Peter Zoll. In his report Cox noted that he had administered "a very severe lecture" to Zoll, who had acknowledged his allegiance to Socialism and pacifism. In short order, the *Leader* printed a front-page story on Zoll's interrogation under the headline, U.S. Sleuth Flashes Gun on Socialist in Quiz. According to the *Leader*, an unnamed "government secret service agent," in accosting Zoll, had displayed a pistol and during the course of the interrogation had said, "You are one of them blank, blank, low-lived, doggy pacifists—one of those who are against the government." Zoll, asserted the *Leader*, had been subjected to a "Humiliating Grilling."[129] The newspaper hammered away at Justice Department misbehavior in other parts of the country as well. In September 1918 the Justice Department helped to coordinate large-scale roundups of potential draft-evaders in New York City—"slacker raids" that netted not only large numbers of innocent men but also a good deal of criticism from Congress.[130] In September, after Attorney General Thomas Watt Gregory conceded that aspects of the raids violated the law, Victor Berger, in a column for his newspaper, compared the roundups to anti-Semitic pogroms in Romanov-era Russia. Blaming Bureau of Investigation head A. Bruce Bielaski for the raids, Berger asserted that old-world ethnic bigotry may have lain at the root of the roundups. "To judge from his name—Mr. Bielaski's father was probably a Russian Cossack," he speculated, adding, "And the son wanted to give the East Side of New York a taste of how his father treated their fathers in the heyday of the rule of the czar."[131]

At the same time, Victor Berger and his Socialist allies recognized the political value of protesting federal abuses of power. Before the April 1918 special election for the U.S. Senate, in which Berger was a candidate, one piece of Socialist campaign material proclaimed that "your vote will also decide between autocracy or a free country, between rule by spies or free speech. It will decide whether you must continue to whisper your innermost thoughts, your deepest desires to your best friends, because you are afraid to speak them out loud."[132] As the September primaries for the general election approached, the *Leader* reflected that "Just at the present moment decent men are almost stifling with the smothered protests which they can not utter," and Berger himself observed in his column that "the ballot box is the only place where a man may still tell his views without danger from some secret service spy."[133]

Indeed, the Socialist strategy of emphasizing the threat to freedom of expression appears to have paid off handsomely at the polls. In the April 1918 special election to fill the seat of the deceased Senator Paul Husting, Victor Berger earned more than a quarter of the vote statewide—more than tripling the party's percentage from the Senate race of 1916. That November, in a three-way race, Berger won election to Congress from the Fifth District, representing part of Milwaukee County. His plurality, 44 percent, was the highest that he or any other Socialist had ever obtained for that district. The party's candidate for the Fourth Congressional District, also representing Milwaukee County, lost in a two-man race but still compiled the largest percentage ever achieved for a Socialist for that seat—42 percent.[134] In races for county offices, the party secured the posts of sheriff, district attorney, county clerk, register of deeds, clerk of courts, county treasurer, and coroner, while the party's candidate for

The Socialist Party of Milwaukee responded to Justice Department investigations and harassment by accusing the federal government of trampling constitutional liberties. A poster from Victor Berger's 1918 campaign for a U.S. Senate seat from Wisconsin depicts him as a champion of freedom of expression. (Wisconsin Historical Society, WHi-1901)

governor, Emil Seidel, took the county. In 1916 the Socialists had won seven of one hundred races for seats in the state assembly; in 1918 the party took sixteen seats.[135]

Analyses of the election results along ethnic lines suggest that the Socialists' message on civil liberties had resonated with the state's German population. In Manitowoc County, on the Lake Michigan coast, the correlation between German ethnicity and support for Socialist gubernatorial candidate Emil Seidel was +.87, while in Marathon County, in the central part of the state, the figure was +.85. In one overwhelmingly German precinct in Marathon County, Seidel garnered more than 89 percent of the vote. Among German Americans, Lutherans were more likely than Catholics to cast a Socialist ticket, which is perhaps a reflection of the long-standing animosity of the Roman Catholic Church toward the party.[136] Conversely, the rise of civil liberties as an issue came at the expense of the party most closely identified with wartime repression—the Democrats. Since the turn of the century, the percentage of the state vote for the Democratic presidential candidate had ranged from 28 percent in 1904 to more than 42 percent in 1916. In 1920, however, Democratic nominee James Cox received only 16.2 percent of the statewide vote, while Republican Warren G. Harding received more than 70 percent of all ballots cast. Socialist Eugene Debs, meanwhile, having been convicted of violating the Espionage Act, campaigned from his cell in the federal penitentiary and won 11.5 percent of the statewide vote.[137] Many issues, such as postwar economic dislocations and animosity toward the Versailles Treaty, help explain the Democratic meltdown that year, but the aggressive methods of Wilson's Justice Department accelerated the party's decline.[138]

Ultimately, the story of the Justice Department in Wisconsin is one of cooperation and resistance. In seeking to shape the churches, journalism, and politics of the Badger State, the department relied on local informants—educators, newspaper employees, town postmasters, average citizens—for guidance, and sometimes those volunteering information may have had ulterior motives. The department's work in the state was not simply a top-down case of repression but rather was subject to the push and pull of those locals who claimed to have special insight into the sources of disloyalty. At the same time, the Justice Department's efforts were so far-reaching that they provoked protests from those people who feared the loss of their freedoms. For a time, the Justice Department became woven into the political fabric of the state.

6

Vigilantism

The First World War saw an explosion of mob violence and vigilantism aimed at dissenters. The Justice Department found itself in competition with this older tradition of extralegal violence. In an effort to weaken the mob impulse, department officials, both high and low, took a tougher stance against dissent. In the field, some enterprising department detectives sought to directly discourage extralegal violence, though at least one investigator came close to excusing vigilantism, and one detective indirectly exploited the threat of mob violence to quell dissent.

The American practice of extralegal violence—punishing of alleged wrongdoers by private groups rather than by government judicial or police authority—dates to colonial times. In the years leading up to the American Revolution, patriotic mobs tarred and feathered officials charged with enforcing unpopular customs regulations, while during the war, the same punishment was meted out to those who seemed loyal to Britain or hostile to the Revolutionary movement.[1] Starting in 1767, South Carolina's Regulators emerged as a powerful vigilante movement that sought to control frontier lawlessness by subjecting alleged criminals to whipping or exile. Similar groups appeared in newly settled territories in the last decade of the eighteenth century, and over the course of the next one hundred years vigilante organizations appeared in the South, the Midwest, the Pacific coast, and the mountain West. In the middle decades of the nineteenth century, vigilantes increasingly resorted to hanging as a penalty. Antebellum lynchings targeted whites,

Mexican Americans, and African Americans, and sought to punish both violent offenses and property crimes. In the South following the Civil War, a massive campaign of extralegal violence aimed at Republicans and politically active blacks hastened the collapse of Republican Reconstruction state governments. By the late nineteenth century, lynching for property crimes had declined, while lynch mobs were increasingly targeting African Americans. In 1893, for example, white lynching parties in ten southern states murdered a total of ninety-nine blacks and eleven whites. By 1917, however, lynching appeared to be extinct or on the wane in much of the nation. Iowa mobs lynched twenty-three people from 1874 to 1900, but only one lynching had occurred in the state since that time. In California, forty-nine individuals had been lynched between 1875 and 1900; by contrast, in the first decade and a half of the twentieth century, nine people had been killed by mobs. In the South, however, lynchings continued, although at a somewhat slower pace than in previous decades.[2]

The revival of vigilantism during the First World War can be traced to a number of factors. From the spring of 1917 on, the increasing emotional commitment of many Americans to the war led them to be less tolerant of dissent. The first American combat deaths occurred in November 1917, and the gradual expansion of the casualty lists brought home the seriousness of the European conflict.[3] When in February 1918 a German submarine destroyed the ship *Tuscania,* carrying American soldiers in the waters off Ireland, resentment toward critics of the war escalated. The *Democrat* of Manson, Iowa, declared,

> Is the war coming close enough to you now, after a Manson boy has been one of those who were on the Tuscania, sunk by a German submarine? If Herbert Gustafson's body is at the bottom of the ocean along the northern coast of Ireland, or washed up along the shores of the Emerald Isle, every pro-German in this country is particeps criminis in his murder.[4]

Anger toward dissenters also stemmed from frustration over the setbacks that dogged the Allies from the summer of 1917 through the spring of 1918. On the eastern front, the Russian Provisional Government's summer offensive of 1917 fizzled amid the collapse of the army's morale.[5] In November, the Bolsheviks, promising a quick end to the war, seized power in Russia, and in the following March signed a peace treaty that left Germany free to shift its forces elsewhere. Aside from the

British successes against Turkish forces in the Middle East, news from other fronts was not encouraging. At Caporetto in October 1917, the Central Powers began an offensive that sent the Italian army reeling in retreat, while on the western front the German offensive in March 1918 threatened to drive a wedge between the British and French armies.[6]

The American government and media blamed many of the reverses on German propaganda. An article presented by the Committee on Public Information, a federal agency tasked with generating popular support for the war, alleged that German propagandists had dampened the morale of Russian servicemen.[7] On 31 October 1917, as the Russian Provisional Government tottered on the verge of collapse, and as the Italian army was in retreat, the *New York Times* argued that Germany had deployed propaganda in an attempt to weaken support for the war among Allied populations. Such efforts, the paper's editors claimed, had been effective in Russia and might bear fruit in Italy as well. Likewise, asserted the *Times,* the United States should be on guard against pro-German propagandists at home:

> Let us no longer treat these agents of disruption and destruction as if they were honest but amiably misguided American patriots, exercising their holy right to express their opinions without let or hindrance. What they are doing is not exercising the right of free speech, but carrying on the demoralizing and disintegrating propaganda concerted in Berlin for the purpose of paralyzing the American national will.

The Russian and Italian experiences, the *Times* maintained, provided another reason for voting against Morris Hillquit, the Socialist candidate in the upcoming New York City mayoral election: "Let us take warning by Russia; let us hope for the best in Italy; and let us see to it that we be not betrayed into the ruinous path which Russia has taken, the ruinous path into which the Italian Hillquits are betraying Italy."[8]

Accompanying this alarm over German propaganda was a fear of subversion of all sorts. The country was awash with rumors of German-backed espionage—of saboteurs hindering military production or otherwise trying to cripple the war effort.[9] Such conspiracies, so the thinking went, could flourish only if the government handled disloyalty leniently, so such rumors diminished public confidence in the competence of the Justice Department.

Indeed, the department came under a hail of criticism in this period. When it paroled some interned enemy aliens from detention in

January 1918, the *New York Times* questioned the department's efforts to control the subversive activities of German citizens living in the United States. An interned alien who had sufficient clout, the *Times* complained, "usually manages to secure a mitigation of sentence, and, under a system of parole, guarded only by an obligation to make weekly appearances before a so-called supervisor, he gains a degree of freedom quite sufficient for the weaving of any plots to which he may be inclined."[10] The American Defense Society (ADS), a private organization dedicated to generating support for the war, echoed such allegations. Asserting that the Justice Department suffered from a shortage of both money and manpower, the society suggested in February 1918 that the department be provided with additional resources; the following April, the ADS accused the department of failing to vigorously hunt down treason. "The complaint of the United States of America against the Department of Justice," claimed the society, "is that it seems to be inherently weak."[11] One cartoon from the *New York Times* in late April 1918, bearing the caption, "He knows it's not loaded," depicted a policeman (labeled "Dep't. of Justice") aiming a pistol at a smiling plotter.[12]

As a solution, some advocated bypassing what they saw as an ineffectual legal system. On 16 April 1918, Senator George Chamberlain (D-OR), introduced a bill that, for certain war-related cases, would have supplanted civilian courts with military tribunals. Under Chamberlain's proposal, anyone who tried to hinder the functioning of the armed forces by distributing treasonous material to servicemen would be tried before a military court, which would have the option of imposing the death penalty. Releasing suspects on bond "makes the criminal courts unfit to handle war crimes," declared the senator, who added that "under the law as it is now we indict a man for making seditious speeches and he is quickly released and is free to go ahead with his seditious work."[13] At hearings on the bill held before the Senate Committee on Military Affairs, witnesses suggested that the legal system was overwhelmed by its wartime responsibilities. The chief of army intelligence, Ralph Van Deman, claimed, "We have got to have summary justice in order to meet the kind of thing we are up against in this country. . . . The ordinary courts . . . are tied up with form and red tape and law which they can not get around." John F. McGee from the Minnesota Commission of Public Safety declared that "the department of justice has been a ghastly failure in prosecuting propagandists, spies, and traitors. The federal district attorneys in many instances have no fighting

Sherlock Holmes: WE ARE NOW ON THE TRACK OF A DANGEROUS GERMAN.
Department of Justice: MARVELOUS! MARVELOUS, HOLMES! I DON'T SEE
HOW YOU DISCOVER THOSE THINGS.

Even as the Justice Department vigorously worked to silence opposition to the war, some critics accused the agency of failing to curb saboteurs and subversives. On 18 July 1918 *Life* magazine, a humor weekly with a circulation of more than 130,000, featured this cartoon depicting a top-hatted and slow-witted Justice Department oblivious to the trail of bombs and propaganda left by "a dangerous German." (courtesy of St. Louis Public Library)

stomach for the work."[14] Although Chamberlain withdrew his proposal in the face of determined opposition from President Wilson, who termed it a threat to civil liberties, Chamberlain had reinforced the notion that the Justice Department was impotent. The *Los Angeles Times'* coverage observed that "even in the brief hearings, Senator Chamberlain has developed in a public way what every one in Washington has known—that the Department of Justice has been and is now incapable of properly punishing spies and traitors."[15]

With newspapers and patriotic societies decrying the Justice Department as lax, many Americans felt justified in turning to vigilantism. Suspected disloyalists were forced to participate in ceremonies, such as kissing the Stars and Stripes, as a means of demonstrating their allegiance to America. "It is impossible to pick up a newspaper these days without finding accounts of angry citizens having forced pro-Germans to march through the streets placarded," complained the *Idaho Daily Statesman* in April 1918, adding, "usually these pitifully useless parades are ended when the victim is forced to kneel and kiss the flag in public."[16] Yellow paint was smeared on the homes and persons of those whose commitment to the war effort seemed lacking.[17] On 12 July 1917, a posse in the Arizona mining town of Bisbee rounded up more than one thousand alleged members and supporters of the radical IWW, placing them on a train bound for New Mexico.[18] In October 1917, the Reverend Herbert Bigelow, an advocate of Socialism and pacifism, was abducted and flogged before a mob in Kentucky; in Oklahoma the following month, a vigilante organization, the Knights of Liberty, whipped, tarred, and feathered sixteen members of the IWW.[19] At least two individuals died at the hands of mobs. On 1 August 1917, vigilantes lynched Frank Little, an IWW organizer, near Butte, Montana, and on 5 April 1918, a mob hanged Robert Prager, a German immigrant suspected of sabotage, just outside of Collinsville, in southern Illinois.[20]

Such lynchings met with widespread criticism in the press. Those responsible for Frank Little's death, argued the *New York Times*, "should be found, tried, and punished by the law and justice they have outraged." The *News-Democrat* of Belleville, Illinois, about ten miles south of Collinsville, denounced Robert Prager's lynchers as "a band of cowardly murderers" whose foreheads now bore "the brand of Cain," while a more restrained editorial in a Georgia newspaper termed the incident "ill-considered and inexcusable."[21] Less violent patriotic vigilantism came in for criticism as well. "White-capping, tarring and feathering, lynching and other kinds of lawlessness are not the right and proper means to inspire and maintain the loyalty of American citizens," declared a South Carolina paper, which in a subsequent editorial asked: "Who could think of Robert E. Lee approving the lynching of an alleged pro-German, as in Illinois the other day, or the tarring and feathering of a woman suspected of pro-German utterances in Michigan?"[22]

Still, editorialists sometimes betrayed a degree of sympathy for vigilantes. Denouncing Prager's murder as "deplorable, to be sure" the *Fort Worth Star-Telegram* nevertheless maintained that "no American with red blood in his veins can criticize the spirit which caused the Collinsville people to lose their temper and commit violence." A North Dakota newspaper called the lynching of Frank Little a "crime not to be excused or palliated in the slightest degree" but also found that "it is easy to understand how the feeling was generated which prompted it." The *Daily News* of Aberdeen, South Dakota, went so far as to claim that the mass November 1917 whipping of IWW members in Oklahoma may have been justified. Condemning the attack as "an atrocious thing," the

A Remedy for the Soap-Box Traitor

On 1 November 1917 *Life* magazine published this comic endorsement of vigilantism. (courtesy of St. Louis Public Library)

News added that "thoughtful persons, however regretful they may be over the incident, will not too hastily condemn the Oklahoma mob" and suggested that perhaps extralegal measures had been needed to curb the Wobblies. "One of the cruelties of war," lamented the paper, "is that it forces otherwise law-abiding persons, all too often, to take the law into their own hands."[23]

Even the well-respected and nationally circulated *McClure's* magazine, famous for its muckraking journalists, in August 1918 celebrated nonlethal vigilantism when it featured Arthur Train's short story "The Flag of His Country," set in an Arizona town. The hero, a fervently patriotic Union Army veteran and prospector, attends a meeting of workers being addressed by seditious, radical union "agitator" Sam Green. Brandishing a "long black pistol," the veteran commands Mr. Green, "Git down on your knees and kiss your country's flag."[24]

Vigilantism put further pressure on the Justice Department, as it was interpreted as a protest against the government's tolerance of sedition. The day after the Collinsville lynching, the editors of the *Chicago Daily Tribune* implicitly blamed Prager's death on the lack of action by the authorities. One should not be too surprised, the editors wrote, if "the irritation and exasperation caused by the unrestrained exhibitions of disloyalty in various parts of the country would flare into a rage somewhere and lead to an act or acts of violence." On the same day, the *Morning Olympian* in Washington State, observing that "mob rule is spreading rapidly throughout the country" and that "the mobs are becoming more and more violent," called for increased vigilance by federal authorities. "The national government can stop this carnival of mob rule easily if it will," the paper wrote, "but no other agency has the power or the authority to do so. Mob rule can be stopped in this instance only by removing the cause—disloyal residents, pro-Germans, Hun propagandists. Shut up the Kaiser's little liars, remove the seditionists, and lock up the rabid pro-Germans and disloyal persons."[25] Newspaper publisher V. S. McClatchy ventured that "in my opinion, it is the apparent unwillingness on the part of the Federal authorities to deal in a spirit of stern and unremitting justice with disloyal utterances that is responsible for lynchings which we must lament and for bringing tar and feathers into play again." In Pennsylvania, the *Wilkes-Barre Times Leader* predicted that "it is very likely that there will be mobs as long as the government handles traitors and spies with velvet gloves and punishes them with slight taps on the wrist."[26]

The increasing number of vigilante acts and growing public clamor put pressure on the Justice Department to take a stronger stance toward allegedly disloyal individuals. In the spring of 1918, for example, Stuart Bolin, a federal prosecutor in Ohio, advised interning Harry L. Lewin, a shopowner whose reputedly seditious comments had "created a very bad feeling" in Columbus. Bolin had already ordered Lewin's detention after discovering that vigilante sentiments were brewing in the community.[27] In Washington, John Lord O'Brian, special assistant to the attorney general, responded with a letter asking Bolin "whether you intended to recommend . . . that Lewin be interned for the duration of the war, or whether or you merely meant that he should be detained for a period and then released upon parole." O'Brian was less concerned about the legal or potential national security issues involved than about the attitudes of local residents: "The Department would be glad to have your view, especially as the matter would seem to depend largely upon public feeling in Columbus." Bolin telegraphed back, "recommend internment Columbus Public would be greatly aroused if paroled." A subsequent department memo to O'Brian, dated 5 August, made the case for interning Lewin: "In view of the fact that he [Lewin] has been in the United States so many years and nevertheless persists in talking for Germany, on all possible occasions to his customers, and by so doing stiring up violent arguments and in view of the fact that if released he might be subjected to violence, I believe that Mr. Bolin's recommendation for internment is warranted and I therefore concur in the same." Three days later, O'Brian notified Bolin that "Lewin . . . has been ordered interned for the duration of the war." Lewin was released from his internment in 1919.[28]

Allegations of Justice Department leniency, as well as a wish to forestall vigilantism, help explain its decision to press for a new, broader version of the Espionage Act. As early as January 1918, the department had signaled its interest in legislation designed to limit criticism of war bonds, but events were to result in the eventual passage of more draconian legislation. A Montanan by the name of Ves Hall was put on trial that month in federal court for violating the Espionage Act. Hall, among other disloyal statements, had supposedly "declared . . . that the United States was only fighting for Wall Street millionaires." Judge George M. Bourquin told the jury to acquit Hall, contending that Hall's alleged words were not in violation of the Espionage Act. "The more or less public impression," declared Bourquin, "that for any slanderous or disloyal remarks the utterer can be prosecuted by the United States is a mistake." Hall's statements, he observed, had been made in a small, isolated town, with "none of the armies or Navy within hundreds of miles, so far as appears." The judge deemed it absurd to think that Hall's attacks on the war could have hurt the armed forces: "It is as if A shot with a .22 pistol with intent to kill B two or three miles away. The impossibility would prevent public fear and alarm of homicide, and A could not be convicted of attempted murder." By requiring prosecutors to demonstrate more specifically how antiwar statements had damaged the capacity of the armed forces to conduct the war, Bourquin's decision set forth a higher burden of proof for securing convictions under the Espionage Act.[29]

Bourquin's decision, announced on 27 January 1918, outraged many Montanans, and the state legislature quickly enacted a law rendering criminal the wartime expression of "disloyal, profane, scurrilous, contemptuous, or abusive language" in regards to the American "form of government," servicemen, or the Stars and Stripes. This Montana sedition act next formed the basis for an amendment to a bill then making its way through Congress designed to penalize critics of war bonds. Backers of the new, strengthened federal sedition bill argued that such strict measures were needed to forestall the wave of extralegal violence aimed at critics of the war.[30]

Likewise, the top leadership of the Justice Department sought to use the strengthened sedition bill wending its way through Congress as a means of both fending off criticism of the department as well as a way of dissipating vigilante impulses. After the lynching of Robert Prager in April 1918, the attorney general wanted to preempt criticism that the murder stemmed from his department's laxity. "While the lynching of Prager is to be deplored," announced Gregory later that day, "it cannot be condemned. The department of justice has repeatedly called upon congress for the necessary laws to prevent just such a thing as happened in the Illinois town." Here Gregory was not speaking of antilynching legislation but of stiffer penalties for the disloyal. One week later, Gregory reemphasized this point in a letter to Republican congressman Gilbert Currie of Michigan. Currie had asked Attorney General Gregory if new laws were needed to combat subversion, noting "the strong feeling throughout the country that our Government authorities are dealing too leniently with spies and dangerous enemies within our confines." Gregory responded that "if such a feeling does exist, it is mainly caused by the lack of Federal statutes" and added that "most of the disorder throughout the country is caused by the lack of laws relating to disloyal utterances."[31]

John Lord O'Brian also saw the sedition bill as a way of forestalling extralegal violence. On 18 April, in hopes of curbing "so far as possible the spread of mob-violence, evidence of which is now appearing in all parts of the Country," O'Brian sent Gregory guidelines for an announcement designed to calm the public's fears about subversion. Such a statement, urged O'Brian, could cite the recent adoption of new national security legislation, as well as "the expected early passage of certain amendments of the Espionage Law," as evidence that the federal government had the legal tools necessary to stifle subversion.[32]

The Justice Department also short-circuited congressional attempts to moderate the stringent language of the bill. In one such effort to prevent potential misuse of the law, Republican senator Joseph France of Maryland successfully offered the following amendment: "Nothing in this act shall be construed as limiting the liberty or impairing the right of any individual to publish or speak what is true, with good motives, and for justifiable ends." The Justice Department then lobbied to strike the moderating France amendment from the final version of the bill. In a letter to North Carolina congressman Edwin Y. Webb, O'Brian claimed that France's amendment would hamstring prosecutors by requiring them to demonstrate that the defendant was not motivated by noble or legitimate concerns.[33] The department's efforts succeeded, and France's amendment vanished from the conference committee's version of the bill. The Senate and House approved the committee version of the bill and on 16 May 1918 President Wilson signed it into law.[34] The bill owed its passage in some part to the department's wish to supplant mobs brandishing tar and feathers with prosecutors wielding indictments. As the Socialist Morris Hillquit declared a week before President Wilson signed the bill: "You have heard about the mobs that lynch people for alleged sedition and we have been given to understand that the sedition law was necessary to prevent this. Why, this law is the nationalization of lynching!"[35]

Dissipating the vigilante spirit by pledging tougher law enforcement was one thing, but actually guarding citizens against extralegal violence was another matter entirely. Even if vigilantes were brought to trial, getting a conviction proved difficult. In 1918 the state of Illinois, cooperating with local authorities, prosecuted eleven men on murder charges for allegedly having participated in the lynching of Robert Prager. To many media observers, the case against the defendants was strong; indeed, one of the mob ringleaders, Joseph Riegel, had admitted to his role in the lynching during the initial coroner's inquiry, although he later recanted his admission in court. The jury deliberated for three-quarters of an hour, then declared all eleven defendants not guilty.[36] To the *New York Times*, the verdict "was evidently a gross miscarriage of justice," while the *Fort Wayne News and Sentinel* argued that "the people of Collinsville, Ill., seem to be possessed of the curious idea that the acquittal of the hoodlums who lynched the unfortunate Prager, vindicates the name of their community and proves its loyalty." Illinois governor Frank Lowden concurred: "The jury seemed to think that it could best show its own loyalty by condoning the crime of those who claimed to act in the name of loyalty. The result was a lamentable failure of justice." Some papers acknowledged that local authorities would inevitably have a difficult time punishing accused lynchers. "It will be a long time before juries will convict men charged with lynching as long as the trial is held in the neighborhood of the crime or alleged crime that provoked it," noted a Georgia newspaper, which also observed, "if any gambler had wanted to make a book on that Collinsville trial he could have with perfect safety laid odds ten or twenty to one they would all be turned loose in short order." The acquittal did not surprise the black-owned *Chicago Defender*, which was engaged in a crusade against southern lynchings. "That members of the mob who took part in the lynching of this man would be detected and punished seemed at the outset only a bare possibility," maintained the *Defender*, especially given the past failure of authorities to punish lynchers: "In turning back the pages of America's day book of similar crimes—especially those staged below the Mason and Dixon line—little if any retribution is meted out to the human brutes who have no respect for the laws of the land, and hold a human life less valuable than the life of a common street cur." Given the failure of states to guard their citizens from vigilantes, the *Defender* argued, it was incumbent on the national government to protect the rights of Americans: "What a great step forward it would be if the federal government had and exercised the power to protect citizens living under the Stars and Stripes, living by the laws of the land, living in one of the states of the Union."[37]

Indeed, there was a significant precedent for vigorous federal action to stop mob violence. When the Justice Department was created in

1870, in the midst of Reconstruction, the Ku Klux Klan was engaged in a campaign of terrorism aimed at curbing the political activities of African Americans and Republicans in the states of the former Confederacy. A set of laws passed by Congress in 1870 and 1871, known as the Enforcement Acts, required election officials to carry out their responsibilities in a fair and honest fashion, and banned the intimidation of voters. Those who conspired together with the goal of depriving the voting rights of others were subject to penalties as well. With the blessing of the attorney general, federal prosecutors embarked on a crusade against the Klan. In northern Mississippi alone, hundreds of individuals were convicted of violating the Enforcement Acts between 1871 and 1884. The armed forces also took a leading role in policing the Klan. The overall result, in the words of Eric Foner, was that "by 1872, the federal government's evident willingness to bring its legal and coercive authority to bear had broken the Klan's back and produced a dramatic decline in violence throughout the South." However, with the fading of the northern commitment to racial equality in the late nineteenth century, the Justice Department abandoned this early effort to suppress vigilantism.[38]

In World War I, the top leadership of the department spoke of the importance of stifling lynching. Even before the declaration of war, the head of the Bureau of Investigation attempted to enlist the APL in curbing potential mob activity. On 2 April 1917, Bureau of Investigation chief A. Bruce Bielaski, in a letter to A. M. Briggs, who at the time was helping to found the APL, warned that if war broke out, "innocent persons may be in danger of losing their lives or of suffering serious property damage at the hands of mobs by more or less irresponsible individuals and possibly also in some instances, at the hands of persons who are ordinarily sober and conservative citizens, but who have temporarily allowed their passions to get the better of their good judgment." American honor was at stake, as "the Department feels very strongly that any violations directed against persons simply because of their nationality or friendly attitude toward a country with which the United States may be at war, would be a serious blot upon the name of this country." Bielaski stressed that noncitizens who did not threaten public safety or violate laws deserved to be left alone, noting, "The protection of peaceful aliens is regarded as an important patriotic duty."[39] And in an address to the American Bar Association roughly a week and a half after the lynching of Robert Prager, Attorney General Gregory called for "the discouragement and suppression of lynch law in every form," suggesting that mob violence put American prisoners of war in Germany at risk.[40]

But in contrast to the 1870s, the Justice Department's efforts to smother vigilantism during the First World War were often halting and tentative. The Justice Department's deference to the notions of local control and states' rights, as well as a limited legal arsenal, hampered its work against extralegal violence. The attorney general's *Annual Report* for 1918, referring to vigilantism, asserted that "this department has made every effort to put down disorders of this character, but most of these activities lay outside of its reach and in control of local authorities."[41] Bureau chief Bielaski, for example, did not think that the September 1918 kidnapping of and attack on Olli Kiukkonen of Minnesota was in violation of federal law. Kiukkonen, an unnaturalized immigrant from Finland, had declared that he no longer wished to become an American citizen. On 18 September two or three men, one dressed in a uniform, had called on Kiukkonen at his rooming house in Duluth; the uniformed man told Kiukkonen that he needed to visit conscription officials. Kiukkonen went outside with his visitors. A telephone call that night to a local newspaper claimed that Kiukkonen, following a quiz about his national loyalties and citizenship status among other things, had been tarred and feathered. On 30 September Kiukkonen's lifeless body, coated with oil or tar, was found hanging from the limb of a tree. Bielaski ordered an "immediate investigation" of the matter; special employee Frank Pelto, who spoke Finnish, took a leading role in the inquiry, interviewing, among others, the last men to see Kiukkonen at his rooming house before his disappearance. Detective John T. Kenny then telegraphed Bielaski with details about the case. Reporting that "Kiukkonen was unemployed easy going Finn not labor agitator or criminal," and that the coroner genuinely thought that Kiukkonen had taken his own life, Kenny confessed that he didn't know "if any federal law violated." Bielaski wired back that "apparently no Federal law violated."[42] Indeed, although there was a federal statute against kidnapping at the time, it applied only to cases in which the intention was to bring about the enslavement of the victim. Bielaski still issued instructions to help "local authorities in any way proper in vigorous investigation."[43]

The department did attempt to bring to justice the perpetrators of the largest extralegal action of the war—the mass IWW deportation from Bisbee, Arizona, in July 1917—charging the defendants with conspiring to violate the rights of the deportees. However, a federal court in

December 1918 dismissed the department's indictments, a decision later upheld by the U.S. Supreme Court.[44]

While the Justice Department was reluctant to become too deeply involved in punishing extralegal violence after the fact, nothing prevented resourceful detectives in the field from working to prevent vigilante attacks from taking place. In Pennsylvania, for example, special agent W. H. Butterworth met with a Rev. Lindemeyer, who allegedly had failed to demonstrate adequate support for the war. After the interview Butterworth met a man "who informed the Agent that he very much feared that violence would be used in dealing with Lindemeyer; that a Mr. Mitchell had informed him that there was a bunch of men who were to gather at the school house to discuss the case and have a committee wait on the minister." (Lindemeyer himself, however, had rejected an offer to attend this meeting.) Butterworth located Mitchell, and together the two went to the conference at the schoolhouse. Sensing that "many of the people there were very much wrought up over the matter," Butterworth warned the group against taking the law into their own hands: "Agent addressed the meeting and advised that utmosr caution should be used ih such matters and that violence should not be resorted to, as the Government preferred that all such matters should be taken up in the proper manner, through the authorized Government officials, who would deal with the matter through the regular channels prescribed by law." With the help of others at the meeting who felt the same way, Butterworth convinced the group that the Lindemeyer case was the responsibility of law enforcement officials. "Several others spoke," wrote Butterworth, "and advised those present that the matter should be handled by the Government authorities, which suggestion was finally agreed to by those present, after which the meeting adjourned."[45]

In a similar case, special agent Charles Petrovitsky sought to dissipate violent sentiments aimed at a F. Schoknecht, a Lutheran pastor from Snohomish, in western Washington State. Army intelligence had been concerned about Schoknecht's loyalty; a letter from the Military Intelligence Branch asserted that evidence pointed to pro-German tendencies of the pastor, who supposedly had "been very inquisitive concerning troop movements in and about Puget Sound."[46] Investigating the matter, Petrovitsky visited a Snohomish bank president, who claimed that Schoknecht had sold numerous war bonds among local German residents. Others, it appeared, were not concerned about Schoknecht's patriotism, although there was some underlying uneasiness with the pastor: "Conservative solid men of Snohomish with whom Agent talked on this date," wrote Petrovitsky, "all agree that subject is above suspicion as to his loyalty and honor as a man generally. They however as a rule do not like the ideas of subject teaching German in his school at this time." Despite the seemingly measured response of the "conservative" town citizens, Petrovitsky did note a report from the mayor that Schoknecht might be in peril: "Mayor, J. W. Hall . . . stated that he understood that the pupils in the school said prayers for the Kaiser and that if the school opens next month there will be trouble. This Agent did not hesitate to press this gentleman for the name of his informand and finally demand the name of the man. Hall stated that Stretch was the man causing the trouble and that he (the Mayor) would not be responsible for what might happen under the leadership of Stretch."

Petrovitsky decided to track down the source of the rumor: "Agent hunted up Stretch who appeared to back up the accusations against the subject and told a lot of rambling tales about the flag and unpatriotic teachings of the subject generally. Stretch stated that if he had given the word about two weeks ago there would have been something doing in the town of Snohomish." Perhaps suspecting that Stretch's allegations were little more than hot air, Petrovitsky "asked Stretch to appear before a Notary Public and put his statements, regarding subject, into writing and under oath to furnish a baisis of prosecution against subject." At this request Stretch balked, and "finally admitted that the matter was all hearsay and did not deny that it all originated in his own mind when Agent accused him of this fact." Characterizing Stretch as a "scoundrel," Petrovitsky issued the following warning: "Agent advised him that if 'anything happened' in Snohomish he probably would be held responsible on account of his malicious prattlings."[47]

Petrovitsky subsequently visited Pastor Schoknecht, describing him as "in all respects, by carriage and speech, an American." In his report, the agent reproduced a letter denouncing vigilantism that had appeared in the Everett, Washington, *Daily Herald* a few months earlier. The author of the letter, J. P. Keaton, advised that "all of us at this critical time . . . watch ourselves that we do not say or write anything that will incite mob violence." Noting that there had been a controversy over German instruction at Snohomish, Keaton defended the patriotism of the city's Lutherans. In his report Petrovitsky observed that the letter of Keaton "has gone on unchallanged. Peace has reigned since at Snohomish except as herein indicated to be still stirred up by Stretch and a few of his followers who have received a hint from Agent which they will no doubt heed."[48]

It is not clear to what extent such warnings were effective, especially after the eleven men charged with Prager's lynching were found not guilty by a Collinsville, Illinois, jury in June 1918. When detective Sydney W. Dillingham looked into conditions in Saline County, Missouri, later that month, he found that the verdict had emboldened one would-be vigilante. A Flare Neal told Dillingham "that he had given Christian Gabler pastor of the Evangelical St. Paul church until Sunday to either stop preaching in German, give us his pulpit or take the consequences and stated that he had sighted the Prager case in Illinois to Gabler and told him it only took a jury of 12 men 39 minutes to acquit the men that hung Prager and said if he doesn't stop preaching in German there is going to be something doing." Dillingham then escorted Neal to a bank and engaged an employee there in a discussion of the attitudes of the local population. The bank employee "accused the members of the German Church of being disloyal and said that they were going to have to cut out their German talk, schools, and preaching in German in their churches o[r] they would be burned and something doing. Agent told him that they had better not start anything like that for the Government was against that and would not stand for it."[49] Then, "Neal asked Agent what he was doing securing evidence to prosecute a mob," at which point Dillingham "told him he was working in the interest of the United States Government and that his Department was for the detection and prosecution of crime." Seemingly unintimidated, "Neal then said there will be something doing all right, but I will have an alibi and besides you have to convict a man by a jury." Dillingham then visited Christian Gabler, a German-born minister, who provided him with an affidavit describing his past statements on the war and also recounting his encounters with patriotic-minded locals. Gabler's affidavit acknowledged that in 1916 he had questioned from the pulpit the morality of the commerce in munitions, but added that those who belonged to his church had invested thousands of dollars in war loans and that his son had joined the navy. His statement also maintained that a small group, including Neal, had earlier that month visited him and "asked me if I would not promise to discontinue the use of the German language in service, school and in all public places." The affidavit further asserted that Neal had paid a threatening return visit later that month: "Mr. F. Neal called upon me Sunday June 23, 1918 at my home and showed with the example of the

Prager case that members of a mob would not be convicted and asked me what I could do if someone would throw a sheet over my head." Dillingham portrayed Gabler's family sympathetically: "Christian Gabler's wife was present, and between sobs she related to Agent about her and her husband giving their written consent for their son to join the United States Navy and showed Agent and old picture of this boy when he was about 5 years of age, dressed in the United States uniform holding a United States flag and told of Neal calling on her husband and asking him how he would like for some one to throw a sheet over her head and drag him out sone night."[50] Dillingham concluded his report by noting that two men who belonged to Saline County's Home Guards told him that "they would have men hid around Blackburn Sunday night to see that the above mentioned parties did not carry out their threats."[51]

Dillingham's report in the Saline County matter sheds light on his motivations in an earlier investigation in Cass County, on the western border of Missouri, where a weekly newspaper, the *Cass County Democrat* of Harrisonville, had been stoking the fires of intolerance. The permissiveness that county residents had displayed "toward some of the expressions of disloyalty that have come from various nooks and corners" would only last so long, wrote the *Democrat* on 11 April 1918. "Some of these times the casualty lists from the battlefields of France will contain the names of Cass county boys, and the gradually-growing anger of Cass county fathers and Cass county brothers and Cass county loyal American citizens is going to break bonds," forecast the paper, adding ominously, "Then, there is going to be 'something doing!'"[52] Less than six weeks later, on the night of 21 May, J. B. Stehman, a Mennonite farmer living a few miles from the Cass County town of Garden City, was tarred and feathered, allegedly for failing to contribute to the Red Cross fund. The mob, reportedly numbering around fifty, seemed to enjoy a good deal of community support. "The party which called on Stehman," claimed the *Cass County Leader*, "was composed of many of the most prominent and mostly highly respected citizens of Garden City and vicinity." The *Democrat* saw little need to tone down its highly charged patriotic rhetoric. On the same day it reported Stehman's tarring and feathering, the following statement, titled "SLACKER!," appeared on its front page:

> Any man or woman in Harrisonville, or any place else, for that matter, who does not make a generous contribution to The American Red Cross

Second War Relief Fund—circumstances permitting—is in exactly the same class with those wretched creatures of feeble brain and jellyfish spine—those cowards we call "SLACKERS."

Such a man or woman isn't worthy to blacken the shoes of an American Soldier, who "goes across" to give his life on the blood-soaked soil of France.

Such men and women . . . are not fit to associate with REAL AMERICANS. Such men and women are not fit to live in this community, or anywhere else in America. They are not fit to live, at all, and SHOULD BE IN HELL.[53]

That night, another county resident, farmer Fred Koeller, who allegedly had been stingy in offering donations to the Red Cross and who supposedly had expressed himself as sympathetic to Germany, was tarred and feathered. "He is probably a better and more valuable citizen now, than he has ever been heretofore, since the true spirit of patriotism, displayed by his captors, could not have been entirely lost on him," observed the following week's *Democrat,* which, along with the *Cass County Leader,* also featured an announcement from county prosecuting attorney J. R. Nicholson pleading with county residents to avoid mob violence. Nicholson himself was imbued with the spirit of 100-percent Americanism—earlier that month he had issued an intemperate letter to a local Lutheran minister requesting that his church stop preaching in German—but his announcement cautioned against vigilante excesses. While asserting that disloyalists were still at large ("there is in this county a handful of yellow curs who are not American, not German, not human, and not even first-class dogs"), Nicholson also cautioned that vigilantism could have serious repercussions, "If, however, righteous indignation against this bunch of curs should lead to such violent extremes as the taking of life, the destruction of property by fire, or other violent means, the consequences might be martial law declared and state troops thrown into our splendid county," he wrote, adding, "may I venture the suggestion that extremes in violence are not warranted or required? May I also venture the suggestion that loyalty, patriotism and good citizenship call for restraint from violent extremes?"[54]

In the spring of 1918, prosecutor Nicholson felt that he would have to consult the federal government, so he, along with an official from the Cass County Council of Defense, informed Dillingham that Joseph Driver, who was a Mennonite clergyman, might be the target of extra-legal violence. Dillingham "advised them that that was the State's

"SLACKER!"

Thousands of you, who read this page, have been filled with LOATHING and CONTEMPT for those SHIRKERS and COWARDS, to whom we apply the epithet, "SLACKER."

But, there are others, in addition to those who are too cowardly to shoulder a gun, to whom that term of BLACK DISGRACE applies.

Any man or woman in Harrisonville, or any place else, for that matter, who does not make a generous contribution to The American Red Cross Second War Relief Fund—circumstances permitting—is in exactly the same class with those wretched creatures of feeble brain and jellyfish spine—those cowards we call "SLACKERS."

Such a man or woman isn't worthy to blacken the shoes of an American Soldier, who "goes across" to give his life on the blood-soaked soil of France.

Such men and women, no matter whether they live in cottages or mansions, are not fit to associate with REAL AMERICANS. Such men and women are not fit to live in this community, or anywhere else in America. They are not fit to live, at all, and SHOULD BE IN HELL.

For, such men and women are perfectly satisfied to continue their selfish pleasures, and go along in their selfish, narrow ruts, while the BEST YOUNG MEN IN AMERICA go across the sea to place their bodies as a barrier of human flesh and blood between us and our enemies.

Such men and women are YELLOW TO THE CORE. By neglecting to help the Red Cross all they can, they're helping the Kaiser; they're making the World-Wide War last longer, and they're helping to drive cold bayonet steel into American Soldiers' breasts.

Such men and women—TIGHTWADS, if you please—may belong to the Church, and attend every service, but they can't fool God Almighty with their WHINING SONGS and HYPOCRITICAL PRAYERS. Their YELLOW, NARROW, "SQUEEZY" SOULS are marked, and they're destined for berths, after life, THREE FLOORS BELOW HELL.

From the front page of the *Cass County Democrat* of Harrisonville, Missouri, of 23 May 1918.

business to give her citizens protection and keep down mob violence and at that they issued a state warrant for Driver and caused his arrest." Dillingham didn't say in his report if he was surprised by this turn of events, but in any case he took the opportunity to talk with Driver, who provided a written declaration noting that his church believed in nonviolence but also acknowledging that "we stand in readiness to help our Government in civilians work."[55] The following day, Dillingham met with Driver once more. A report by the county attorney included in the file seems to imply that Dillingham had pushed the pastor to soft-pedal the pacifism: "Driver admitted that he had told . . . a Mennonite boy that if he put on the United States uniform and did military duty that he would have to take steps to exclude him from the church. After a lengthy interview with Driver by Mr. Dillingham and myself he promised not to teach or preach such matters."[56] Dillingham noted in his own report that he "had Driver to call in the leading men of the Church which he did." Conferring with the Mennonites, Dillingham was told that when an assemblage had approached the wife of a church bishop, questioning her in reference to Red Cross contributions, members of the group had suggested applying tar to her person. The conference then engaged in some creative thinking as to how the Mennonites could help the nation without sacrificing their pacifist ideals. Driver noted that "the Mennonite religion doesn't allow their members to assist in war, therefore they won't purchase Liberty Bonds, but they asked Agent about Farm Loan Bonds and stated that they would be pleased to assist the Government by purchasing same." By buying Farm Loan Bonds instead of war bonds, the Mennonites would be investing in a federally managed program that provided rural credits to farmers, instead of directly subsidizing the armed forces. The Mennonites "also upon suggestion of Agent to give Liberally to the Red Cross giving systematically once each month." Indeed, Dillingham noted that "Driver gave $25.00 to Red Cross June 4, 1918." The *Kansas City Star* appeared to suggest that the Justice Department had actively pushed the Mennonites into shifting their attitudes toward the war. Noting that Driver had been arrested, the *Star* claimed that: "through the influence of a Department of Justice official the colony has changed its attitude to one of full support to all war measures, and has organized to make monthly contributions to the Red Cross. Mr. Driver, after giving a substantial sum to the Red Cross, and the sentiment against him having subsided, was released from jail."[57]

Dillingham also cautioned locals against mob violence—a task made easier by the fact that the Mennonites were willing to support the country in some fashion. He met with "ten business men of Garden City, Missouri, and they advised Agent they would do everything in their power to keep down mob violence." Dillingham "advised them frankly that the Government had laws under which to prosecute disloyal citizens and that the Government wasn't going to have mob violence."[58] Still, it seems that even these concessions by the Mennonites failed to mollify their critics in Cass County. In August 1918 Dillingham was notified by officials from the county war bond sales program and the county Council of Defense that residents wished that the Mennonites would make more of a contribution to the war effort. Dillingham then authorized a panel of nine to "represent the citizens of Cass County" and a panel of eight, including Joseph Driver, "to represent the Mennonites," and "advised committee of citizens to ask for $1500.00 per month of the Mennonites for the Red Cross." The two panels then agreed on a contract under which Mennonites would contribute $1,500 monthly to the Red Cross starting in September. The *Cass County Leader,* printing the contract on its front page, pronounced it "highly creditable to the Mennonites of the county."[59]

Most likely, Dillingham regarded pushing Mennonites to contribute to the country as a worthy accomplishment, but his actions in the entire Cass County episode were probably also guided by his personal repugnance for mob violence. In both the Saline County and Cass County episodes he issued admonitions against vigilantism, and in his reports for both cases he allowed the potential victims of mob violence (or someone speaking on their behalf) the chance to allege that they had been threatened by extralegal violence.

Admonitions against mob violence proved ineffectual, however, when Justice Department investigator T. E. Campbell, responding to reports that farmers allied with the Nonpartisan League were subjected to intimidation, issued a warning in June 1918 against efforts to evict residents from Rock County, Minnesota. The *Eau Claire Daily Telegram* reported that Campbell "had before him newspaper accounts of 376 farmers of Rock county being forced to register and disavow their political affiliation under threat published in a posted notice that they would be deported from the state if they insisted upon remaining members of the league." The *Telegram* added that Campbell "said that no action would be permitted which would be considered a parallel for the Bisbee, Ariz., incident."[60] The publicity given Campbell's declaration may explain why, on 6 August, John Meintz of Rock County visited Justice Department headquarters in St. Paul and told Campbell about his experiences at the hands of vigilantes. Meintz related that on 21 June, a mob had driven him from Rock County and had escorted him to the Iowa state line. Meintz provided the names of more than twenty people who he said were members of this mob. Several weeks after this incident, Meintz recounted, he had come back to Rock County, and, on 3 August, had managed to dodge the clutches of another mob that had been lying in wait for him. Presumably as a way of demonstrating his loyalty, Meintz told Campbell that he did not belong to the Nonpartisan League and that he had bought war bonds.[61] After his meeting with Campbell, Meintz returned to Rock County. On 21 August 1918, Meintz reappeared at the St. Paul office and told Campbell that on the previous evening vigilantes wearing masks had tarred and feathered him. A member of the mob had threatened him with lynching, telling him that that would be his fate if he ever returned to Minnesota again. "Mr. Meints took off his coat and vest and opened his shirt and showed United States Attorney Jaques and Agent the tar and feathers, which were still on his body," noted Campbell, adding, "He is well coated." Somewhat abashed over his failure to follow up on Meintz's earlier visit, Campbell wrote, "This case should have been investigated some time ago, and it was Agents intention, as stated in his former report to give it prompt attention, but have been so busy with work along other lines that this case has been neglected."[62]

One investigator in Arizona seemed more or less resigned to accept vigilantism as inevitable. Detective Justin C. Daspit looked into the case of Marco Benderach, who was being detained by police in Bisbee and who had been moved to a jail in the nearby town of Lovell. Benderach, it seemed, had been one of those evicted from Bisbee earlier that summer, and had since returned. At some point, a local policeman had claimed that shortly before the deportation in July, Benderach had "stated in his presence that he intended to sell out his business and go and fight with the Germans." But Daspit found that Benderach was actually a Serbian with limited English facility who apparently wanted to fight Germany. The policeman "was frank enough to admit that he might have misunderstood Benderach," but Daspit, presumably concerned that a clueless vigilante might at some point again threaten the Serbian's life, seems to have concluded that Benderach would not be safe in Bisbee. "I could see nothing in the case to justify any action against the accused," wrote Daspit, "but advised him that it would be best for him to leave Bisbee, which he agreed to do."[63]

Another department detective, J. Reese Murray, when confronted with an example of vigilantism, blamed the victim. When Ulysses Hale, an African American labor activist who was working on a campaign to unionize steelworkers in Birmingham, Alabama, was tarred and feathered in June 1918, Murray did order an investigation but was probably not too enthusiastic about efforts to track down the perpetrators.

As Murray explained to a visiting Labor Department official, who had come to confer about the matter and about how to avoid similar events in the future, Hale had brought his punishment on himself. "I suggested to him," wrote Murray in his report, "that the <u>causa causans</u> of this incident seemed to be that the negro <u>Hale,</u> had made many and repeated remarks inciting race predjudice among the negroes, and that this was, in my opinion directly responsible for his being tarred and feathered, and that the treatment of <u>Hale</u> was in no wise directed at <u>Labor</u>." Murray did offer his help to the Labor Department representative.[64]

Murray's indifferent attitude comes as little surprise, given the fact that he was completely unsympathetic to Hale's message. "Some days" before the vigilante attack, Murray had personally met with Hale and two other black men, lecturing them that while it was fine "to organize labor to their heart's content," it was not permissible to push for work stoppages. Murray explained that efforts to challenge segregation were doomed to fail and would result in violence:

> I further told Hale that it had been reported to me that he had been preaching "social equality,"—that is that the negroes should be permitted to have all the privileges that the white people had, be permitted to send their children to white schools and churches, etc. etc. and stated to him that if such conduct on his part were true, it was certainly bound to result in the failure of the very object he was sent here to attain, because the negroes of the south know that these things are impossible for him at this time, and such ambitions on the part of the negro race would certainly end in blood-shed if an attempt were made to realize them, and that furthermore, any negro sent south to organize labor, would, if such ideas were advanced by him, become the object of suspicion.[65]

For Murray, this was not just an issue of questionable labor activism; in his mind Hale was challenging the racial caste system. Hale was just one of many Americans in 1918 and 1919 worried about an increasingly assertive African American voice, and such fears led to a sharp rise in violence against blacks. According to one study, the number of African Americans lynched nationwide rose from 36 in 1917 to 60 in 1918 to 76 in 1919.[66]

While some investigators worked to discourage vigilantism, one detective indirectly exploited the threat of extralegal violence as a means of silencing dissent. In Oakland, Illinois, detective W. H. Kerrick raised the specter of vigilantism to try and stifle W. C. Carpenter, an allegedly unpatriotic Socialist. In a conference attended by Kerrick and other locals,

Carpenter "agreed finally that he would never speak another word on Socialism hereafter at least during the period of War," and "promised that he and his wife would both join the Red Cross the next day." The day after, a postmaster told Kerrick that "from what he had learned of the meeting the night before he felt certain that CARPENTER would make no more trouble in Oakland." Toward the conclusion of his report, Kerrick acknowledged that he had indirectly deployed the threat of vigilante violence: "CARPENTER was told not only by myself but by others that it was just such conduct toward the Government coming from such persons as he was that started Mobs and that he was in danger of even the good people of Oakland using violence toward him."[67]

In addition to accelerating the rise of a national police force headquartered in the nation's capital, the First World War also briefly rejuvenated an older practice of extralegal violence in which communities administered penalties ranging from tarring and feathering to lynching. These two means of enforcing the law—one centralized, professional, and legal, the other local, amateur, and extralegal—coexisted uneasily in a kind of rivalry. The upsurge in vigilantism pushed the department into taking a harder line against critics of the war, and at the same time the danger posed by patriotic mobs probably enabled investigators to more effectively manipulate those who dissented from the attitude of patriotic enthusiasm for the war effort. When detective Sydney Dillingham spoke with Mennonites of Cass County, Missouri, about ways in which they could contribute to the nation, he was speaking to a community living under the threat of mob violence. Likewise, detective Kerrick warned a resident of Oakland, Illinois, of the violence that could befall dissenters. At the same time, department officials sought to discourage local communities from engaging in extralegal violence.

In the long run, the rash of vigilantism in 1917 and 1918 strengthened the power of what would, in 1935, become the Federal Bureau of Investigation. During the era of the Second World War, the Justice Department and the FBI cited the mob violence of the era of the First World War as a reason for centralizing counter-subversive efforts at the federal level. "Twenty years ago inhuman and cruel things were done in the name of justice; sometimes vigilantes and others took over the work," observed Attorney General Frank Murphy in September 1939, adding "we do not want such things done today, for the work has now been localized in the FBI." In June 1941, an Iowa newspaper recorded that an FBI official speaking to an audience in Waterloo had "said many innocent persons had suffered at the hands of vigilante groups during the world war."[68] In the summer of 1943, J. Edgar Hoover boasted that "we have, by planning and coordination, avoided the hysteria which prevailed in World War I when innocent persons were persecuted and harmed as the result of ill-advised vigilante activities." The Justice Department and FBI bolstered their own legitimacy by presenting themselves as more orderly and judicious than the mobs of the First World War.[69]

Epilogue

Previous studies of the wartime activities of the Department of Justice have depicted prosecutions under the Espionage and Sedition Acts as the chief instrument by which the department sought to stifle dissent. But the focus on prosecutions has had the effect of understating the scope of the department's activities. Far more commonly, department investigators watched, warned, and reprimanded suspected seditionists. The bad-tendency test gave the department's detectives a tremendous degree of latitude in determining whether speech interfered with the war effort and set the tone for the informal campaign to browbeat dissenters into submission. Even though some investigators showed restraint, others, believing that any critique of the nation's leadership could weaken morale, treated criticism of the president as illegal. Using a similar logic, some detectives treated criticism of the nation's economic or racial inequalities as criminal. This wartime campaign served as a rehearsal for Justice Department and Bureau of Investigation surveillance and harassment of groups considered disloyal in subsequent decades.

The experience of the Justice Department during the war was profoundly shaped by the tendencies of the Progressive Era. For some time progressives had advocated creating centralized government agencies to deal with the increasing complexities of national life, and during the war Attorney General Thomas Watt Gregory and his special assistant John Lord O'Brian established a centrally directed office for the suppression of dissent. Progressives had also long advocated educating and, to varying degrees, fostering the assimilation of immigrants. In 1917 and

1918 Justice Department detectives, in the interest of wartime unity, took an analogous approach, instructing immigrants not only about the risks of remaining loyal to their homelands but also on their civic duties as Americans.

Indeed, during the war the federal government adopted both progressive methods and goals. Progressives had long argued for a more assertive federal role in the economy and in particular for regulation of transportation and industry. New agencies appeared in 1917 and 1918 to manage the wartime economy. The Railroads War Board took command of the nation's train network, the War Industries Board worked to boost the output of war materiel in the nation's factories, and the Food Administration sought to maximize agricultural output and to minimize the consumption of vital foodstuffs.[1] Progressives had for a long time pushed for a more active governmental involvement in combating prostitution as well; the Wilson administration, fearing that soldiers who consorted with prostitutes would become infected with sexually transmitted diseases, devoted considerable wartime effort to curbing the sex trade. In the spring of 1917, under section 13 of the Selective Service Act, Congress empowered the secretary of war to shut down houses of prostitution in the vicinity of military bases, while the Wilson administration created the Commission on Training Camp Activities (CTCA), one of whose missions was to make sure that red-light districts close to military camps were abolished.[2]

For his part, J. Edgar Hoover ensured that the Bureau of Investigation would more fully embrace the progressive model of bureaucracy. Hoover had joined the department in 1917, working in that section devoted to dealing with enemy aliens. Assuming control of the bureau in 1924, Hoover reshaped it into a very highly centralized agency in which agents, tightly bound by regulations as to their conduct, were expected to supply detailed reports of their activities to their superiors. Putting his faith in trained experts, Hoover sought to staff his bureau with college graduates. But Hoover's progressivism meant more than simply espousing managerial innovations—his crucial role in organizing the dragnet of suspected radical immigrants after the war indicates that he shared the nativism common to many progressives.[3]

At the same time, the links between the Justice Department and progressivism should not be overstated. While the Justice Department embraced progressive methods and much of its respective agenda, it was often at odds with much of the movement itself. Many progressives,

NEW HUNTING GROUNDS

The Justice Department continued to target radicals after the end of World War I, as the above editorial cartoon, appearing in the *Rockwell City* (Iowa) *Gazette* of 20 November 1919, suggests.

such as Senator Robert La Follette, argued that the federal government was trampling on constitutional liberties, and the department's campaign against dissent estranged progressives from Woodrow Wilson and the Democratic Party. Since 1912, Wilson's calls for reform and his success during his first term at shepherding liberal legislation through Congress had brought many progressives into the Democratic fold, but his administration's repressive policies during the war sparked confusion and discord within the progressive camp. Three days after Republicans had seized control of both houses of Congress in the 1918 midterm elections, the progressive journalist Oswald Garrison Villard complained to presidential secretary Joseph Tumulty, "I am dismayed by the defeat, because you in the White House have not built up a liberal party and have permitted [Postmaster General] Burleson and Gregory to scatter and intimidate such liberal forces as have existed."[4] Gregory stepped down as attorney general in 1919; his replacement, A. Mitchell Palmer, supervised postwar raids on suspected immigrant radicals that further alienated many progressives from the Democratic Party and helped doom Wilson's campaign for American membership in the League of Nations. Wilson's proposal for an international organization to guard the peace did appeal to liberal opinion-makers, who could have provided Wilson with another base of support for his battle for American membership in the League. As it happened, however, the administration's continued imprisonment and prosecutions of dissenters meant that liberals, instead of rallying behind Wilson's drive for the League, spent much of their time attacking the president's policies on civil liberties. The failure of progressives to press vigorously for U.S. membership, according to historian Thomas J. Knock, helps explain the failure of the League to make it past Republican opposition in the Senate.[5]

Two of the progressives who oversaw the campaign against dissent— Alfred Bettman and John Lord O'Brian—would later demonstrate a genuine commitment to civil liberties. In 1930, for example, Bettman lent his talents to the legal defense of three Communists who, attempting to proselytize Ohioans, had been arrested and convicted under that state's criminal syndicalism law.[6] The previous year, Bettman asked President Herbert Hoover to restore the rights of those convicted of violating the Espionage Act during the war. Bettman defended the wartime prosecutions on the grounds that they had helped to funnel the nation's repressive tendencies into nonviolent, legalized forms. "On analysis," he wrote, "I think that the Department of Justice and its War Division would be given credit as an agency of moderation rather than aggravation of an emotionalism which might otherwise have resulted in violence and as having conserved, under difficulties, fundamental civil liberties." At the same time, Bettman more or less conceded that the prosecutions themselves had often violated principles of the rule of law, as "they arose, with a very few exceptions, out of expressions of opinion about the war, and while the text of the statute did not contemplate the creation of a political type of offense, in actual practice, due to war atmosphere, there can be no doubt that a large portion of the offenses which resulted in prosecution and conviction were of a type properly denominated as political, a type of offense which is considered as contrary to the American theory of public justice."[7]

After leaving the Justice Department in 1919, John Lord O'Brian repeatedly warned against the dangers of government repression. In 1920 he publicly criticized the decision of the New York state legislature to bar five elected Socialist representatives from taking their seats.[8] As war loomed in the summer of 1941, O'Brian noted that the public's escalating fear of foreign subversion had created an environment in which "the legislative branches of government throughout the country have been more and more inclined to favor extreme restraints upon private utterance," and pointed to the recently adopted Alien Registration Act (also known as the Smith Act) as containing the potential for abuse.[9] At the height of the McCarthy era in 1952, O'Brian stated that the search for subversion since 1940 was eroding traditional freedoms. Government repression, according to O'Brian, typically came not in response to a clear and present danger to national security but as a reaction to inflamed public opinion. Drawing on his own experience at the Justice Department during World War I, O'Brian praised his superiors Wilson and Gregory for (at least as he recalled) having tried to maintain a sense of public calm about the extent of German influence, and he contended that the current crop of national leaders lacked any such restraint. "During the First World War there were always public officials of the first rank who were seeking to minimize war excitement and to quiet unjustified apprehension," he maintained, adding that "in contrast, during the recent war and, to a greater degree, since the recent war, the legislation of Congress, the attitude of the Executive Department, and the arbitrary acts of administrative officials have almost unanimously operated in the opposite direction and have steadily tended to encourage the growth of distrust, suspicion, and fear." O'Brian implied that the FBI's extensive public relations apparatus nourished exaggerated fears of the extent of the Communist threat: "No study of the influences affecting public opinion can omit reference to the Federal Bureau of Investigation. Few realize how constantly its activities are publicized daily in the press, in the films and on the radio. So great is the popular interest that fictitious spy stories have become a daily diet for millions of readers." O'Brian further raised the possibility that the agency might abuse its authority. Observing that the FBI "is now one of the most powerful agencies in the Federal Government," O'Brian asserted that "the usefulness or advisability . . . of using this agency to investigate the private lives of citizens and to accumulate thousands of files dealing with them is open to question." O'Brian, however, seasoned his warnings with praise for the bureau's "able and intelligent director," J. Edgar Hoover, who "has wisely opposed further extension of its powers."[10] Hoover's FBI, as a later generation would discover, had few qualms about targeting and harassing dissenters.

Appendix

Biographical Information of Justice Department Investigators in Wisconsin

I was able to find biographical information on eleven Justice Department investigators who worked in Wisconsin. Generally, Justice Department investigators belonged to the middle or upper middle class. At least three investigators—John E. Ferris, Frank F. Wolfgram, and Willard Nathan Parker—had earned college degrees, the possession of which placed them in the upper echelons of the middle class. According to one calculation, as of 1920 fewer than 4 percent of Americans had attended college for four years or more.[1] Ferris, a native of St. Louis, had attended Cornell University before obtaining a degree in pharmaceutical chemistry from the University of Michigan, while Wolfgram had been awarded a law degree from Marquette University in Milwaukee in 1915.[2] Parker's prominence in state affairs probably qualified him as a member of the state elite. A native of Fond du Lac, Parker, after receiving a Bachelor of Science at the University of Wisconsin, had held a series of administrative positions in various school districts. Later, he had served as assistant state superintendent of public instruction and as Wisconsin State Teachers' Association president.[3] In addition, Parker was president of the Parker Educational Company, which published the *Wisconsin Journal of Education*.[4] With American entrance into the war, the *Journal* advocated that the state's students should undergo a patriotic regimen. In the April 1917 issue of the *Journal*, Parker advised that teachers should "open school every morning with a salute to the flag and repeating the oath of allegiance as given elsewhere in this issue. Sing the patriotic songs and sing them over and over again." Unpatriotic educators deserved to be fired, he insisted: "proof of disloyalty should be sufficient grounds for the dismissal of any teacher. All for America!"[5] Personally, Parker tried to assist the war effort as best he could, joining the Wisconsin Loyalty Legion, a patriotic organization. As secretary of the Madison Club, Parker helped cancel Senator Robert La Follette's club membership in December 1917; along with a majority of the club's directors, Parker had endorsed a declaration accusing the senator "of giving aid and comfort to the enemy of his country in this great crisis when this country is fighting for its very existence and to make the world safe for democracy."[6]

Two other detectives—Charles I. Rukes and Lewis E. Sawyer—I categorized as middle class, since they had either graduated from high school or had attended high school for at least four years. (At the time, high school graduates could generally count themselves as being members of the middle class; by one estimate, fewer than 20 percent of Americans in 1920 had attended high school for four years or longer.)[7] After graduating from high school in Indiana, Rukes had served as a U.S. government farmer on the Bad River Indian reservation in northern Wisconsin, where he had also been an agent with the U.S. Indian Service. His application for employment with the Justice Department stated that he had confiscated alcohol on dozens of occasions.[8]

Wisconsin-born Sawyer had attended high school for four years and had also gone to art school in Minneapolis. Sawyer had worked a variety of occupations—artist, art dealer, and overseer of the art section of the Milwaukee Gimbel Brothers Store. He claimed experience at detective work, asserting on his application that he had worked "as spotter for Lt. Railway in catching men not doing duty and keeping tab on conductors," and he further said that he had worked "on Police force as plain clothes man." Sawyer also boasted of his ability to masquerade as a member of the opposite sex: "If necessary can make up and carry off part of a woman. (have done this without being detected)."[9]

I was not able to ascertain the educational background of three investigators—Charles Bodenbach, Charles L. Harris, and Charles Woida—but their experience in managerial or clerical positions qualifies them as members of the middle class. Bodenbach was a sales representative who at one point had been secretary-treasurer of the John Meunier Gun Company in Milwaukee. Harris been employed as a clerk for the Northwestern Mutual Life Insurance Company in Milwaukee, while Charles Woida, the son of Polish-speaking immigrants, had worked as a clerk.[10]

One employee, Kajetan Charles Jakoubek, seems to have had more of a working-class background, in terms of education and employment. On his employment application, he stated that he had received "Public school education, up to first year high school," while a background check conducted for his employment application for the department had turned up one acquaintance who "seemed to think that Jakoubek's limited education would be a drawback to his success in some ways." Jakoubek had worked in the logging industry, helping to assess the lumber potential in stands of timber. Still, Jakoubek's background in law enforcement—he had served as a county under-sheriff and was employed by the state conservation agency as a warden—plus his apparent knowledge of languages—he claimed to be able to speak German, Bohemian, and Slavonian, and to some extent Magyar and Polish—probably explain the decision of the Justice Department to hire him.[11]

I was not able to find any biographical information on some detectives, and on a few I was able to find only a few scraps—not enough to really classify them as belonging to any particular stratum of society. Henry Hugh Stroud apparently worked for the Pinkerton detective agency and as a sheriff, while Ralph Izard had worked for the Immigration Bureau.[12] The APL served as a kind of farm team for Justice Department investigators. Four men—Lewis Sawyer, Henry Stroud, Charles Harris, and Walter Cox, all of whom eventually became Justice Department employees—had earlier spent some time serving in the APL.[13] A fifth, Willard Parker, had at some point enjoyed some kind of an affiliation with the APL.[14]

Notes

Prologue

1. For examples of work that examine prosecutions under the Espionage and Sedition Acts, see Peterson and Fite, *Opponents of War;* Polenberg, *Fighting Faiths;* Preston, *Aliens and Dissenters;* and Murphy, *World War I and the Origin of Civil Liberties.* Numerous articles, such as Scott Merriman's "'Intensive School of Disloyalty'" have detailed prosecutions under the Espionage and Sedition Acts. The prosecutions of the radical labor union the IWW have been treated in Dubofsky, *We Shall Be All,* in Philip Taft, "The Federal Trials of the IWW," and in Clayton Koppes, "The Kansas Trial of the IWW." Joan M. Jensen's *Price of Vigilance* has examined the investigations made by the Justice Department's volunteer auxiliary, the American Protective League (APL). Justice Department undercover investigations have received attention from Charles H. McCormick's *Seeing Reds.* McCormick's focus, however, is limited to the Pittsburgh area and does not extensively explore efforts to silence nonradical opponents of the war. Regin Schmidt's *FBI and the Origins of Anticommunism* uses reports from the bureau's Investigative Case Files to depict the department's wartime attitudes concerning African Americans and radicals, but mainly focuses on the postwar Red scare. In *Race, War, and Surveillance,* Mark Ellis explored the Justice Department's role in monitoring blacks for alleged subversion, while Theodore Kornweibel Jr.'s *"Investigate Everything": Federal Efforts to Compel Black Loyalty during World War I* not only analyzed the national government's larger struggle against antiwar sentiment among African Americans but also detailed efforts of Justice Department investigators along these lines. In *Becoming Old Stock,* Russell A. Kazal noted that the Bureau of Investigation investigated cases of suspected disloyalty among Philadelphia's German American community. For other portrayals of the investigative aspect of the wartime Justice Department, see Cary, "The Bureau of Investigation and Radicalism in Toledo, Ohio," and Levy, "The American Symphony at War."

2. *Statistical Abstract of the United States, 1916,* 252.

3. *Congressional Record,* 65th Cong., 2nd sess., 5542.

4. As quoted in Peterson and Fite, *Opponents of War,* 8–9.

5. *Belleville* (IL) *News-Democrat,* 26 March 1918, [4].

6. *Philadelphia Inquirer,* 16 August 1917, 1.

7. *New York Times,* 29 September 1917, 10.

8. U.S. Census Bureau, *Thirteenth Census of the United States,* vol. 3, 1075.

9. *New York Times,* 27 March 1918, 11.

10. N. W. Ayer and Sons, *American Newspaper Annual and Directory* (Philadelphia: N. W. Ayer and Son, 1914–19), 1188.

11. Pfeifer, *Rough Justice,* 94–121.

12. Theoharis and Cox, *The Boss.*

13. Kornweibel, *"Seeing Red."*

14. Schrecker, *No Ivory Tower.*

15. O'Reilly, *"Racial Matters";* Garrow, *FBI and Martin Luther King, Jr.*

16. Cunningham, *There's Something Happening Here.*

17. Doyle, "USA PATRIOT Act: A Legal Analysis"; Doyle, "National Security Letters in Foreign Intelligence Investigations"; Barton Gellman, "The FBI's Secret Scrutiny," *Washington Post,* 6 November 2005, A01; Federal Bureau of Investigation, "Comprehensive Guidance on National Security Letters" (1 June 2007), available from Electronic Privacy Information Center, http://www.epic.org/privacy/nsl.default.html; "My National Security Letter Gag Order," *Washington Post,* 23 March 2007, A17; testimony of Justice Department Inspector General Glenn Fine before Senate Judiciary Committee, 21 March 2007, Federal News Service.

18. Testimony of Glenn Fine.

19. Rood, "FBI Proposes Building Network."

20. *Pittsburgh Post-Gazette,* 15 March 2006, B-1; *Buffalo* (NY) *News,* 15 March 2006, A1; the released documents are available via the American Civil Liberties Union website, at http://www.aclu.org/safefree/spyfiles/.

21. *Investigative Case Files of the Bureau of Investigation, 1908–1922,* 2. The FBI had originally microfilmed the reports and records in the early 1950s.

Chapter 1. Setting the Stage

1. *Census of Iowa for the Year 1915,* compiled and published under direction of the Executive Council of the State of Iowa, 53, 462; *Pomeroy Herald,* 10 June 1915, 27 April 1916; for U.S. Census Bureau data from Calhoun County for the year 1910, see Historical Census Browser at the Geospatial and Statistical Data Center of the University of Virginia Library, available at http://fisher.lib.virginia.edu/collections/stats/histcensus/php/state.php.

2. *Pomeroy Herald,* 2 September 1915; *Chicago Sunday Tribune,* 5 September 1915; *Chicago Daily Tribune,* 6 and 7 September 1915; *New York Times,* 7 September 1915; Luebke, *Bonds of Loyalty,* 137–38.

3. *Pomeroy Herald,* 13 August 1914.

4. Robinson to Lansing, 5 March 1917, and Chief to Eberstein, 19 March 1917, file OG ("Old German") 3688, *Investigative Case Files of the Bureau of Investigation, 1908–1922,* National Archives Microfilm Publication M1085. Files from this publication will be identified as either being from the OG (Old German) subsection or from the MISC (Miscellaneous) subsection. For information on the depot agent, see entry for Fred Robinson in *Census of Iowa for the Year 1915,* microfilm roll IA1915–69.

5. Reports of A. P. Sherwood, 30 October 1917 and 3 November 1917, OG 78958. Edwin Wattonville served as postmaster at Pomeroy's post office from 1913 until after the conclusion of the war. Letter dated 13 February 1997 from Jennifer Lynch, research assistant, Postal History, U.S. Post Office, Washington, D.C. It is possible that the department had also recruited Wattonville to monitor the pastor. One of Sherwood's reports from early September 1917 concerning Pomeroy states that "the postmaster also report that Rev. Schuman, the German Evangelical Minister whom he had been requested to watch stated prior to the declaration of war that his five borthers were in the German Army." Report of Sherwood, 4 September 1917, OG 3688.

6. Narrative of Hanni contained in report of Marshal Eberstein, 28 November 1917, OG 78958; a more legible copy of this report is found in folder 10332-6/1 to 10332-20/1, box no. 3070, Military Intelligence Division Correspondence, 1917–41, Records of the Military Intelligence Division, RG 165, National Archives, Washington, D.C. Information on Hanni is from his employment applications of 16 April 1921, 9 November 1923, and 1935(?) contained in personnel file released by FBI.

7. Report of J. F. McAuley, 1 December 1917, OG 78958.

8. Warrant for arrest of Wm. Schumann, Records of the District Courts of the United States, RG 21, National Archives, Central Plains Region, Kansas City, MO.

9. *Pomeroy Herald,* 6 December 1917; *Fort Dodge Messenger and Chronicle,* 4 December 1917.

10. *Pomeroy Herald,* 6 December 1917.

11. *Pomeroy Herald,* 20 December 1917.

12. *Pomeroy Herald,* 3 January 1918; *Rockwell City Advocate,* 3 January 1918; *Lake City Graphic,* 17 January 1918.

13. *Rockwell City Advocate,* 10 January 1918; *Fort Dodge Messenger and Chronicle,* 9 January 1918.

14. *Calhoun County Republican,* reprinted in *Lake City Graphic,* 17 January 1918.

15. *Rockwell City Advocate,* 10 January 1918.

16. *Coon Rapids Enterprise,* 10 May 1918.

17. U.S. v. Schumann, trial transcript, Records of the District Courts of the United States, RG 21, National Archives, Central Plains Region, 2–8. Hereafter referred to as U.S. v. Schumann.

18. The Evangelical Churches and the Reformed Churches joined together in 1934 to become the Evangelical and Reformed Church, which in 1961 joined with the Congregational Christian Churches to form the United Church of Christ.

19. U.S. v. Schumann, 14–15.

20. Ibid., 20, 56–58.

21. Ibid., 64–76.

22. Ibid., 84–86, 95–103.

23. Schumann appealed the assault conviction to the Iowa State Supreme Court, which rejected his appeal. See *Abstracts and Arguments,* Iowa State Supreme Court, September term, 1919; *Pomeroy Herald,* 7 November 1918; *Fort Dodge Messenger and Chronicle,* 4 November 1918; *Rockwell City Advocate,* 21 November 1918, 5 December 1918, and 6 February 1919. In December 1918, the Justice Department received a handwritten note from Schumann in which he stated that a "bunch of outlaws" had attacked his home: "The windows were smashed, bricks thrown into the bedroom and shots fired into the house, where I slept. Plaster fell on my face and bullets were picked up right from the bed. According to the testimony of a neighbor about fifty shots were fired." Schumann to Attorney General (undated, but received 29 December 1918) in Classified Subject File (CSF) on Wilhelm Schumann, file no. 9-19-910, General Records of the Department of Justice, RG 60, National Archives, College Park, MD.

24. *Rockwell City Advocate,* 1 May 1919, 20 November 1919; appellate records of U.S. v. Schumann, in Records of the U.S. Courts of Appeals (Eighth Circuit), RG 276, National Archives, Central Plains Region; *Pomeroy Herald,* 16 October 1919.

25. *Rockwell City Advocate,* 20 November 1919, 29 December 1921.

26. *New York Times,* 1 February 1915, 8; Luebke, *Bonds of Loyalty,* 83–95, 119–23, 130–31; Higham, *Strangers in the Land,* 195–97; Berthoff, *British Immigrants in Industrial America,* 205–7.

27. McAdoo, *Crowded Years,* 323–30; Link, *Wilson: The Struggle for Neutrality,* 554–58; *New York Times,* 16 August 1915, 1; 17 August 1915, 2; 20 August 1915, 7.

28. Link, *Wilson: The Struggle for Neutrality,* 645–50; *New York Times,* 6 September 1915, 1, 3, and 6 October 1915, 3; *Sun* quoted in *New York Times,* 7 September 1915, 3.

29. *New York Times,* 29 December 1915, 1. In May 1917 the German naval officer and two other conspirators were convicted and sentenced to prison. See

New York Times, 21 May 1917, 1, and 22 May 1917, 7. After the war, Rintelen acknowledged that he had indeed encouraged strikes among dockworkers. See Rintelen, *Dark Invader*, esp. 166–75.

30. *New York Times*, 3 February 1915, 1, and 4 February 1915, 1. Horn's effort had been part of a larger plan to attack several Canadian bridges. The man in charge of this larger operation, a Captain Böhm, received money and instructions to sabotage Canadian railroads from Franz von Papen, then German military attaché in the United States. At the last moment, Böhm decided to abort the plan, but Horn hadn't received word of this before setting off on his mission. Kitchen, "German Invasion of Canada in the First World War."

31. *New York Times*, 25 October 1915, 1; 26 October 1915, 1; 9 November 1915, 1; 4 May 1916, 3; 5 May 1916, 3; 6 May 1916, 20; 9 May 1916, 1.

32. *New York Times*, 18 December 1915, 1; 18 April 1916, 1; 4 May 1916, 1; 27 June 1916, 22; Link, *Wilson: Confusions and Crises*, 56–59. Papen acknowledged his role in the Canadian canal conspiracy in his autobiography. See Papen, *Memoirs*, 33–34.

33. *New York Times*, 13 April 1916, 1; 14 April 1916, 1; 29 April 1916, 4. In a subsequent trial that concluded in April 1917, six defendants were found guilty. *New York Times*, 3 April 1917, 7. For more on German intrigues during the period of American neutrality, see Spence, "K. A. Jahnke and the German Sabotage Campaign in the United States and Mexico," and Reinhard R. Doerries, introduction to Rintelen, *Dark Invader*.

34. Quoted in Link, *Wilson: The Struggle for Neutrality*, 558–64.

35. Quoted in Luebke, *Bonds of Loyalty*, 144. See also ibid., 115–94, for his examination of the relationship between nativism and politics in these years.

36. Wilson, "State of the Union Message," 7 December 1915, Lexis-Nexis Primary Sources in U.S. Presidential History.

37. Luebke, *Bonds of Loyalty*, 157–71.

38. Quoted in ibid., 178.

39. Quoted in ibid., 174.

40. Ibid., 172–83.

41. Tuchman, *Zimmermann Telegram*, 132–99; *New York Times*, 15 March 1917, 1; *Hartford* (CT) *Courant*, 19 March 1917, 1.

42. *Congressional Record*, 65th Cong., 1st sess., 102–4; Harries and Harries, *Last Days of Innocence*, 71–73. For an examination of Wilson's prewar record on civil liberties, see Link, "That Cobb Interview."

43. Some statewide studies have attempted to gauge public attitudes regarding the war. One historian, after sampling the commentary in Maine's newspapers, concluded that the state's residents "wanted war in the spring of 1917—and wanted it fervently" (Costrell, *How Maine Viewed the War*, 1–2, 81–91). Missouri's attitude toward the war has been the subject of two works: John Clark Crighton, *Missouri and the World War, 1914–1917: A Study in Public Opinion*,

and Christopher C. Gibbs, *The Great Silent Majority: Missouri's Resistance to World War I*. Crighton, relying heavily on newspapers, argued that Missourians supported the decision to enter the war, while Gibbs, tapping a variety of sources, claimed that "there is evidence that most people in Missouri opposed the war." See Crighton, *Missouri and the World War*, 5, 161–87, and Gibbs, *Great Silent Majority*, 38–49.

44. Falk, "Public Opinion in Wisconsin during World War I," 394–95.

45. *Congressional Record*, 65th Cong., 1st sess., 362. Earlier, in February 1917, a Pennsylvania congressman reported the returns of a mail poll among his constituents: 80 votes in support of going to war and 796 votes in opposition. *Congressional Record*, 64th Cong., 2nd sess., appendix, 515.

46. Capps, *From Isolationism to Involvement*, 31–58; Wittke, *German-Americans and the World War*, 112–42.

47. Shannon, *Socialist Party of America*, 93–104.

48. Kennedy, *Over Here*, 144–45.

49. Dubay, "The Opposition to Selective Service."

50. *New York Times*, 6 June 1917, 1; Emmons, *Butte Irish*, 364; Chrislock, *Watchdog of Loyalty*, 133–36.

51. *New York Times*, 5 June 1917, 1; Peterson and Fite, *Opponents of War*, 25.

52. Woodward, *Tom Watson*, 451–58.

53. Sealander, "Violent Group Draft Resistance in the Appalachian South"; Jeannette Keith notes that "opposition to the draft in the South began as a political movement, and it reached such a level that governors of three southern states asked for federal troops to put down armed bands of deserters." See Keith, "The Politics of Southern Draft Resistance."

54. Sellars, *Oil, Wheat, and Wobblies*, 77–92; Green, *Grass-Roots Socialism*, 357–61.

55. Vaughn, *Holding Fast the Inner Lines*, 16–20, 78–81, 116–17; *Saturday Evening Post*, 3 August 1918, 23.

56. For more on the Alien and Sedition Acts, see James Morton Smith, *Freedom's Fetters*.

57. For an examination of efforts to silence dissent during the Civil War, see Neely, *Southern Rights* and *Fate of Liberty*.

58. An act to regulate the immigration of aliens into the United States, 32 Stat. 1213–22 (3 March 1903); see also Preston, *Aliens and Dissenters*, 32–33.

59. Rabban, *Free Speech in Its Forgotten Years*, 27–44; Horowitz, "Victoria Woodhull, Anthony Comstock, and Conflict over Sex in the United States in the 1870s," 433–34.

60. Gutman, "The Tompkins Square 'Riot' in New York City on January 13, 1874"; Donner, *Protectors of Privilege*, 7–35; Goldstein, *Political Repression in Modern America*, 23–101; Genini, "Industrial Workers of the World and Their Fresno Free Speech Fight."

61. Quoted in Donner, *Protectors of Privilege*, 29.

62. Rabban, *Free Speech in Its Forgotten Years*, 129–76.

63. Morn, *Eye That Never Sleeps*, 94–99, 152, 158–61, 167; Fink, *Fulton Bag and Cotton Mills Strike;* Robert M. Smith, "Spies against Labor: Industrial Espionage Agencies," 65–68, and "Industrial Espionage Agencies," 93–105; Holter, "Labor Spies and Union-Busting in Wisconsin."

64. Wiebe, *Search for Order.*

65. See the *Annual Report of the Attorney General of the United States* for the following years: for the year ended 30 June 1910, 25–26; for 1911, 22–25; for 1912, 46–53; for 1913, 44–51; for 1914, 45–51; for 1915, 47–51; for 1916, 62–66. Though the bureau was formed in 1908, it only received the formal appellation Bureau of Investigation in 1909 during the administration of William H. Taft. Rosenfeld, "Organization and Day-to-Day Activities," 207.

66. Beckman, "The White Slave Traffic Act," 1111–24; McCormick, *Seeing Reds*, 9–11; Roy Lubove, "The Progressives and the Prostitute."

67. I was able to locate information on the educational backgrounds of twenty Justice Department investigators, ten of whom had received degrees in law. Arthur L. Barkey and Joseph Kropidlowski had earned law degrees at the University of Michigan, John A. Dowd, Thomas Marshall, and Donald D. Lamond had been awarded Bachelors of Law from Georgetown University, while Charles G. Petrovitsky, Diego E. Ramos, Edward Wright Byrn, Jr., Frank Wolfgram, and James Francis Terry had been awarded law degrees by the University of Iowa, Howard University, George Washington University, Marquette University, and the Evening School of Law of the Boston YMCA (later Northeastern College), respectively. Three other detectives had earned diplomas from four-year colleges in fields other than law: Willard N. Parker had obtained a B.S. from the University of Wisconsin, Max M. Schaumburger had been awarded a B.A. from Tulane University, and John E. Ferris had earned a pharmaceutical chemistry degree from the University of Michigan. Another detective, Joseph Polen, had graduated from Davis-Wagner Business College, but part of his course of study there included stenography, so his alma mater may have been more of a professional school than a liberal arts college. Of the remaining detectives, Charles I. Rukes was a high school graduate, Lewis E. Sawyer had gone to high school for four years and also to an art school, Dave L. Gershon had spent two years at a "Manual Training High School" and one year at a commercial college, Kajetan Charles Jakoubek, by his own account, had a "public school education, up to first year high school," and Albert E. Farland had a "common school" education. Werner Hanni had attended public schools and a gymnasium (roughly equivalent to an American high school) in his native Switzerland, and claimed to have attended a commercial school (though receiving no degree) in Europe. The above biographical information came from the following sources: Arthur L. Barkey, e-mail to author from Marilyn McNitt,

Reference Assistant, Bentley Historical Library, University of Michigan, 24 August 2007; Edward Wright Byrn, Jr., e-mail from Christopher Walker, Archives and Manuscript Specialist, Special Collections and University Archives, Melvin Gelman Library, George Washington University, 18 May 2007; John Ambrose Dowd, employment application, 19 April 1921, in personnel file released by FBI, and 1914 Commencement program of Georgetown University, Special Collections, Georgetown University Library; Albert E. Farland, employment application, 16 June 1917, in personnel file released by FBI; Dave L. Gershon, employment application, 2 October 1916, in personnel file released by FBI; Werner Hanni, employment applications of 16 April 1921 and 9 November 1923, and 1935(?), and letter Hanni to director, 1 February 1954, all in personnel file released by FBI; Joseph Kropidlowski, employment application, 3 April 1914, in personnel file released by FBI, and e-mail from Marilyn McNitt, 9 August 2007; Donald D. Lamond, employment application, 12 June 1923, in personnel file released by FBI, and 1916 Commencement program of Georgetown University, Special Collections, Georgetown University Library; Thomas S. Marshall, employment application, 28 August 1912, in personnel file released by FBI, and 1913 Commencement program of Georgetown University, Special Collections, Georgetown University Library; Charles G. Petrovitsky, e-mail from Sarah N. M. Harris, Senior Associate Director, Enrollment Services, University of Iowa, 23 August 2007, and e-mail from Denise Anderson, Special Collections Archives Assistant, University of Iowa Libraries, 24 August 2007; Joseph Polen, employment applications, 12 April 1921 and 20 December 1933, in personnel file released by FBI; Diego E. Ramos, employment applications, 1 March 1917 and 25 March 1924, in personnel file released by FBI, and *Directory of Graduates Howard University*, ed. Frederick D. Wilkinson (Washington, D.C., 1965), 303; Max M. Schaumburger, e-mail from Ann E. Smith Case, Assistant University Archivist, Tulane University Library, 18 May 2007; James Francis Terry, e-mail from Caitlin Stevens, Archives Reference, Northeastern University, 5 October 2007 and e-mail from Marisa Hudspeth, Assistant Archivist, Northeastern University, 2 January 2008. For information and sources on Ferris, Jakoubek, Parker, Rukes, Sawyer, and Wolfgram, see the Appendix on Investigators from Wisconsin. For statistics on educational levels, see "Educational Attainment by Sex," pdf file at http://www.census.gov/compendia/statab/hist_stats.html.

68. Higham, *Strangers in the Land*, 38–39; Hofstadter, *Age of Reform*, 176–81.

69. O'Brian, *Reminiscences*, 119–34; *New York Times*, 5 November 1913, 2.

70. Mink, *Wages of Motherhood*. Progressives had varying degrees of tolerance for immigrants. While many viewed them as threats to the fabric of national life, some, such as Jane Addams, celebrated certain aspects of immigrant culture. However, almost all native-born progressives believed that immigrants needed some kind of enlightening influence. In her study of Addams's Hull

House, Rivka Shpak Lissak notes that Addams and other progressives sought to incorporate newcomers into a culture that was simultaneously internationalist and American. "In short," Lissak writes, "Hull House was not an immigrant institution in the sense that it represented a pluralist cultural view of society. It was, rather, an American institute that sought to integrate individual newcomers of different backgrounds into a cosmopolitan, America-oriented society by breaking down ethnic barriers and ending segregation." While Addams felt that immigrants should not be intimidated into assimilating, the Hull House organization championed public education as a means of drawing immigrant children into the larger society. Accordingly, Hull House hoped that public schools would supplant the religious (and sometimes bilingual) private schools that catered to immigrant families. Lissak, *Pluralism and Progressives*, 47.

71. Anders, "Thomas Watt Gregory and the Survival of His Progressive Faith"; *American National Biography*, s.v. "Gregory, Thomas Watt" (by Charles Howard McCormick).

72. *American National Biography*, s.v. "O'Brian, John Lord" (by Michal Belknap); O'Brian, *Reminiscences*, 17–22, 57–58; Hughes, *Autobiographical Notes of Charles Evans Hughes*, 138. For more on Hughes's progressive record, see Wesser, *Charles Evans Hughes*.

73. On the Plattsburg camps, see O'Brian, *Reminiscences*, 215–16, and Kennedy, *Over Here*, 146.

74. *New York Times*, 2 May 1917, 5; 21 May 1917, 1; O'Brian, *Reminiscences*, 223–29; *Register of the Department of Justice and the Courts of the United States*, 1918, 24.

75. Wright, "Alfred Bettman: The Making of a Civil Libertarian, 1917–29," 59–61; Nelson, *Zoning and Property Rights*, 9, 59; Power, "Advocates at Cross-Purposes."

76. Harris and Sadler, "The 1911 Reyes Conspiracy: The Texas Side"; Raat, *Revoltosos*, 227–50.

77. *New York Times*, 14 April 1916, 1; *Annual Report of the Attorney General*, 1916, 52–54.

78. For an overview of the Justice Department's wartime responsibilities, see the *Annual Report of the Attorney General*, 1918.

79. For a discussion of the Espionage Act and its wartime usage, see Rabban, *Free Speech in Its Forgotten Years*, 254–61.

80. Kohn, *American Political Prisoners*, 8–9.

81. The figure is derived from statistics in Scheiber, *Wilson Administration and Civil Liberties*, 61–63.

Chapter 2. Methods and Ideology

1. *Investigative Case Files of the Bureau of Investigation, 1908–1922*, 2. This 955-roll collection of microfilm has been available to the public at the National

Archives since 1977 and includes a 111-roll index of the names of individuals and organizations who appear in the files. In researching for this book, I used the index to look up promising entries and also scrolled through reels looking for relevant material. Recently, the National Archives, working together with a private firm, Footnote.com, has digitally scanned much of the collection and in 2007 placed it on a subscriber-only web site, Footnote.com. In the final stages of my project, I used the Footnote web site to locate relevant files in the Bureau of Investigation collection. See "National Archives and Footnote Launch Project to Digitize Historic Documents," 10 January 2007, press release available at http://www.archives.gov/press/press-releases/2007/nr07-41.html.

2. *Providence* (RI) *Journal,* 3 November 1917, 8; *Hartford* (CT) *Courant,* 13 November 1917, 10; *Wellsboro* (PA) *Agitator,* 30 January 1918, 8; *Miami* (FL) *Herald,* 17 December 1917, 4; *Cass County Democrat* (Harrisonville, MO), 14 February 1918, [10]; *Grand Forks* (ND) *Herald,* 16 February 1918, 4; *Albuquerque* (NM) *Morning Journal,* 30 November 1917, 2; *Lowell* (MA) *Sun,* 17 June 1918, 6.

3. *Annual Report of the Attorney General,* 1918, 21.

4. For an overview of the department's wartime responsibilities, see *Annual Report of the Attorney General,* 1918, esp. 14–58.

5. Bryon to A. B. Bielaski, 2 October 1918, OG 80140.

6. Reports of M. M. Schaumburger, 1[8?] July 1918 and 20 July 1918, both in OG 241189.

7. Report of Henry W. McLarty, 29 June 1918, OG 231571.

8. Reports of John E. Burke, 24 June 1918, OG 227834, and 29 June 1918, OG 231295.

9. Report of H. D. Bishop, 11 January 1918, OG 125430; report of E. J. Geehan, 16 February 1918, OG 32303.

10. Report of Denis S. Kilmer, 15 July 1918, OG 243502.

11. Report of Chas. H. Lane, Jr., 29 August 1917, OG 51205.

12. Report of Bernard Kahn, 1 July 1918, OG 231762. In Chicago, investigator J. E. Wheeler reported that a suspected disloyalist was an elderly veteran whose duty in the Civil War had soured his opinion of military conflict. Wheeler cautioned the man, who "agreed to be more careful in the future." Wheeler reports, 26 October and 30 October 1917, OG 73014.

13. Report of F. Gosling, 3 November 1917, OG 95561. In a similar case, an Arizona woman who had allegedly made antiwar remarks found herself being escorted "to the office of the United States Attorney where she was released after a lecture." Report of Chas. S. Oliver, 7 June 1918, OG 213212.

14. Report of Edward R. Willcox, 19 July 1918, OG 115556.

15. Report of L. S. Perkins, 24 June 1917, OG 30255.

16. Report of L. S. Perkins, 24 July 1917, OG 48944.

17. Report of Mark Hanna, 2 October 1917, OG 42325.

18. In his report, detective George Holman asserted his belief that the

"frank interview . . . will make her a better citizen in the future than she has been in the past." Holman report, 8 March 1918, OG 157830.

19. Report of P. J. Fergus, 22 November 1917, OG 98173. Other suspects, it seems, proved more resistant to the department's entreaties. In Fort Wayne, Indiana, special agent Simon Nash had little luck in trying to win Bertha Eickels, who was "in a very defiant state of mind," to the cause; he "tried hard to make her understand what we were fighting for, but made little or no impression on her." Nash report, 10 July 1918, OG 231535.

20. Reports of J. P. Folsom, 4 June and 28 June 1918, OG 213842. In a similar case, an investigator, failing in his efforts to meet an older woman who allegedly voiced unpatriotic statements, met with the suspect's daughter and "requested that she talk to her mother, and personally see that she did not repeat her actions." Report of O. L. Tinklepaugh, 12 June 1918, OG 213560. For yet another example in which an investigator sought to deliver a warning to a possible disloyalist via a member of the suspect's family, see report of B. Kahn, 16 August 1917, OG 51298.

21. Report of Joseph Polen, 1 January 1918, OG 115395.

22. Holman report, 30 January 1918, OG 91060.

23. Burke report, 29 June 1918, OG 231295.

24. Burke reports, 29 June 1918, OG 230970, and 24 June 1918, OG 227834.

25. Report of D. D. Lamond, 15 January 1918, OG 125325.

26. Report of E. D. Kirk, 16 November 1918, OG 326206; *San Francisco Chronicle*, 8 November 1918, 9; 14 November 1918, 1; 15 November 1918, 4; 16 November 1918, 2.

27. For more on the APL, see Joan M. Jensen, *Price of Vigilance*. For examples of the APL providing information to the Justice Department, see report of William H. Steiner, 13 July 1917, OG 35861; report of A. A. Viall, 10 February 1918, OG 146083; report of Chas. L. Harris, 1 December 1917, OG 97632; report of G. W. Green, 6 June 1918, OG 214092; report of L. M. Cantrell, 25 June 1918, OG 213596; report of B. H. Littleton, 24 September 1917, OG 64486.

28. Report of L. M. Cantrell, 5 July 1918, OG 228900.

29. Report of T. S. Marshall, 29 July 1917, OG 5265; report of Arthur J. Devlin, 6 November 1917, OG 86375.

30. Report of Geo. W. Lillard, 31 October 1918, OG 64173.

31. Report of APL, 27 June 1918, OG 73992.

32. Jensen, *Price of Vigilance*, 154–55.

33. Report of William W. Roat, 26 August 1917, OG 54595.

34. Reports of C. E. Woida, 18 July and 19 July 1918, OG 243722.

35. Holman report, 29 June 1918, OG 214109.

36. Report of C. E. Argabright, 29 September 1918, OG 228632.

37. Report of W. A. Weymouth, 12 April 1918, OG 179214. In a similar case in Indiana, a veteran was interviewed for allegedly having exaggerated the evils

of life on the front line. Investigator G. W. Green noted that a local APL official had complained that the soldier, among other statements, "has enlarged upon the horrors of trench life to such an extent as to discourage enlistments." On being summoned for questioning, the soldier, a Peter Michaelson, claimed to be a Canadian veteran. Michaelson protested that since returning to Indiana he had lent his support to war bond drives. He acknowledged "that he has talked considerably in Hobart about his life in the trenches and that he has no doubt showed the horrible side of same at times, but has not uttered an untruth concerning his exepriences in the service." In his report, Green expressed his belief in the man's patriotism. Although Green made no mention of issuing a warning to Michaelson, such an interview may have had a quieting effect on the ex-soldier's comments about the war. Green report, 6 June 1918, OG 214092.

38. Burke report, 28 June 1918, OG 228716. In 1918 a Pittsburgh firm came under investigation for having produced an advertisement suggesting that the war would continue at least until the conclusion of the year. The ad asserted that German soldiers who had previously been serving on the eastern front could now be shifted westward, and asked, "If the Germans on the West Fron could not be beaten last Summer, can we beat them next Summer when there will be twice as many." The ad predicted price increases and forecast some kind of allotment system for steel. Report of W. H. Butterworth, for period of 8 April 1918, OG 179348.

39. Report of C. L. Keep, 24 December 1917, OG 115552.

40. Report of W. H. Valentine, 22 April 1918, OG 179533.

41. Memo from Alfred Bettman to A. B. Bielaski, 19 April 1918, memo of Bielaski to Bettman, 11 May 1918, and reports of Pasquale Pigniuolo, 3 May 1918 and 6 May 1918, all from OG 184258.

42. Report of W. S. Carman, for period of 1 April 1918, OG 160374. Typically, DOJ reports listed two dates: the date on which the events described in the report took place and the date on which the report was made. I have used the date of the writing of the report in my references, but if for some reason the date when the report was made was obscured or missing, I have used the date on which the events described transpired, and indicate this by using the phrase "for period of."

43. Reports of Paul Hofherr, 23 June and 25 June 1917, OG 33622.

44. Report of M. J. Murray, 28 October 1917, OG 72975.

45. Carroll, "Freedom of Speech and of the Press in War Time," 648–51.

46. Report of Chas. Schmid, 9 April 1918, OG 176242.

47. Report of Denver H. Graham, for period of 28 May 1918, OG 179560.

48. Report of Charles J. Bodenbach, 6 April 1918, OG 176044.

49. Graham report, May 1918 (specific date unclear), OG 183022.

50. Report of A. E. Farland, 24 July 1918, OG 30324.

51. Schaumburger report, 7 July 1918, OG 231183 . A Justice Department

investigator issued a similar warning in Hammond, Indiana, after two Red Cross workers reported a family as having been uncooperative. When one of the Red Cross workers had called on the family, the wife, a Mrs. Wolf, allegedly had appeared to suggest that she and Mr. Wolf favored the German cause and that the Red Cross suffered from corruption. Another Red Cross worker alleged that on a later visit the couple had likewise hinted at venality on the part of the Red Cross leadership. Investigator G. W. Green met with Mr. Wolf, who "stated that he had three nephews in the United States Army" and that he had invested in war bonds. Green seemed somewhat convinced of the suspect's sincerity, noting that he "seemed willing to do anything in his power to show his loyalty to the United States." Deciding that none of Mr. Wolf's expressions had been illegal, Green simply noted that the suspect "was warned to be extremely careful what he said regarding the Red Cross funds or liberty bonds." Green report, 6 June 1918, OG 213512.

52. Report of Leo J. Brennan, 12 September 1918, and report of W. N. Parker, 12 October 1918, OG 286467.

53. Report of Edward Oechsle, 4 December 1918, OG 335867.

54. See George W. Ellis, "Political Institutions in Liberia" and "Liberia in the Political Psychology of West Africa"; *Chicago Defender,* 17 June 1916, 6; 1 September 1917, 6; 8 December 1917, 10; and 22 April 1933, 11.

55. Sturgis also asserted that Ellis's future orations would be monitored as well. Report of F. M. Sturgis, 18 September 1918, OG 286075.

56. Feldman, "Prostitution, the Alien Woman and the Progressive Imagination,"192–98; Beckman, "The White Slave Traffic Act," 1111–24; Powers, *Secrecy and Power,* 134.

57. *New York Times,* 31 March 1918, sec. 4, 8.

58. Report of N. H. Castle, 28 June 1918, OG 231261.

59. Report of T. A. Matheson, 16 August 1918, OG 46382.

60. Holman report, 22 August 1917, OG 48907.

61. Report of Raymond Littell, for period of 11 May 1918, OG 195495.

62. Schaumburger report, 3 August 1917, OG 42096. One of the Hondurans interviewed was a Joaquin Salgado. See *Passenger and Crew Lists of Vessels Arriving at New Orleans, LA, 1910–1945* (Microfilm Publication T905, National Archives, Washington, D.C), roll 50.

63. Report of Arthur M. Allen, for period of 9 January 1918, OG 58962.

64. *New York Times,* 31 March 1918, sec. 4, 8; Higham, *Strangers in the Land,* 217; Zecker, "The Activities of Czech and Slovak Immigrants during World War I."

65. *Chicago Daily Tribune,* 20 January 1918, 10.

66. Report of Arthur M. Allen, 21 July 1918, OG 58962.

67. Report of P. P. Mindak, 12 November 1918, OG 326003.

68. Kennedy, *Over Here,* 281–83.

69. As quoted in Beaver, *Newton D. Baker and the American War Effort*, 31.

70. For an account of the riot and its aftermath, see Robert V. Haynes, *A Night of Violence.*

71. Chambers, *To Raise an Army*, 222–26.

72. Report of E. O. Irish, 25 June 1918, OG 227046.

73. Report of E. J. Kerwin, 2 May 1918, OG 195498.

74. Report of Claude McCaleb, 16 December 1918, and report of Lewis H. Henry, 31 December 1918, both in OG 336400.

75. Report of J. B. Rogers, [14?] May 1917, OG 18414.

76. Report of Manuel Sorola, 16 December 1917, OG 119064; *Register of the Department of Justice*, 1917, 190.

77. Report of J. H. Harper, 27 August 1917, OG 55088; e-mail from Rachel Howell, assistant manager, Texas/Dallas History and Archives Division, Dallas Public Library, 31 August 2007; the 1917 *Dallas City Directory* (Dallas: John F. Worley Directory Company) helped identify the participants in the affair.

78. For more on southern suspicions of radicalism in the twentieth century, see Williamson, *Rage for Order*, 238–47.

79. Harper report, 29 August 1917, OG 57042.

80. Gordon, "Onward Kitchen Soldiers."

81. *New York Times*, 16 April 1917, 1.

82. *New York Times*, 22 July 1915, 1.

83. Zeiger, "She Didn't Raise Her Boy to be a Slacker."

84. Report of Paul J. Kelly, 29 June 1918, OG 203619.

85. Gere, *Intimate Practices*, 151–52; General Federation of Women's Clubs Eleventh Biennial Convention (25 June to 5 July 1912, San Francisco, CA), *Official Report*, ed. and comp. Mrs. George O. Welch, 1912, 400–416.

86. Gere, *Intimate Practices*, 152–54; *Los Angeles Times*, 13 January 1912, [1]0; 26 February 1958, A10; *Evening News* (San Jose, CA), 29 October 1914, 3.

87. Report of C. L. Keep, 24 December 1917, OG 115653; Lillian B. Goldsmith to Judge Trippet, 21 December 1917, E. M. Blanford to A. B. Bielaski, 28 December 1917, and Chief to C. L. Keep, 7 January 1918, all in OG 115642; entry for Oscar A. Trippet, *History of the Federal Judiciary*, http://www.fjc.gov, web site of the Federal Judicial Center, Washington, D.C.

88. Blanford to A. B. Bielaski, 28 December 1917, and Chief to C. L. Keep, 7 January 1918, all in OG 115642.

89. Report of Lena R. Smith contained in report of C. L. Keep, 1[6?] January 1918, OG 30749.

90. Peabody's daughter, in a biographical sketch of her mother from 1943, noted that "the causes of woman suffrage and peace always found her a zealous and hard-working ally, even when such movements were not popular." See "Mrs. Frederick W. Peabody (Anna Greenough May)," sketch by Mrs. J. Leslie Hotson, in Memorial Biographies file of Radcliffe Alumni Association. For

more on Peabody, see Gill, *Mary Baker Eddy*, 436–38, and 674 n.29. For coverage of the fight, see *Philadelphia Inquirer*, 3 April 1917, 1, 14; *Boston Daily Globe*, 3 April 1917, 1, 6; *Atlanta Constitution*, 3 April 1917, 4; *The State* (Columbia, SC), 3 April 1917, 1, 3. Lodge's biographer notes that "later Bannwart brought suit against the Senator, charging assault and defamation of character, but withdrew his case when Lodge published a statement admitting he had started the fight. In later years Lodge always claimed the 'credit' of having opened the fracas." Garraty, *Henry Cabot Lodge*, 305–34. Reports of Donald B. Clark, 29 and 30 July 1918, 1 and 15 August 1918, and 11, 18, 25, and 27 September 1918, OG 243526.

91. Reports of Donald B. Clark, 29 July 1918 and 18 September 1918, OG 243526.

92. Report of C. S. Vial, 21 April 1918, OG 33504.

93. Report of L. O. Thompson, 21 October 1918, and report of R. E. Monroe, 25 October 1918, both from OG 285994.

94. Kauffman to AG, 8 October 1918; memo from Harold F. Hanes to Alfred Bettman, 17 February 1919; Thomas D. Slattery to the AG, 17 February 1919, both contained in CSF on Elizabeth Watkins, file no. 9-19-1103.

95. Report of W. R. Bryon, 9 January 1918, OG 125392.

96. Report of P. J. Fergus, 25 October 1917, OG 72652.

97. Littleton report, August 1917 (precise date obscured), OG 54438.

98. Report of Louis Loebl, 28 June 1918, OG 228887.

99. Report of Leonard M. Stern, 14 June 1918, OG 213110.

100. Reports of William E. Hill, 19 September 1918 and 14 October 1918, OG 254283.

101. Bodenbach report, 1 July 1918, OG 228034.

102. Report of Leonardis Augustus, 8 August 1918, OG 249352; *Harvard Encyclopedia of American Ethnic Groups*, s.v. "Greeks" (by Theodore Saloutos).

103. Woods, "The Problem of the Black Hand"; *New York Times*, 20 February 1909, 2, and 14 March 1909, 2.

104. Reports of Billups Harris and Alex Vonnegut, 4 May 1918, OG 195444; e-mail from reference staff, Harvard University Archives, 26 February 2007.

105. Report of F. B. Pond, 27 April 1918, OG 179924; von Mücke, *The Emden*; König, *Voyage of the Deutschland*; *New York Times*, 29 May 1915, 1; 15 July 1916, 2; 26 August 1916, 3.

106. Reports of Fifty, for period of 8 January 1918, OG 80140, and for period of 13 February 1918, OG 137269; *New York Times*, 25 November 1914, 4, and 16 June 1915, 14. See also reports of Elton Watkins, 23 January 1918 and 15 May 1918, OG 80140, which specifically identify her as an informant.

107. Fifty reports, for period of 30 January 1918 and for period of 19 January 1918, both in OG 80140.

108. Fifty reports, for period of (date unclear, probably the twenty-eighth) June 1918, OG 227510.

109. Fifty report, for period of 20 June 1918, OG 231053.

110. Fifty reports, for period of 27 April 1918, OG 179944; for period of 13 February 1918, 137269; for period of 20 February 1918, OG 72778; and for period of 1 May 1918, OG 179395; *New York Times*, 16 April 1917, 1. Ellen Schrecker's study of the post–World War II Red scare found that informants played an important role in the FBI's crusade against Communism. See Schrecker, *Many Are the Crimes*, 227–31.

111. Report of H. F. Edson, 18 July 1918, OG 243436.

112. Report of Harry F. Meurer, 8 July 1918, OG 231569.

113. Report of L. H. Van Kirk, 31 July 1917, OG 54961.

114. Report of V. W. Killick, 13 January 1918, OG 125409.

115. Report of E. H. Waterhouse, June 1918 (precise date unclear), OG 227237. In a similar case in Kansas, investigator C. E. Argabright, in inquiring about a man who had allegedly made disloyal comments, was told by some farmers that the suspect was poorly educated and not very bright. Judging the suspect to be "a harmless and irresponsible sort of man," Argabright asked two farmers to "report any disloyal action on his part." Argabright report, August 1918 (precise date unclear), OG 254983.

116. Report of E. B. Speer, 2 August 1918, OG 249193.

117. Report of Joseph F. Purcell, 12 November 1917, OG 80180.

118. *Seattle Directory* (Seattle: R. L. Polk and Co., 1914–21); e-mail from Sarah N. M. Harris, senior associate director, Enrollment Services, University of Iowa, 24 August 2007.

119. Report of Charles Petrovitsky, 11 November 1917, OG 55115.

120. Reports of B. F. Alford, 31 December 1917, and Roy H. Pickford, 26 January 1918, OG 115396.

121. Kelly report, 1 July 1918, OG 241429.

122. Allen did add that "if it develops that the party complained against is guilty of making disloyal statements, he will be given a warning to desist." Report of Harry B. Allen, [5?] September 1917, OG 53415.

123. Report of F. J. Weyand, 3 December 1917, OG 97634.

124. Mindak noted that the company "keeps a complete record of each employe as to his education, nationality, sympathies on the war, particularly as to purchase of Liberty bonds,—in fact all information they can gather through their own under-cover men working in the plant." Mindak report, 30 December 1918, OG 213465.

125. Report of Geo. W. Hartz, 2 August 1917, OG 46244.

126. Report of G. J. Willett, 17 April 1918, OG 179766.

127. Tinklepaugh report, 12 October 1918, OG 229057.

128. Speer report, 25 July 1918, OG 241275. After examining allegations

against a New Jersey man, an investigator "closed the case as one . . . due to personal antagonism." Report of John S. Read, 8 August 1918, OG 254649.

129. Wilson, "Spurious versus Real Patriotism in Education," 602–3.

Chapter 3. Policing the Clergy

1. Sessions, "Espionage in Windsor"; Joseph, "The United States vs. H. Miller"; *San Antonio Light,* 17 December 1918. One study of the American religious experience during World War I asserts that "fifty-five ministers of the gospel from various denominations and sects [were] arrested for alleged violation of one or more of the espionage and sedition laws." This total appears not to have included members of the Russellite sect. See Abrams, *Preachers Present Arms,* 211–19.

2. Peterson and Fite, *Opponents of War,* 119–20; *Brooklyn Daily Eagle,* 21 June 1918.

3. For more on how Lutheran churches viewed the war, and how others viewed the Lutheran church from 1914 through 1918, see the following articles from the *Concordia Historical Institute Quarterly:* Koch, "Friedrich Bente on World War I in *Lehre und Wehre*"; Johnson, "The Patriotism and Anti-Prussianism of the Lutheran Church-Missouri Synod"; Nohl, "The Lutheran Church—Missouri Synod Reacts to United States Anti-Germanism during World War I"; Scheidt, "Some Effects of World War I on the General Synod and General Council"; Manley, "Language, Loyalty, and Liberty." For more on how religious communities nationwide responded to the onset of war, see Abrams, *Preachers Present Arms.*

4. M. Churchill / G. C. Van Dusen to Bielaski, 26 July 1918, OG 243145.

5. R. H. Van Deman / W. C. Smiley to Bielaski, 1 June 1918, OG 207639. A similar letter from the Military Intelligence Branch requesting an investigation claimed that "rumors have reached this office that tend to show that Rev. W. H. C. Lauer of Summit Hill, Penna., appointed Lutheran Chaplain at Camp Greene, N.C., cannot be fully trusted as to loyalty. We have received information that Rev. Lauer has returned to his home at Summit Hill, Pennsylvania." R. H. Van Deman / W. C. Smiley to Bielaski, 8 May 1918, OG 191472.

6. Linkh, *American Catholicism and European Immigrants,* 133–44; Cuddy, "Pro-Germanism and American Catholicism"; Esslinger, "American German and Irish Attitudes Toward Neutrality"; O'Keefe, "*America,* the *Ave Maria,* and the *Catholic World* Respond to the First World War."

7. Report of James R. Magee, 14 September 1918, OG 288829. The draft registration being referred to was scheduled for 12 September 1918 and was the third national registration for the draft. See Chambers, *To Raise an Army,* 198.

8. Report of Charles J. Bodenbach, 10 June 1918, OG 210493.

9. Report of Irving Best, 16 March 1918, OG 160323.

10. Ibid.

11. Reports of S. W. Dillingham, 1 July 1918, 2 July 1918, OG 29159.

12. Report of W. N. Zinn, 22 September 1918, OG 286279; *Annual of the Southern Baptist Convention* (Nashville, TN: Marshall and Bruce, 1917–18), 534.

13. Report of W. N. Zinn, 22 September 1918, OG 286279.

14. Ibid.

15. Report of Denver H. Graham, 15 July 1918, OG 100205.

16. Ibid.

17. Report of Ralph Izard, 21 May 1917, OG 16652. The 1917, 1918, and 1919 editions of the *Official Catholic Directory* list Father Pop's church, St. Michael's, as Romanian.

18. Billington, *Protestant Crusade,* 362–65; Higham, *Strangers in the Land,* 5–7, 178–80.

19. Report of Ralph Izard, 21 May 1917, OG 16652.

20. Report of William Roat, 9 May 1918, OG 126085.

21. Ibid.; 1917 *Official Catholic Directory,* 1007.

22. Report of John Dowd, 1[1?] September 1918, OG 222910.

23. Report of James F. Terry, 18 October 1918, OG 222910.

24. Report of Ward E. Thompson, 29 June 1917, OG 30785.

25. Ibid., and reports of J. C. Drautzburg, 3 July and 12 July 1917, all in OG 30785.

26. Report of Lenoidas Augoustos, 1[5?] August 1918, OG 63296.

27. Hanni employment applications of 16 April 1921, 9 November 1923, and 1935(?); Hanni to McAuley, 25 February 1919; and Hanni to director, 1 February 1954, all in personnel file released by FBI.

28. Hanni's narrative is contained in report of Marshal Eberstein, 10 August 1917, OG 44308.

29. Eberstein report, 10 July 1917, OG 37705.

30. Eberstein report, 14 March 1918, OG 159368.

31. Eberstein report, 3 August 1917, OG 44676; 1918 *Official Catholic Directory.*

32. Eberstein report, 3 August 1917.

33. Eberstein report, 13 June 1918, OG 173400.

34. Eberstein report, 29 January 1918, OG 133065; unsigned original version of Hanni's report appears in CSF on H. Athrop, file no. 9-19-585.

35. Eberstein report, 13 June 1918, OG 213990.

36. Eberstein report, 9 May 1917, OG 13517.

37. Eberstein report, 22 May 1917; report of Wade A. Wilson, 18 May 1917. Both reports in OG 13517.

38. Eberstein report, 5 and 7 July 1917, OG 29239; 1917 *Annual Report of the Attorney General,* 57–59.

39. Thomas Allen to AG, 11 July 1917; Charles Warren to Thomas Allen, both contained in CSF on William Krauleidis, file no. 9-16-12-524.

40. *Kearney* (NE) *Daily Hub*, 26 July 1917; CSF on William Krauleidis, file no. 9-16-12-524.

41. Petition of Krauleidis congregation, CSF on William Krauleidis, file no. 9-16-12-524.

42. Allen to AG, 15 August 1917; CSF on William Krauleidis, file no. 9-16-12-524; Krauleidis was released sometime in 1919 (apparently in June). See Summary Sheet for Disposal of Alien Enemy; Diggs to DOJ, 16 December 1919; John Hanna to Diggs, 8 January 1920; all contained in CSF on William Krauleidis. See also entry for Krauleidis, Wm., in Dockets of Presidential Warrants Issued, 1918–19, Records of the War Emergency Division, General Records of Department of Justice, RG 60, National Archives, College Park, MD.

43. Report of Marshal Eberstein, for period of 8 January 1918, OG 95309. See also Summary Sheet for Disposal of Interned Alien Enemy, CSF on Paul Hempel, file no. 9-16-12-2362.

44. Telegram from Taubman to AG, 16 January 1918; Paul Hempel to Swiss Legation, 1 April 1919; both contained in CSF on Paul Hempel, file no. 9-16-12-2362.

45. Report of Marshal Eberstein, 25 May 1918, OG 203878. I am indebted to Clara Rolen of the National Archives for finding the Espionage Act case of William Windolph in the Records of the District Courts of the United States, RG 21, National Archives, Central Plains Region. *Official Catholic Directory*, 1917, 1918.

46. Hanni to McAuley, 26 November 1918, in personnel file.

47. Hanni to Eberstein, 21 April 1919, in personnel file.

48. Bossard-Borner, "Village Quarrels and National Controversies"; Evans, *The Cross and the Ballot*, 78–92; Steinberg, *Why Switzerland?*, 218.

49. Wust, *Zion in Baltimore*, 87, 89, 99–101.

50. Report of Alex Vonnegut, 1 September 1918, OG 18415. Tagore's 1917 book *Nationalism* had blamed the modern nation-state for fostering brutality and selfishness.

51. Vonnegut reported that Hofmann's spouse said the following: "'Why,' she asks, 'won't the Americans see that Germany had to force her way through Belgium?'" Report of Alex Vonnegut, 30 September 1918, and report of Billups Harris, 8 October 1918, OG 18415.

52. *Hartford Courant*, 8 August 1914, 13; 16 July 1918, 5; and 26 October 1919, 2A; *Hartford Times*, 16 July 1918, 12.

53. *Hartford Times*, 15 July 1918, 1, 3; *Hartford Courant*, 16 July 1918, 5; criminal case 768, U.S. District Court for the District of Connecticut, National Archives, Northeast Region, Waltham, Massachusetts. I am indebted to George P. Young of the archives for locating the records in this case.

54. According to the *Courant* article, Woodruff stated "that the Kerrs received no compensation for their labors, but admitted that Mr. Kerr was

employed by him at the New Departure Manufacturing Company at Bristol."
Hartford Courant, 16 July 1918, 5.

55. *Hartford Courant,* 16 July 1918, 5.

56. *Hartford Courant,* 18 July 1918, 5; and *Hartford Times,* 17 July 1918, 1, 11.

57. *Hartford Times,* 19 July 1918, 1. In March 1919, President Wilson reduced Beussel's sentence so that he would be released that April, but in October of that year his U.S. citizenship was canceled. *Hartford Courant,* 6 March 1919, 1, and 26 October 1919, 2A.

58. Memo to Glavin, 26 March 1954, and Assignment History of Werner Hanni, in personnel file.

59. Vonnegut, *Slapstick,* 8–10.

60. Reports of V. L. Snyder, [2?] December and 5 December 1918, OG 331830.

61. I am indebted to archivist Barbara Rust of the National Archives for locating Pluenneke's arrest record and sending it to me. U.S. Commissioners case 1408, vol. 13 of Record of Proceedings (entry 48W142A), RG 21, Records of U.S. District Courts, Western District of Texas, San Antonio Division, National Archives, Southwest Region, Fort Worth, TX; report of V. L. Snyder, 5 December 1918, OG 331830.

62. *San Antonio Express,* 11 December 1918; Robertson to AG, 14 December 1918, and O'Brian to Robertson, 26 December 1918, in Justice Department CSF 9-19-496.

63. *San Antonio Light,* 17 December 1918.

64. Linkh, *American Catholicism and European Immigrants,* 19–31, 133–62.

65. Luebke, *Bonds of Loyalty,* 38–39, 315–16.

Chapter 4. Policing the Left

1. Weinstein, "The Socialist Party" and *Decline of Socialism in America,* 93–118.

2. Bissett, *Agrarian Socialism in America,* 125–26.

3. Weinstein, *Decline of Socialism in America,* 93, 107, 107, n.248.

4. Ibid., 119–29; Shannon, *Socialist Party of America,* 81–98.

5. Peterson and Fite, *Opponents of War,* 8–9.

6. Weinstein, *Decline of Socialism in America,* 119–76; Lorence, "'Dynamite for the Brain.'"

7. Weinstein, *Decline of Socialism in America,* 149–54; *New York Times,* 5 November 1917, 3; advertisement, "Three Letters of Interest . . ." appearing in *New York Times,* 5 November 1917, 3.

8. Peterson and Fite, *Opponents of War,* 184–86.

9. *New York Times,* 10 March 1918, sec. I, 1, and 29 October 1918, 9; Sally Miller, *Victor Berger and the Promise of Constructive Socialism,* 204–6.

10. Report of James C. Tormey, 6 July 1917, OG 32625; *Register of the Department of Justice*, 1919, 115.

11. Reports of John E. Ferris, 12 December and 14 December 1917, OG 118541.

12. Report of Pearce, 14 September 1918, OG 289279 (the U.S. Commissioner's report indicates that the charges against Gilmore were dropped. See U.S. Commissioner Transcripts 1915–1920, U.S. District Court, Northern District of Ohio, Eastern Division, Cleveland, RG 21, Records of the District Courts of the United States, National Archives, Great Lakes Region, Chicago); report of Todd Daniel, 7 October 1918, OG 313815.

13. Bassett, "The American Socialist Party and the War"; Weinstein, *Decline of Socialism in America*, 162–66; Shannon, *Socialist Party of America*, 119–21.

14. Report of John Read, for period of 30 July 1918, OG 249500.

15. Report of J. F. Kropidlowski, 9 January 1918, OG 98089. In Illinois, William Roat was not alarmed at having discovered a Socialist whose allegiance to the party stemmed from innocuous factors. Referring to the suspect, Roat reported, "I do not consider him rank. The Socialist party is the dry party in Central city that is the reason why he is a Socialist. I don't think that economic conditions come into his Socialism at all." A local resident, observed Roat, "explained . . . that the Socialist party always put up Dry candidates for office and the drys voted for them." Report of William W. Roat, 27 June 19[year unclear], OG 32528.

16. Report of E. W. Byrn, Jr., 23 January 1918, OG 130351.

17. Byrn report, 22 April 1918, OG 203865.

18. Report of W. N. Parker, 20 July 1918, OG 248898.

19. Reports of Fred S. Dunn, 12 and 13 November 1918, OG 325538.

20. Lyon to AG (two letters with same date), 23 November 1918; AG to U.S. attorney, 29 November 1918. All cites from CSF 9-19-662.

21. Report of S. J. Adams, 26 June 1918, OG 231315.

22. Report of [W?] H. Jones [5?] October 1917, and report of W. L. Furbershaw, 24 September 1917, OG 13392.

23. Report of Norman L. Gifford, 30 April 1918, OG 13726.

24. Interview with William Gallo, in Avrich, *Anarchist Voices*, 153–57.

25. Report of E. T. Drew, 20 September 1918, OG 289493.

26. Drew report, 24 September 1918, OG 289493; *U.S. v. Fermino Gallo, alias Frank Gallo* (docket sheet and indictment), Crim. 1426, Records of the U.S. District Court of New Jersey, RG 21, National Archives, Northeast Region, New York City.

27. *U.S. v. Fermino Gallo*, docket sheet; e-mail from Gregory J. Plunges to William Thomas, 21 March 2001; E. T. Drew report, 28 November 1918, and memo of Vera C. Brungart, 20 February 1920, OG 289493.

28. Preston, *Aliens and Dissenters*, 35–62; Dubofsky, *We Shall Be All*, 350–52.

29. Dubofsky, *We Shall Be All,* 353–58. For more on Gompers's attitude toward the war and the role of the AFL in the conflict, see Larson, *Labor and Foreign Policy,* and Grubbs, *Struggle for Labor Loyalty.*

30. Preston, *Aliens and Dissenters,* 122–28; Dubofsky, *We Shall Be All,* 358–81, 393–97.

31. Dubofsky, *We Shall Be All,* 404–6; Taft, "The Federal Trials of the IWW."

32. Marc Karson's *American Labor Unions and Politics* examines both the AFL's relationship with the Democratic Party and its wartime stances. For the Rintelen trial, see the *New York Times,* 29 December 1915, 1; 2 May 1917, 5; 21 May 1917, 1; as well as O'Brian, *Reminiscences,* 223–27.

33. Report of John Dillon, for period of 10 October 1917, OG 51511.

34. Report of Charles H. Lane Jr., 16 October 1917, OG 72587.

35. Report of F. A. Watt, 27 June 1917, OG 30490.

36. Report of G. C. Outlaw, 16 April 1918, OG 176244.

37. Supposedly, the four victims of the vigilantes had been intimidating agricultural workers. Report of E. J. Kerwin, 27 September 1917, clippings from Stuttgart *Booster,* 26 September 1917, and Stuttgart *Daily Free Press,* 26 September 1917, all in OG 64436.

38. Report of J. F. McDevitt, 24 July 1918, and report of W. S. Carmen, 24 July 1918, OG 243334.

39. Report of Robert S. Judge, 17 October 1917; report of John Dillon, 2[3?] October 1917, OG 72750; *American National Biography* 8, s.v. "Garfield, Harry Augustus," 713–15.

40. Reports of E. D. Strickland, 27 and 2[8?] October 1917, OG 86812.

41. Strickland report, 8 October 1917, OG 58639; report of William L. Buchanan, 21 September 1917; and report of Arthur L. Barkey, 21 September 1917; all three reports in OG 58639. The investigators may have been joined on this venture by a representative of the Niagara Frontier Defense League, or by a representative or two from the APL, but the reports are unclear and possibly contradictory on this point.

42. Report of William L. Buchanan, 21 September 1917, OG 58639. Community backers of labor activism likewise could come under pressure from the department. In Hibbing, Minnesota, investigators met with a barber who allegedly "had attempted to induce others not to enlist or work in the mines." One investigator "advised him what he could and could not do, intimating strongly that if he had any part in bringing about a strike which would impair the manufacture of munitions such action would border on treason." The barber vowed "that he would not talk war in any manner again." Report of John T. Kenny, 23 May 1917, OG 13582.

43. Report of E. D. Strickland, 8 October 1917, OG 58639.

44. The investigator pointed out "the nature of the periodical" to an

owner of a shop where the *Liberator* was available, and the owner promptly pulled his copies of the magazine. Report of H. Nathan, 11 September 1918, OG 136944.

45. Taft, "The Federal Trials of the IWW," 57–76; Dubofsky, *We Shall Be All,* 407, 423–37.

46. Taft, "The Federal Trials of the IWW," 76–80; Dubofsky, *We Shall Be All,* 438–43.

47. Report of William L. Buchanan, 4 January 1918, OG 118487. Whether Murphy was telling his inquisitor the truth is another question. A later report filed by the Justice Department suggested that Jack Murphy was perhaps also John Murdoch, who supposedly had sought to enroll others in the IWW the previous year. The author of this later report noted that "In view of the report by Mr. Buchanan of the Buffalo office, I am convinced that Murphy, or Murdoch, is either honestly trying to do better or is trying to put one over." Report of Finch, 17 January 1918, OG 118487.

48. Report of W. B. Holliday, 12 April 1918, OG 176671.

49. Holliday report, 16 April 1918, OG 176671. Holliday mistakenly referred to Howell as the U.S. attorney, whereas in fact Howell was assistant U.S. attorney. See *Register of the Department of Justice,* 1919, 169.

50. Reports of Chas. L. Tyman, 3 July 1918, OG 231496.

51. Reports of E. O. Reading, 15 July 1918 and 20 July 1918, OG 228525.

52. Reading report, 30 July 1918, OG 228525.

53. Reading reports, 22 July 1918 and 30 July 1918, OG 228525. In his report of 30 July, Reading noted that Silva "had been classified in 4 on account of having two minor children." According to an historian of the conscription system, draft class four "included married men whose dependents had no other means of support." See Chambers, *To Raise an Army,* 191.

54. Morn, *"The Eye That Never Sleeps,"* 94–99, 152, 158–61, 167.

55. Report of Diego E. Ramos, for period of 3 December 1917, OG 97502.

56. Report of S. Guzman, 1[3?] July 1918, OG 13726.

57. Heale, *American Anticommunism,* 9–51, and Higham, *Strangers in the Land,* chaps. 1–5, 7.

58. Report of Norman L. Gifford, 24 July 1918, OG 51125.

59. Report of Claude McCaleb, 18 December 1917, OG 13332-a.

60. Report of L. S. Perkins, 18 May 1918, OG 72817.

61. Perkins report, 30 August 1918, OG 72817.

62. Ibid.

63. Ibid.

64. Singerman, "The American Career of the *Protocols of the Elders of Zion*"; Higham, *Strangers in the Land,* 279–85; Dinnerstein, *Antisemitism in America,* 75–83.

65. Higham, *Strangers in the Land,* 202–3, 221; Preston, *Aliens and Dissenters,* 73–85, 181–207.

66. Weinstein, *Decline of Socialism in America,* 129–33.

67. For accounts of the postwar left-right fissure, see Shannon, *Socialist Party of America,* 126–49, and Weinstein, *Decline of Socialism in America,* 177–233.

68. Historians offer different perspectives as to the consequences of the federal trials upon the IWW. Melvyn Dubofsky suggests that the prosecutions wrought long-lasting damage to the union by depriving it of seasoned leadership. In Dubofsky's judgment, the leaders who replaced the jailed Wobbly chiefs were bereft of common sense and made foolish decisions that helped ensure the demise of the IWW. In contrast, Nigel Sellars's more recent study of the IWW in Oklahoma points to the continued postwar resilience of the union, acknowledging that while "federal prosecutions essentially decapitated the union leadership . . . the IWW still had a core of veteran members and organizers." Dubofsky and Sellars agree, however, that the legal defense operation was a substantial financial burden on the IWW. Dubofsky, *We Shall Be All,* 445–57; Sellars, *Oil, Wheat, and Wobblies,* 141–62, 183.

69. Dubofsky, *We Shall Be All,* 461–62.

70. Ibid., 410–14, 446–47, 461–62; for example, two key Finnish leaders of the IWW, convicted in the Chicago trial, became adherents of communism and eventually left for Bolshevik Russia. See Kivisto, *Immigrant Socialists in the United States,* 156–57.

71. Sellars, *Oil, Wheat, and Wobblies,* 143–62, 175–83; Dubofsky, *We Shall Be All,* 447–48.

72. McCormick, *Seeing Reds,* 103–4; Powers, *Secrecy and Power,* 56–148; Gentry, *J. Edgar Hoover,* 75–143; Belknap, "The Mechanics of Repression."

Chapter 5. Policing Wisconsin

1. U.S. Census Bureau, *Thirteenth Census of the United States; Sheboygan* (WI) *Press,* 2 April 1917, 1, 6, and 3 April 1917, 1. For information on Judge Bassuener, see *Sheboygan Press,* 27 January 1917, 11. That Adam Trester was a Justice of the Peace is indicated by items in the *Sheboygan Press* of 7 April 1915, 1, 27 February, 1917, 5, and 13 December 1917, 6. For a recent scholarly overview of the period, including an account of Wisconsin's view of the war during the period of neutrality, see Glad, *History of Wisconsin,* 1–23.

2. "Peace Day, May 18," *Educational News Bulletin* 6 (30 March 1914), Madison. See also the Peace Day announcements in the 24 April 1911, 22 April 1912, and 21 April 1913 *Bulletins.*

3. *Wisconsin Memorial Day Annual 1915,* 78, 81–82; Zeiger, "Teaching Peace: Lessons from a Peace Studies Curriculum of the Progressive Era." For more examples of pacifist materials, see the *Memorial Day Annual 1913,* 64–78.

4. *Wisconsin State Journal,* 18 May 1915, 2.

5. Trattner, "Julia Grace Wales and the Wisconsin Plan for Peace," 203–13; Frooman, "The Wisconsin Peace Movement 1915–1919," 74–77.

6. U.S. Census Bureau, *Thirteenth Census of the United States,* vol. 3, 1075, 1096; Historical Census Browser, University of Virginia Geostat Center, http://fisher.lib.virginia.edu/collections/stats/histcensus/.

7. *Milwaukee Journal,* 29 August 1914, 10.

8. *Milwaukee Free Press,* 3 March 1916, 1, 5, and 6 March 1916, 5; *Milwaukee Journal,* 8 March 1916, 14

9. *Milwaukee Journal,* 7 March 1915, 5, and 8 March 1916, 14; *Milwaukee Free Press,* 6 March 1916, 5.

10. *Milwaukee Free Press,* 10 August 1914, 4, and 12 August 1914, 4.

11. Child, *German-Americans in Politics,* 69. The following year, editor Emil von Schleinitz was tapping nails into the bazaar's iron cross (see the *Free Press,* 3 March 1916, 1). For more evidence of von Schleinitz's pro-German attitude, see his "War Forced on Germany," *Milwaukee Free Press,* 10 August 1914, 4.

12. *Milwaukee Free Press,* 9 May 1915, part 2, 4. For another example of the *Free Press*'s pro-German attitude, see its editorial of 28 August 1914, 4.

13. Wachman, *History of the Social-Democratic Party of Milwaukee,* 53; *Milwaukee Sentinel,* 6 April 1904, 10.

14. Miller, "Casting a Wide Net"; Miller, *Victor Berger,* 35–39, 84; N. W. Ayer and Sons, *American Newspaper Annual and Directory* (Philadelphia: N. W. Ayer and Son, 1914–19), 1188.

15. Ueberhorst, "Turners and Social Democrats in Milwaukee," 8–13; Wachman, *History of the Social-Democratic Party of Milwaukee,* 9–13; Olson, "The Milwaukee Socialists," 6–12; Miller, "Casting a Wide Net," 25.

16. Miller, "Casting a Wide Net," 25–29, 34; Niven, *Carl Sandburg: A Biography,* 2–3, 132–229; Pienkos, "Politics, Religion, and Change in Polish Milwaukee," 185–95; Gregory, *History of Milwaukee, Wisconsin,* vol. 4, 201–3.

17. Meta Berger, *A Milwaukee Woman's Life on the Left,* 3; Stevens and Goldlust-Gingrich, *Family Letters of Victor and Meta Berger,* 1–9, 47–49.

18. *Milwaukee Leader* editorials, 7 August, 21 August, and 26 August 1914.

19. *Milwaukee Journal,* 3 March 1916, 1; *Milwaukee Free Press,* 7 August 1914, 4. For more on Berger's stance on the war, see Miller, *Victor Berger,* chap. 6, and Hamilton, "A Victor Without Peace."

20. Miller, *Victor Berger,* 120; Stevens and Goldlust-Gingrich, *Family Letters of Victor and Meta Berger,* 184–85; Berger to Untermann, 26 April 1916, reel 51, Victor L. Berger Papers; Kreuter and Kreuter, *American Dissenter,* 155–60; Simons, "The Future of the Socialist Party."

21. La Follette, "Take the Profit Out of War."

22. La Follette, "Consult the People!"

23. Finnegan, "The Preparedness Movement in Wisconsin," 10–19.

24. *Milwaukee Journal*, 24 May 1916, 6.

25. *Milwaukee Sentinel*, 17 June 1916, 1; *Milwaukee Leader*, 17 June 1916, 5. For background on Lizzie Black Kander, see Waligorski, "Social Action and Women."

26. *Milwaukee Journal* owner Lucius W. Nieman chaired the committee that was in charge of Wilson's reception during the president's 1916 visit to the city, while assistant editor Henry C. Campbell served on the arrangements committee. See Jean L. Berres, "Local Aspects of the 'Campaign for Americanism,'" 77, and *Milwaukee Journal*, 29 January 1916, 1, 2. Since its founding in 1882, the *Journal* had never endorsed a Republican presidential nominee and had consistently endorsed Democratic nominees save in those years where William Jennings Bryan was the party standard-bearer. For a record of the *Journal*'s presidential endorsements and for more on the ties between the paper and Wilson, see Conrad et al., *The Milwaukee Journal*, 85–86, 214, and the *Milwaukee Journal* editorial of 7 November 1916.

27. *Milwaukee Journal* editorial, 14 February 1916. See also the *Milwaukee Journal* of 10 February 1916, 1, 8.

28. *Milwaukee Journal* editorial, 15 June 1916.

29. *Milwaukee Journal* editorial, 16 October 1916. See also the critical front-page coverage devoted to German American political activities on 24 and 25 October 1916 and 3 November 1916.

30. Conrad et. al., *Milwaukee Journal*, 87–88.

31. Olds, "'Kultur' in American Politics"; e-mail from reference staff of Harvard University Archives to William Thomas, 26 February 2007.

32. *Milwaukee Journal*, 14 October 1916, 1, 5, and editorial; *Germania-Herold* editorials of 20 and 28 March 1916. To see if the *Journal* had accurately translated these two editorials, I consulted with Gregor Mieder, a native-born German speaker and a student at the University of Wisconsin–Madison. After comparing the source of the translations (the *Germania-Herold* editorials of 20 and 28 March 1916) and the *Journal* translations, Mr. Mieder reported that "Overall, both translations are flawless—I could detect no bias in the way they were translated." E-mail from Gregor Mieder to William Thomas, 7 March 2005.

33. *Milwaukee Journal*, 8 November 1918, 10.

34. *Milwaukee Journal*, 1 April 1917, 2; for more on Guy Goff, see his entry in the *Biographical Directory of the United States Congress*.

35. *Milwaukee Leader*, 17 February 1917, 1.

36. *Milwaukee Free Press*, 28 February 1917, 1–2; *Milwaukee Leader*, 28 February 1917, 1, 12. The *New York Times* had reported that "federal investigators who have been working on the persistent rumors that the agitation against the high food prices was the direct result of an extensive plot by officials and sympathizers of the Central Powers have become satisfied, it was learned yesterday, that the rumors had no basis in fact." *New York Times*, 24 February 1917, 3.

37. *Milwaukee Leader*, 13 March 1917, 1.

38. The rules committee gave its approval to the plan. *Milwaukee Leader*, 23 March 1917, 9; *Milwaukee Free Press*, 23 March 1917, 1.

39. Eventually, Hoan's stance on the war led to his dismissal as joint chair of the council, but he continued as a member of the bureau of food control. Reinders, "Daniel W. Hoan and the Milwaukee Socialist Party."

40. *Milwaukee Leader* editorial, 20 June 1917.

41. *Milwaukee Leader*, 4 March 1918, 1; Glad, *History of Wisconsin*, 45.

42. *Milwaukee Leader*, 6 March 1918, 1.

43. Quoted in Unger, *Fighting Bob La Follette*, 254.

44. Thelen, *Robert M. La Follette*, 128–48; Unger, *Fighting Bob LaFollette*, 242–61.

45. *Congressional Record*, 65th Cong., 1st sess., 6 October 1917, 7878–979.

46. Ibid., 7886–895.

47. *Milwaukee Journal* editorial, 8 October 1917.

48. For biographical information on Wisconsin investigators, see the appendix.

49. Reports of C. Bodenbach, 6 April 1918, OG 176044, and 12 September 1918, OG 289141.

50. Report of Chas. I. Rukes, 19 July 1918, OG 240900 (taken from retakes section of microfilm roll 654).

51. The Phoenix Knitting incident is recorded in the report of W. C. Juneau, 3[1?] December 1917, OG 1105. For examples of admonitions or warnings, see the following reports:

> C. J. Bodenbach, 6 April 1918, OG 176044; 3 June 1918, OG 203542; 12
> September 1918, OG 289141; 21 November 1918, OG 326207;
> John E. Burke, 28 June 1918, OG 228716; 29 June 1918, OG 231295; 24 June
> 1918, OG 227834;
> W. E. Cox, 25 February 1918, OG 149676;
> John E. Ferris, 12 and 14 December 1917, OG 118541;
> Paul J. Kelly, 29 June 1918, OG 203619;
> Henry W. McLarty, 29 June 1918, OG 231571; 27 July 1918, OG 264748 (taken
> from retakes of microfilm roll 676);
> W. N. Parker, 9 April 1918, OG 16291; 24 June 1918 (including transcript,
> "Interrogation of Jessica Colvin"), OG 159796; 20 July 1918, OG 248898;
> Chas. I. Rukes, 19 July 1918, OG 240900 (taken from retakes of microfilm
> roll 654);
> L. Sawyer, 1 February 1918, OG 103313; 21 February 1918, OG 335827; and
> Wm. H. Steiner, 13 December 1917, OG 103312; 10 January 1918, OG
> 125369.

In addition to the cases listed above, a Conrad Weinig received two separate warnings from two different detectives and eventually was the subject of an indictment. See reports of Wm. H. Steiner, 31 July 1917, A. A. Viall, 10 January 1918, and W. E. Cox, 29 November 1918, all in OG 41019. A significant proportion of those receiving these admonitions or warnings were members of the clergy, which I have listed separately here:

A. A. Viall, 28 November 1917, OG 103407; 10 February 1918, OG 146083;
Julius Rosin, 23 October 1917, OG 75379; 24 October 1917, OG 72089; 30 October 1917, OG 73648;
Julius Rosin, 5 November 1917, in folder 10332-6/1 to 10332 20/1, MID Correspondence, 1917–41, RG 165, National Archives;
L. E. Sawyer, 30 January 1918, OG 125447;
R. B. Spencer, 11 September 1917, OG 51262;
Wm. H. Steiner, 2 August 1917, OG 42592.

In addition to the thirty-one individuals who received admonitions in the reports listed above, there were also three workers (N. P. Gaffney, Albert Tetzlaff, and William Williston) in Marinette who received warnings from A. A. Viall. I have not included them in the above tally because their admonitions concerned their alleged labor activism at the place where they worked, and as such are of a somewhat different nature than the cases listed above. For more on the experiences of these workers, see pages 136–37 of this chapter.

52. Virtually all of these cases were found in the Old German (OG) files, a 594-reel collection of microfilm containing more than 380,000 files on individuals and organizations. I was able to use the alphabetical index (a separate 111-reel index that catalogues other microfilm holdings as well) to some benefit to locate investigations that took place in Wisconsin. Under the heading of Wisconsin, the index contains listings for the names of numerous towns and cities. The files listed under a particular locality will typically contain investigations of conditions in that particular place, and Milwaukee's index number contained a large cluster of reports from that city. Still, these listings by locality for Wisconsin cover only a small minority of total reports filed from that state, and tracking down most of the reports from Wisconsin would be an immense task. An index listing for a person or organization typically indicates the state where the target of the investigation was located, so someone could scroll through the entire index, noting (and subsequently looking up) all the files listed as relating to Wisconsin.

53. In six additional cases clergy were investigated and interviewed, but the reports for these six cases make no mention of a warning or admonition being provided. See the following reports:

W. C. Juneau, 15 January 1918, OG 134528;
W. N. Parker, 29 September 1918, OG 116672;
Julius Rosin, 2[4?] October 1917, OG 72815;
R. B. Spencer, 8 June 1917, OG 22996;
Wm. H. Steiner, 4 September 1917, OG 57198; and 22 October 1917, OG 71804.

I should note here that clergy are probably overrepresented in my survey of Justice Department activities in the state. At an earlier stage of this project (before I had started research for the Wisconsin chapter), I scanned through portions of the microfilm index specifically looking for clergy who were investigated—a search facilitated by the fact that the microfilm name index typically indicated when a particular person listed happened to be a clergyman. While doing this index search, I found the names of a number of pastors from Wisconsin who were interviewed and/or reprimanded, and I have included their names in tabulating my figures.

54. Report of Julius Rosin, 24 October 1917, OG 72089.

55. Rosin report, 30 October 1917, OG 73648.

56. Report of Chas. L. Harris, 12 April 1918, OG 176977; for the ad, see the issues of the Racine *Correspondent* for 5 January 1918, 23 February 1918, 9 March 1918, 23 March 1918, 30 March 1918, and 6 April 1918.

57. Parker reports, 15 March 1918 and 5 April 1918, OG 157865.

58. *Racine Times-Call*, 4 April 1918, 7, and 6 April 1918, 4; Burke report, 4 June 1918, OG 205546; George F. Kull, "The Wisconsin Loyalty Legion," in *The Wisconsin Blue Book, 1919*, 415, available at http://digital.library.wisc.edu/1711.dl/WI.WIBlueBK1919. The report refers to a William Goodland, but this is a mistake, as the *Guide to Wisconsin Newspapers, 1833–1957*, 213, lists Walter S. Goodland as the editor. See also the *Wisconsin State Journal*, 13 March 1947, 1.

59. For examples of postmasters providing information on specific persons, see the following reports:

T. H. Stacy, 25 October 1917, OG 64821;
Wm. H. Steiner, 31 July 1917, OG 41019;
Julius Rosin, 1[6?] October 1917, OG 81815;
W. E. Cox, 24 September 1918, OG 294562;
W. N. Parker, 5 April 1918, OG 157865;
L. E. Sawyer, 30 January 1918, OG 135593.

For examples of postmasters or other postal officials providing information on overall loyalty situation of a locality, see reports of Julius Rosin, 11 June 1917, OG 23709; 20 October 1917, OG 81360; 1 May 1917, OG 295512; and 23 October 1917, OG 47531; and report of Wm. H. Steiner, 7 May 1918, OG 190605.

60. Harris report, 27 December 1917, OG 119633. I have not found any other examples of postal officials opening domestic (as opposed to overseas) letters anywhere in the country. For another example of a postmaster forwarding accusations of a lack of patriotism, see Burke report, 29 June 1918, OG 230970.

61. Viall report, 1 April 1918, OG 137433; report of F. J. Payson, 1 November 1918, OG 317258; Cox report, 26 August 1918, OG 197482.

62. Sawyer report, 14 January 1918, OG 51592.

63. Rosin report, 11 June 1917, OG 23464.

64. Rosin report, 11 June 1917, OG 23465 and OG 23463.

65. For examples of consultations or cooperation with representatives of county councils of defense, see report of H. [H.?] Stroud, 4 September 1918, OG 4107; report of D. H. Barry, [2?]8 November 1917, OG 105080; and report of Leo J. Brennan, 13 July 1918, OG 47557. For examples of the above with local law enforcement, see Rosin report, 1 May 1917, OG 295512; Rosin report, 20 October 1917, OG 81360; report of Harry Gordon, 8 May 1918, OG 40991; Steiner report, 28 June 1917, OG 23256; Sawyer report, 1 February 1918, OG 103313.

66. Report of J. E. Ferris, 16 January 1918, OG 125391.

67. Unger, *Fighting Bob LaFollette*, 257.

68. For accounts of the event, see the *Capital Times,* the *Wisconsin State Journal,* and the *Madison Democrat* for 30 March 1918.

69. The group originally called itself the "Bascom Forum." See entries for 18 December 1916, 7 January 1917, 16 January 1917, 4 March 1917, and 19 April 1917, in Minutes of the Wisconsin Forum, as well as Curti and Carstensen, *University of Wisconsin,* 73–75.

70. Spencer report, [21?] February 1918, OG 151297.

71. Parker reports, 11 March 1918, 24 June 1918, OG 151297; Parker report, 24 June 1918, and transcript, "Interrogation of Jessica Colvin," in OG 159796.

72. Izard to Mark Catlin, 19 December 1917, OG 1105. In a letter sent to a postmaster previously, Izard acknowledged using disorderly conduct statutes for punishing "outspoken disloyal utterances." See Izard to postmaster, 1[2?] November 1917, OG 493.

73. Cox report, 2 September 1918, OG 274842.

74. Reports of Charles J. Bodenbach, 8 June 1918, 19 June 1918, and 24 June 1918, OG 213414.

75. *Milwaukee Journal,* 18 June 1918. The *Journal* noted that the clerk of court earlier "wrote to Washington complaining that seditious remarks cases were being prosecuted in the district court." The other defendant that day, a Gottfried Froeming, allegedly had been very critical of the government and had expressed his wish "that the Germans are going to come over here and take everything." Froeming was facing a disorderly conduct charge, and was later found guilty in a trial in which the investigating Justice Department detective also served as a witness. Sawyer reports, 14 June 1918, 17 June 1918, and 12 July 1918, in OG 217548. For more on the role played by local and state authorities in Wisconsin, see John D. Stevens, "Suppression of Expression in Wisconsin during World War I."

76. Ralph Izard to Wm. H. Steiner, 25[?] January 1918, and report of Wm. H. Steiner, 30 January 1918, OG 493.

77. Izard to Charles Harris, 25[?] January 1918, OG 16361, and report of Chas. L. Harris, 12 February 1918, OG 92108. For other examples of juror

investigations, see reports of Chas. L. Harris, 10 February 1918; John [M?] Carter, 11 February 1918; and John E. Burke, 30 April 1918, all in OG 80515.

78. Report of Harry Gordon, 23 Jan 1918, OG 116672.

79. Gordon reports, 23 January 1918 and 8 May 1918, OG 116672.

80. Report of Irving Best, 28 June 1918, OG 116672.

81. Best report, 28 June 1918, OG 166672.

82. Gordon report, 14 March 1918, OG 116672.

83. The data on national origins is found in U.S. Census Bureau, *Fourteenth Census of the United States*. In Wisconsin were Kalandyk (Oneida Co.), O'Mahoney (Washburn Co.), and Rice (Oneida Co.); Father Iciek was listed as living in St. Louis Co., MN, and Father Arts was in Monroe Co., MI. The *Official Catholic Directory* for the years 1917–20 was useful in correcting spellings and tracking down clergymen.

84. John Hanna, memorandum for John Lord O'Brian, 6 July 1918, and John Hanna, supplementary memorandum for John Lord O'Brian, 24 July 1918, both contained in CSF on Joseph Koudelka, file no. 9-5-1243; *Register of the Department of Justice*, 1919, 24.

85. Best report, 1 August 1918, and Parker report, 29 September 1918, both in OG 116672.

86. *Wisconsin State Journal* editorial of 23 August 1917, as well as editorials of 31 March 1917, 3 April 1917, 6 April 1917, and 17 December 1917.

87. Evjue, *Fighting Editor*, 242–55, and Fola La Follette, *Robert M. La Follette*, vol. 2, 824.

88. *Wisconsin State Journal*, 6 December 1917, 7. Jones himself may have supplied Adams with allegations against the *Capital Times*. In the fall of 1917, La Follette had sued the *State Journal* for libel, and during pretrial questioning Jones acknowledged having known Adams for more than a dozen years and appears to have admitted that he had passed along to Adams an allegation that the *Capital Times* subscribers were pro-German. The cross-examination of Jones, printed in the *Capital Times* of 29 January 1918, contained the following exchange:

> A [Jones] Well, I had the information from one of my solicitors who encountered a man who told him that the [*Capital Times*] stock was practically all subscribed for at that time and that it would go into the home of every pro-German in the state and started out with a circulation of about thirty thousand.
> Q You furnished that information to Mr. Adams?
> A I told Mr. Adams what this solicitor told me.

See also *Wisconsin State Journal*, 29 January 1918, 1; and Unger, *Fighting Bob La Follette*, 258.

89. *Wisconsin State Journal* editorial, 8 December 1917; Unger, *Fighting Bob LaFollette*, 249.

90. Spencer report, 25 October 1917, and letter from Chief to George R. Mayo, 2 November 1917, both in OG 85502.

91. Mayo report, 1 May 1918, OG 85502.

92. Mayo offered to try and see "if the same arrangement with one of the official family of La Follettes in Washington can not be made." Justice Department headquarters responded to Mayo's memo with a cautionary instruction, "Referring to your report of the 4th instant, regarding the Capitol City Times, I do not think it advisable for you to go any further in the matter of the arrangements mentioned by you." Presumably the department was referring to an expansion of the documentary surveillance program, although it might have also been advising Mayo to be careful in secretly drawing on sources from the law office. Mayo report, 4 December 1917, OG 85502. See also letter Chief to Mayo, 8 December 1917, OG 85502 (in retakes section of reel 457). For more of Mayo's investigation, see his reports of 1 December 1917, 11 December 1917, 17 December 1917, and 1 April 1918, all in OG 85502.

93. I am relying here on Evjue, *Fighting Editor*, 293–96. *Capital Times*, 10 May 1918, 1, has a slightly different version of the encounter between Mayo and Evjue.

94. Mayo reports, 1 April 1918 and 9 April 1918, OG 85502.

95. Evjue, *Fighting Editor*, 295–96; *Capital Times*, 10 May 1918, 1, and *Capital Times* editorial, 18 December 1918 (clipping contained in OG 85502).

96. Report of Geo. H. Bragdon, 12 February 1916, OG 20117.

97. See *Coshocton* (OH) *Morning Tribune*, 27 March 1917, 1; reports of Wm. S. Fitch, 29 March 1917 and 3[0?] March 1917, OG 20117. A report by the same investigator later that month, apparently referring to the same interview, phrased Seaman's attitude slightly differently: "As stated in my report for the 20th inst., Dr. Seaman is confident that [German] Ambassador von Bernstorff did not contribute the $40,000 put up for the purchase of the paper when it was sold about two years ago; but he is not confident that a subsequent contribution of $40,000 did not come from von Bernstorff." Harold Dudley, a former *Free Press* official who felt that the publication was unpatriotic, likewise didn't seem to think that it was receiving subsidies from Germany. "Dudley," noted the investigator, "had heard rumors on the street a number of times that the paper was bought by German money, but heard nothing in the office to lead him to believe this and from the fact that the inspection of the corporations records would show that there was a large number of stock holders, he was of the opinion that it was not bought by German money, although he had never actually seen the stock certificate book." Spencer report, 30 June 1917, OG 20117.

98. Fitch reports, 29 March 1917, 3[0?] March 1917, OG 20117; and *Coshocton* (OH) *Morning Tribune*, 27 March 1917, 1.

99. The note stated that the *Free Press* files "will not be given to the public unless public interests should demand it." Justice Department to Theodore

Kronshage, 29 January 1918, in Theodore Kronshage Papers, Box 3, State Historical Society of Wisconsin; Mayo report, 14 January 1918, OG 20117; *Free
Press,* 1 December 1918, 1; Foss, "Theodore Kronshage, Jr."

100. Mayo report, 14 January 1918, OG 20117; *Milwaukee Free Press,* 1 December 1918, 1; *Guide to Wisconsin Newspapers,* 162.

101. *Milwaukee Journal,* 3 June 1919, 1.

102. Parker report, 27 August 1918, OG 286162.

103. Report of Frank Wolfgram, 31 August 1918, OG 275702.

104. Viall report, 5 June 1918, OG 212233.

105. Viall reports, 5 June 1918 and 1[0?] June 1918, both contained in OG
212233; letter from Albert Tetzlaff and statements of N. P. Gaffeny and William
Williston, MISC 24437, *Investigative Case Files of the Bureau of Investigation.* Tetzlaff
refers to the meeting as having taken place on 8 June, but it seems clear that his
questioning by Viall took place a week earlier.

106. See Viall reports, 1[0?] June 1918, 1 July 1918, and [5?] August 1918, all
in OG 212233; R. B. Spencer to A. B. Bielaski, 20 August 1918, MISC 24437,
roll 232.

107. Wolfgram report, 28 June 1918, and 11 October 1918; report of John S.
Couillard, 30 December 1918; and Sawyer report, 6[?] September 1918; all in
OG 3341.

108. Report of Frank F. Wolfgram, 18 June 191[8?], OG 3341.

109. Wolfgram report, 13 June 1918, and 19 June 1918, OG 3341.

110. Wolfgram report, 22 April 1918, OG 3341.

111. Kreuter and Kreuter, *American Dissenter,* 157–67; Korman, *Industrialization, Immigrants, and Americanizers,* 171–91.

112. Wolfgram report, 13 May 1918, and Simons's accompanying report
"The Pro-Prussian Socialist Machine," OG 3341.

113. Report of L. F. Millar, 31 July 1918, OG 3341; Niven, *Carl Sandburg,*
229, 299–302.

114. Ferris report, 12 March 1918, OG 3341.

115. *Milwaukee Journal,* 14 July 1918, 1.

116. *Milwaukee Journal,* 3 November 1917, 1; *Proceedings of the Sixty-Fifth Annual Session of the Wisconsin Teachers' Association, Held at Milwaukee, November 1 to 3,
1917* (Madison: Democrat Printing Company, 1918), 9–10.

117. *Milwaukee Leader,* 17 October 1917, 1, 2; *Milwaukee Journal,* 17 October
1917, 8. The *Journal* seems to have reported Potter's remarks somewhat differently. "If there were [those who did not support the petition]," he is quoted as
saying, "they ought to be ashamed of it. If I had it to do, I would let the teachers sign and circulate it and have every child in school sign it—willingly, of
course."

118. *Milwaukee Leader,* 31 January 1918, 2; and *Milwaukee Free Press,* 31 January 1918, 2.

119. *Milwaukee Leader* editorial of 6 February 1918.

120. The "subjects" to which Potter referred also included a Josephine E. Murphy, who headed an organization of teachers; Wolfgram report, titled, "IN RE META BERGER ELIZABETH H. THOMAS AND JOSEPHINE E. MURPHY Possible Violation of the Espionage Act," 31 August 1918, OG 265647. See also report of Wolfgram, 28 June 1918, OG 3341.

121. See Wolfgram, "IN RE ELIZABETH H. THOMAS, META BERGER AND JOSEPHINE E. MURPHY Alleged Violation of the Espionage Act," 25 September 1918, OG 318295.

122. Stevens and Goldlust-Gingrich, *Family Letters of Victor and Meta Berger,* 212, 233–34, 253–54, 256–57.

123. Ibid., 34–35, 242–44; Miller, *Victor Berger,* 198–201.

124. According to the *Leader,* the proposal would have penalized "disloyal remarks, statements tending to hinder the government's war work or utterances inciting sympathy for the country's enemies." *Milwaukee Leader,* 26 February 1918, 1, and 7 March 1918, 5.

125. Later in the conversation, King did state that the ring could be reclaimed subsequent to the end of the war. See *Leader,* 14 February 1918, 1, 10; 16 February 1918, 1, 10. In a report, Ralph Izard referred to Harry King as "an A.P.L. investigator who is working upon alien enemy cases under the direction of this office." Izard report, 18 February 1918, OG 22355. For evidence that Izard's formal title was special agent in charge, see Harris report, 10 February 1918, OG 80515, and special agent in charge to Wm. H. Steiner, 2[5?] January 1918; Steiner report, 30 January 1918, both in OG 493; and *Milwaukee Leader,* 16 February 1918, 10.

126. *Leader,* 14 February 1918, 1, 10; 16 February 1918, 1, 10. A *Leader* reporter had provided Izard's office with a copy of Huettlin's affidavit, as well as a note "stating that Mrs. Huettlin wished Izard to investigate her charge of brutal treatment."

127. *Leader,* 15 February 1918, 1; 16 February 1918, 1, 10. Yet a third statement (this one from an office employee) provided by Izard left out any mention of the ring.

128. *Leader* editorial, 19 February 1918.

129. Cox report, 25 February 1918, OG 149676; and *Milwaukee Leader,* 23 February 1918, 1. I should note here that there is a chronological discrepancy between Cox and the *Leader* in their accounts of the episode. The *Leader* stated that the interview had taken place on 23 February, while Cox's report, filed on the twenty-fifth, said that it had taken place on the twenty-second. Technically, it is possible that the *Leader* article could have been referring to a separate warning delivered to Zoll by a government agent other than Cox, but I think that such a coincidence is highly improbable.

130. For more on the slacker raids, see Jensen, *Price of Vigilance*, 198–215.

131. *New York Times,* 12 September 1918, 10; *Leader,* 13 September 1918, 1.

132. Letter from Socialist Campaign Committee, file folder 49841, Box 144, Entry 40, Office of the Solicitor, Records Relating to the Espionage Act, World War I, 1917–1921, RG 28, Records of the Post Office Department, National Archives, Washington, D.C.

133. *Leader,* 29 August 1918, 1, editorial page.

134. Ettenheim, *How Milwaukee Voted,* 94–99, 114–18; *Wisconsin Blue Book 1919,* 155. The U.S. House of Representatives moved to prevent Berger from serving in Congress and in November 1919, following hearings that delved into the topic of Berger's attitude toward the war, voted to bar the Socialist, who was out on bail and appealing his Espionage Act conviction through the court system, from taking his seat in the House. In a special election held that December to fill the vacant seat, the voters of the fifth district again elected Berger, and the following January the House again voted to bar him from serving as a congressman. In 1921 the U.S. Supreme Court reversed Berger's Espionage Act conviction, and he won election to the House the following year, finally being seated in 1923. Muzik, "Victor L. Berger."

135. *Milwaukee Sentinel,* 7 November 1918, 4; *Wisconsin Blue Book 1917,* 294–99; *Wisconsin Blue Book 1919,* 160–63.

136. See Lorence, "Socialism in Northern Wisconsin, 1910–1920," and "'Dynamite for the Brain'"; Brye, *Wisconsin Voting Patterns,* 265–69, 386–91.

137. Brye, *Wisconsin Voting Patterns,* 371.

138. Margulies, "The Election of 1920 in Wisconsin," and *Decline of the Progressive Movement in Wisconsin,* 277–82.

Chapter 6. Vigilantism

1. In the pre-Revolutionary period, tar and feathers were applied to those who reputedly had informed the authorities about alleged customs violations. See Irvin, "Tar, Feathers, and the Enemies of American Liberties."

2. Brown, "History of Vigilantism in America"; Brown, *Strain of Violence;* Brundage, *Lynching in the New South,* 1–8; Pfeifer, *Rough Justice,* esp. pp. 122–47 and 156–83; statistics on southern lynchings are from Tolnay and Beck, *Festival of Violence,* 271–72; Carrigan and Webb, "*Muerto por Unos Desconocidos* (Killed by Persons Unknown)."

3. Harries and Harries, *Last Days of Innocence,* 3–5.

4. *New York Times,* 8 February 1918, 1; *Manson* (IA) *Democrat,* quoted in *Pomeroy* (IA) *Herald,* 21 February 1918.

5. Lincoln, *Passage Through Armageddon,* 397–411.

6. Stokesbury, *Short History of World War I,* 246–48, 254–56, 261–67.

7. *New York Times*, 10 March 1918, sec. I, 6.

8. *New York Times*, 31 October 1917, 12.

9. Luebke, *Bonds of Loyalty*, 243–44; *New York Times*, 31 March 1918, sec. I, 16.

10. *New York Times*, 5 January 1918, 18; 7 January 1918, 12; 9 January 1918, 12.

11. *New York Times*, 25 February 1918, 4; Davison to Currie, 17 April 1918, in *Congressional Record*, 65th Cong., 2nd sess, 5364–65.

12. *New York Times Magazine*, 28 April 1918, 2.

13. *New York Times*, 17 April 1918, 12; *Los Angeles Times*, 17 April 1918, 15.

14. Van Deman quoted in Talbert, *Negative Intelligence*, 45–48; *Chicago Daily Tribune*, 20 April 1918, 1, 4.

15. Wilson and Link, *Papers of Woodrow Wilson*, vol. 47, 381–82; *New York Times*, 20 April 1918, 8, and 24 April 1918, 4; *Los Angeles Times*, 24 April 1918, 14.

16. *New York Times*, 20 July 1918, 4; *Belleville* (IL) *News-Democrat*, 28 February 1918; *Idaho Daily Statesman*, 9 April 1918, 4.

17. Stevens, "Suppression of Expression in Wisconsin during World War I," 179–80; *Kansas City Star*, 16 April 1918, 1, and 28 April 1918, 1.

18. Dubofsky, *We Shall Be All*, 385–87.

19. *New York Times*, 30 October 1917, 3; Weinstein, "Anti-War Sentiment and the Socialist Party," 223; Sellars, *Oil, Wheat and Wobblies*, 105–9.

20. Peterson and Fite, *Opponents of War*, 57–58; Luebke, *Bonds of Loyalty*, 3–11. For more on vigilantism during the war, see Capozzola, "The Only Badge Needed Is Your Patriotic Fervor."

21. *New York Times*, 4 August 1917, 6; *Belleville* (IL) *News-Democrat*, 6 April 1918, [4]; *Macon Daily Telegraph*, 7 April 1918, 6.

22. *State* (Columbia, SC), 5 April 1918, 4, and 17 April 1918, 4.

23. *Fort Worth Star-Telegram*, 6 April 1918, 4; *Grand Forks* (ND) *Herald*, 2 August 1917, 4; *Aberdeen* (SD) *Daily News*, 12 November 1917, 2.

24. Train, "The Flag of His Country," 9–11, 45–46, 52.

25. *Morning Olympian*, 6 April 1918, 2; *Chicago Daily Tribune*, 6 April 1918, 8.

26. *New York Times*, 19 April 1918, 15; *Wilkes-Barre Times Leader*, 9 April 1918, 12.

27. The prosecutor noted that "I learned on Friday that statements had been made by persons who were hanging about his [Lewin's] place that an example was to be made of him on Friday night in the State house yards." Bolin to AG, 22 April 1918, CSF 9-5-798.

28. O'Brian to Bolin, 29 May 1918; telegram Bolin to AG, 2 August 1918; memo Morgan to O'Brian, 5 August 1918; O'Brian to Bolin, 8 August 1918. Harry Lewin was released from his internment in 1919. Summary sheet for disposal of interned alien enemy; letter Porter to Lewin, 12 June 1919. All cites from CSF 9-5-798.

29. Polenberg, *Fighting Faiths*, 27–28; *Congressional Record*, 65th Cong., 2nd sess., 4559–60.

30. Polenberg, *Fighting Faiths*, 29–35; Gutfeld, "The Ves Hall Case, Judge Bourquin, and the Sedition Act of 1918," 163–75; *Congressional Record*, 65th Cong., 2nd sess, 4560–61; Kohn, *American Political Prisoners*, 9.

31. Luebke, *Bonds of Loyalty*, 3–13; *Chicago Daily Tribune*, 6 April 1918, 4; Currie to Justice Department, 2 April 1918, and Gregory to Currie, 12 April 1918, both in *Congressional Record*, 65th Cong., 2nd sess., 5095–96.

32. Wilson and Link, *Papers of Woodrow Wilson*, vol. 47, 363–65.

33. Polenberg, *Fighting Faiths*, 32–33; *New York Times*, 25 April 1918, 12; *Congressional Record*, 65th Cong., 2nd sess., 5542. Department officials, including Attorney General Gregory, did object to a provision of the bill allowing the post office the right to cease delivering mail to supposedly disloyal persons. See Polenberg, *Fighting Faiths*, 35, and Wilson and Link, *Papers of Woodrow Wilson*, vol. 48, 12–14.

34. Polenberg, *Fighting Faiths*, 33–36.

35. *New York Times*, 10 May 1918, 7.

36. Carl R. Weinberg's analysis of the Prager lynching concludes that Riegel was a key participant, but also found that at least four of the men put on trial were not present when Prager was murdered. See Weinberg, *Labor, Loyalty, and Rebellion*, 112–53. See also Hickey, "The Prager Affair," and Luebke, *Bonds of Loyalty*, 3–11. News reports suggested that the Justice Department would most likely conduct some kind of inquiry into the affair. See *Chicago Daily Tribune*, 6 April 1918, 4, and the *New York Times*, 6 April 1918, 15.

37. *New York Times*, 3 June 1918, 10; *Fort Wayne News and Sentinel*, 5 June 1918, 9; *Belleville* (IL) *News-Democrat*, 4 June 1918, 2; *Macon Daily Telegraph*, 7 June 1918, 6; *Chicago Defender*, 22 June 1918, 16.

38. Cresswell, "Enforcing the Enforcement Acts"; Kaczorowski, *Politics of Judicial Interpretation*, 50, 79–113; Foner, *Reconstruction*, 342, 454–59.

39. Bielaski to A. M. Briggs, 2 April 1917, folder for Goldsboro, NC, in Correspondence with Field Offices, 1917–19, records of the APL, records of the FBI, RG 65, National Archives, College Park, MD; Jensen, *Price of Vigilance*, 22–31.

40. *Congressional Record*, 65th Cong., 2nd sess., 6233–35.

41. *Chicago Daily Tribune*, 6 April 1918, 4; *Annual Report of the Attorney General of the United States for the Year 1918*, 23.

42. *Duluth Sunday News Tribune*, 19 September 1918, 1; *Duluth News Tribune*, 1 October 1918, 1; reports of Frank O. Pelto, 8 October and 9 October 1918; reports of John T. Kenny, 11 October 1918, in OG 309719.

43. A broader federal ban on kidnapping would come in 1932, in the wake of the abduction of aviator Charles Lindbergh's son, but it only applied in cases where the victim had been transported across state lines; a 1934 revision to the law allowed federal authorities to assume that a presumed abductee who had been missing for seven days had indeed crossed state lines. "Federal Power to Prosecute Violence against Minority Groups"; Bomar, "The Lindbergh

Law"; Cushman, "Judicial Decisions on Public Law"; Kenny report, 11 October 1918, OG 309719.

44. *New York Times*, 16 May 1918, 13, and 29 May 1918, 7; Dubofsky, *We Shall Be All*, 390–91; Cushman, "Judicial Decisions on Public Law," 283; Edward S. Corwin, "Constitutional Law in 1920–1921."

45. Report of W. H. Butterworth, 17 April 1918, OG 183758.

46. W. C. Smiley to A. Bruce Bielaski, 24 July 1918, OG 155860.

47. Report of Charles Petrovitsky, 16 August 1918, OG 155860.

48. Ibid. My quotation from Keaton's letter is taken from Petrovitsky's report. For a copy of Keaton's original letter, see *Everett Daily Herald*, 11 May 1918. There are some minor differences between Keaton's original letter and Petrovitsky's copy.

49. Report of Sydney W. Dillingham, 29 June 1918, OG 218274.

50. Ibid.

51. Ibid.

52. *Cass County Democrat* (Harrisonville, MO), 11 April 1918, [10].

53. *Cass County Democrat*, 23 May 1918, [1]; *Cass County Leader* (Harrisonville, MO). 23 May 1918, [1].

54. *Cass County Leader*, 30 May 1918, [1], [2], [3], [7]; *Cass County Democrat*, 30 May 1918, [1], [7], [10].

55. Dillingham report, 4 June 1918, OG 136731; *Cass County Democrat*, 6 June 1918, [1].

56. Dillingham report, 5 June 1918, OG 212170.

57. Ibid.; *Kansas City Times*, 5 June 1918, 9. For a description of the Federal Farm Bond program, I relied on articles in the *Charlotte Observer*, 17 August 1916, 5, and the *Grand Forks* (ND) *Herald*, 15 April 1917, 3.

58. Dillingham report, 5 June 1918, OG 212170.

59. Dillingham report, 15 August 1918, OG 29159; *Cass County Leader*, 15 August 1918, [1].

60. *Eau Claire* (WI) *Daily Telegram*, 25 June 1918, 5.

61. Report of T. E. Campbell, for period of 6 August 1918, OG 30630.

62. Campbell report, 21 August 1918, OG 30630.

63. Report of Justin C. Daspit, 30 August 1917, OG 54675.

64. Reports of L. H. Harrison, 15 June 1918, and of J. Reese Murray, 17 June 1918, in OG 216775; McCartin, *Labor's Great War*, 149–56.

65. Murray report, 17 June 1918, OG 216775.

66. The figures are from Zangrando, *NAACP Crusade against Lynching*, 6–7.

67. Report of W. H. Kerrick, 8 April 1918, OG 171916.

68. *New York Times*, 1 October 1939, 38; *Waterloo* (IA) *Daily Courier*, 5 June 1941, 8.

69. *Maryville* (MO) *Daily Forum*, 17 July 1943, 2; Steele, "Fear of the Mob and Faith in Government in Free Speech Discourse."

Epilogue

1. Hawley, *Great War and the Search for a Modern Order,* 16–23; Kester, "The War Industries Board."

2. *Statutes at Large of the United States of America from April 1917 to March 1919* (Washington: Government Printing Office, 1919), 83; Brandt, *No Magic Bullet,* 52–95; Connelly, *Response to Prostitution in the Progressive Era,* 136–50.

3. For more on Hoover's management methods and their relation to progressivism, see Powers, *Secrecy and Power,* esp. 144–57.

4. Wilson and Link, *Papers of Woodrow Wilson,* vol. 51, 646.

5. Knock, *To End All Wars,* 158–61, 185–88.

6. Sterling, "The 'Naïve Liberal,' The 'Devious Communist' and the Johnson Case."

7. Wright, "Alfred Bettman"; Bettman to Hoover, 19 April 1929, box 48, Alfred Bettman papers, University of Cincinnati archives.

8. *New York Times,* 18 January 1920, 1.

9. O'Brian, "Restraints upon Individual Freedom in Times of National Emergency."

10. O'Brian, "Changing Aspects of Freedom," 137–97. On Hoover's incessant efforts to tout the achievements of his bureau to the public, see Powers, *Secrecy and Power.*

Appendix

1. "Educational Attainment by Sex," pdf file at http://www.census.gov/compendia/statab/hist_stats.html, 2006 Statistical Abstract, U.S. Census Bureau.

2. E-mail, 25 August 2004, from Marquette University Alumni Office; e-mail, 12 July 2006, from Michael Luther, Division of Rare and Manuscript Collections, Cornell University Library; e-mail, 18 July 2006, from Mark Mullins, Alumni Records Office, University of Michigan; "John E. Ferris" entry in *History of Milwaukee, City and County,* vol. 3, 484.

3. Thwaites, *University of Wisconsin,* 582.

4. Transcript of trial, Robert M. La Follette v. F. W. Montgomery, E. J. B. Schubring, and W. N. Parker, 2–4, in Robert M. La Follette papers; *Wisconsin Journal of Education* (November 1915), 262.

5. Willard N. Parker, "By Way of Current Comment and Casual Inquiry," *Wisconsin Journal of Education* 49 (April 1917): 111. See also *Wisconsin Journal of Education* 49 (November 1917).

6. *Capital Times,* 11 January 1918, 2; *Wisconsin State Journal,* 29 December 1917, 1.

7. "Educational Attainment by Sex."

8. Charles I. Rukes, employment application for special agent of the Department of Justice, 28 May 1918, in Bureau of Investigation personnel file.

9. Lewis E. Sawyer, employment applications, 8 November 1923 and 3 May 1917, in Bureau of Investigation personnel file.

10. For information on Charles Woida, see *Wright's Directory of Milwaukee* for 1915, 1916, 1917, 1918, and in 13th and 14th U.S. Censuses for Milwaukee County, Wisconsin. For information on Charles J. Bodenbach, see *Wright's Directory of Milwaukee* for 1907, 1915, 1916, 1917, 1918, and in 13th and 14th U.S. Censuses for Milwaukee County, Wisconsin. For information on Charles L. Harris, see *Wright's Directory of Milwaukee* for 1915, 1916, 1917, and in 14th U.S. Census for Milwaukee County, Wisconsin, as well as Chas. L. Harris to A. Bruce Bielaski, 24 September 1918, OG 278252; and oath of Charles Lee Harris, 12 December 1924, in personnel file released by FBI.

11. Employment applications, 20 March 1917 and 18 April 1918; W. K. Parkinson to AG, 8 March 1917, and report of F. J. Payson, 7 May 1918, all in Bureau of Investigation personnel file of Kajetan Charles Jakoubek.

12. R. B. Spencer to Bielaski, 3 October 1918, OG 278252; Ralph Izard to Chief, Bureau of Investigation, 21 March 1925, in personnel file of Ralph Izard, released by FBI.

13. W. E. Cox to Bielaski, 28 September 1918; Henry H. Stroud to Bielaski, 24 September 1918; Lewis E. Sawyer to Bielaski, 24 September 1918; Chas. L. Harris to Bielaski, 24 September 1918, all in OG 278252.

14. Trial transcript of Robert M. La Follette v. F. W. Montgomery, E. J. B. Schubring, and W. N. Parker, 21–22, in Robert M. La Follette papers.

Bibliography

Archives

National Archives, College Park, Maryland.
General Records of the Department of Justice, RG 60:
   Appointment Letter Books.
   Classified Subject Files.
   Docket of Presidential Warrants Issued, 1917–18.
Records of the Federal Bureau of Investigation, RG 65:
   Records of the American Protective League.
National Archives, Washington, D.C.
Investigative Case Files of the Bureau of Investigation, 1908–1922. Microfilm
      Publication M1085.
Records of the Military Intelligence Division, RG 165:
   Military Intelligence Division Correspondence, 1917–41.
Records of the Post Office Department, RG 28.
National Archives, Central Plains Region, Kansas City, Missouri.
Records of the District Courts of the United States, RG 21.
Records of the U.S. Court of Appeals, RG 276.
National Archives, Great Lakes Region, Chicago, Illinois.
Records of the District Courts of the United States, RG 21.
National Archives, Northeast Region, New York City.
Records of the District Courts of the United States, RG 21.
National Archives, Northeast Region, Waltham, Massachusetts.
Records of the District Courts of the United States, RG 21.
National Archives, Southwest Region, Fort Worth, Texas.
Records of the District Courts of the United States, RG 21.
Library of Congress, Washington, D.C.
Papers of Thomas Watt Gregory.
**Schlesinger Library, Radcliffe Institute for Advanced Study, Harvard
      University.**
Radcliffe Alumni Association Memorial Biographies File.

University of Cincinnati Archives, Cincinnati, Ohio.
Alfred Bettman papers.
University of Wisconsin–Madison Archives.
File on The Forum.
File on Scott H. Goodnight.
Wisconsin Historical Society, Madison, Wisconsin.
Council of National Defense papers.
Victor L. Berger papers.
Theodore Kronshage papers.
Robert M. La Follette papers.
Personnel files of the following investigators, released by Federal Bureau of Investigation, Washington, D.C., pursuant to Freedom of Information Act request.
Albert E. Farland
Dave L. Gershon
Werner Hanni
Charles L. Harris
Ralph Izard
Kajetan Charles Jakoubek
Joseph F. Kropidlowski
Benjamin H. Littleton
Thomas S. Marshall
Joseph Polen
Diego E. Ramos
Charles Rukes
Lewis E. Sawyer
James Francis Terry
Personnel files of the following investigators, released by National Personnel Records Center (Civilian Personnel Records), St. Louis, Missouri.
Ralph Izard
Donald D. Lamond

Sources

Abrams, Ray H. *Preachers Present Arms*. Scottdale, PA: Herald Press, 1969. First published 1933 by Round Table Press.

American National Biography. Edited by John A. Garraty and Mark C. Carnes. New York: Oxford University Press, 1999.

Anders, Evan. "Thomas Watt Gregory and the Survival of His Progressive Faith." *Southwestern Historical Quarterly* 93 (July 1989): 1–24.

Annual Report of the Attorney General of the United States. Washington: Government Printing Office, 1910–18.

Avrich, Paul. *Anarchist Voices: An Oral History of Anarchism in America.* Princeton: Princeton University Press, 1995.

Bassett, Michael. "The American Socialist Party and the War 1917–1918." *Australian Journal of Politics and History* 11 (December 1965): 277–91.

Beaver, Daniel R. *Newton D. Baker and the American War Effort, 1917–1919.* Lincoln: University of Nebraska Press, 1966.

Beckman, Marlene D. "The White Slave Traffic Act: The Historical Impact of a Criminal Law Policy on Women." *Georgetown Law Journal* 72 (February 1984): 1111–42.

Bedford, Henry Frederick. "A Case Study in Hysteria: Victor L. Berger, 1917–1921." Master's thesis, University of Wisconsin, 1953.

Belknap, Michal R. "The Mechanics of Repression: J. Edgar Hoover, the Bureau of Investigation and the Radicals 1917–1925." *Crime and Social Justice* 7 (Spring/Summer 1977): 49–58.

Berger, Meta. *A Milwaukee Woman's Life on the Left: The Autobiography of Meta Berger.* Edited by Kimberly Swanson. Madison: State Historical Society of Wisconsin, 2001.

Berres, Jean L. "Local Aspects of the 'Campaign for Americanism': The *Milwaukee Journal* in World War I." PhD diss., Southern Illinois University–Carbondale, 1978.

Berthoff, Rowland Tappan. *British Immigrants in Industrial America, 1790–1950.* New York: Russell and Russell, 1968. First published 1953 by Harvard University Press.

Billington, Ray Allen. *The Protestant Crusade, 1800–1860: A Study of the Origins of American Nativism.* New York: Rinehart, 1952. First published 1938 by The Macmillan Company.

Bissett, Jim. *Agrarian Socialism in America: Marx, Jefferson, and Jesus in the Oklahoma Countryside, 1904–1920.* Norman: University of Oklahoma Press, 1999.

Bomar, Horace L., Jr. "The Lindbergh Law." *Law and Contemporary Problems* 1 (October 1934): 435–44.

Bossard-Borner, Heidi. "Village Quarrels and National Controversies: Switzerland." In *Culture Wars: Secular-Catholic Conflict in Nineteenth-Century Europe,* edited by Christopher Clark and Wolfram Kaiser, 255–84. New York: Cambridge University Press, 2003.

Branch, Taylor. *Parting the Waters: America in the King Years, 1954–63.* New York: Simon and Schuster, 1988.

Brandt, Allan M. *No Magic Bullet: A Social History of Venereal Disease in the United States since 1880.* Expanded edition. New York: Oxford University Press, 1987.

Brown, Richard Maxwell. "The History of Vigilantism in America." In *Vigilante Politics,* edited by H. Jon Rosenbaum and Peter C. Sederberg, 79–109. Philadelphia: University of Pennsylvania Press, 1976.

———. *Strain of Violence: Historical Studies of American Violence and Vigilantism.* New York: Oxford University Press, 1975.

Brundage, W. Fitzhugh. *Lynching in the New South: Georgia and Virginia, 1880–1930*. Urbana: University of Illinois Press, 1993.

Brye, David L. *Wisconsin Voting Patterns in the Twentieth Century, 1900 to 1950*. New York: Garland, 1979.

Burner, David. *The Politics of Provincialism: The Democratic Party in Transition, 1918–1932*. New York: W. W. Norton, 1975. First published 1967 by Knopf.

Cappozzola, Christopher. "The Only Badge Needed Is Your Patriotic Fervor: Vigilance, Coercion, and the Law in World War I America." *Journal of American History* 88 (March 2002): 1354–82.

Capps, Finis Herbert. *From Isolationism to Involvement: The Swedish Immigrant Press in America, 1914–1945*. Chicago: Swedish Pioneer Historical Society, 1966.

Carrigan, William D., and Clive Webb. "Muerto por Unos Desconocidos (Killed by Persons Unknown): Mob Violence against Blacks and Mexicans." In *Beyond Black and White: Race, Ethnicity and Gender in the U.S. South and Southwest*, edited by Stephanie Cole and Alison M. Parker, 35–74. College Station: Published for the University of Texas at Arlington by Texas A&M University Press, 2004.

Carroll, Thomas F. "Freedom of Speech and of the Press in War Time: The Espionage Act." *Michigan Law Review* 17 (June 1919): 621–65.

Cary, Lorin Lee. "The Bureau of Investigation and Radicalism in Toledo, Ohio: 1918–1920." *Labor History* 21 (Summer 1980): 430–40.

———. "The Wisconsin Loyalty Legion, 1917–1918." *Wisconsin Magazine of History* 53 (Autumn 1969): 33–50.

Chambers, John Whiteclay, II. *To Raise an Army: The Draft Comes to Modern America*. New York: Free Press-Macmillan, 1987.

Child, Clifton James. *The German-Americans in Politics, 1914–1917*. Madison: University of Wisconsin Press, 1939.

Chrislock, Carl H. *Watchdog of Loyalty: The Minnesota Commission of Public Safety during World War I*. St. Paul: Minnesota Historical Society Press, 1991.

Coben, Stanley. *A. Mitchell Palmer: Politician*. New York: Columbia University Press, 1963.

Conrad, Will C., Kathleen F. Wilson, and Dale Wilson. *The Milwaukee Journal: The First Eighty Years*. Madison: University of Wisconsin Press, 1964.

Corwin, Edward S. "Constitutional Law in 1920–1921. I: The Constitutional Decisions of the Supreme Court of the United States in the October Term, 1920." *American Political Science Review* 16 (February 1922): 22–40.

Costrell, Edwin. *How Maine Viewed the War, 1914–1917*. Orono, ME: University Press, 1940.

Cresswell, Stephen. "Enforcing the Enforcement Acts: The Department of Justice in Northern Mississippi, 1870–1890." *Journal of Southern History* 53 (August 1987): 421–40.

Crighton, John Clark. *Missouri and the World War, 1914–1917: A Study in Public*

Opinion. Vol. 21, no. 3 of the University of Missouri Studies. Columbia: University of Missouri, 1947.

Cuddy, Edward. "Pro-Germanism and American Catholicism, 1914–1917." *Catholic Historical Review* 54 (October 1968): 427–54.

Cunnigham, David. *There's Something Happening Here: The New Left, the Klan, and FBI Counterintelligence.* Berkeley: University of California Press, 2004.

Curti, Merle E., and Vernon Carstensen. *The University of Wisconsin: A History.* Madison: University of Wisconsin Press, 1949.

Cushman, Robert E. "Judicial Decisions on Public Law." *American Political Science Review* 2 (May 1919): 281–92.

Dictionary of Wisconsin Biography. Madison: State Historical Society of Wisconsin, 1960.

Dinnerstein, Leonard. *Antisemitism in America.* New York: Oxford University Press, 1994.

Donner, Frank. *Protectors of Privilege: Red Squads and Police Repression in Urban America.* Berkeley: University of California Press, 1990.

Doyle, Charles. "National Security Letters in Foreign Intelligence Investigations: Legal Background and Recent Amendments." *Congressional Research Service* report, available from Federation of American Scientists website, http://fas.org/sgp/crs/intel/RL33320.pdf.

———. "The USA Patriot Act: A Legal Analysis." *Congressional Research Service* report, 15 April 2002, available from Electronic Privacy Information Center, http://www.epic.org/privacy/terrorism/usapatriot/.

Dubay, Robert W. "The Opposition to Selective Service, 1916–1918." *Southern Quarterly* 7 (April 1969): 301–22.

Dubofsky, Melvyn. *We Shall Be All: A History of the Industrial Workers of the World.* New York: Quadrangle, 1969.

Durham, Weldon B. "'Big Brother' and the 'Seven Sisters': Camp Life Reforms in World War I." *Military Affairs* 42 (April 1978): 57–60.

Ellis, George W. "Liberia in the Political Psychology of West Africa." *Journal of the Royal African Society* 12 (October 1912): 52–70.

———. "Political Institutions in Liberia." *American Political Science Review* 5 (May 1911): 213–23.

Ellis, Mark. *Race, War, and Surveillance: African Americans and the United States Government during World War I.* Bloomington: Indiana University Press, 2001.

Emmons, David M. *The Butte Irish: Class and Ethnicity in an American Mining Town, 1875–1925.* 1989. Urbana: University of Illinois Press, 1990.

Esslinger, Dean R. "American German and Irish Attitudes Toward Neutrality, 1914–1917: A Study of Catholic Minorities." *Catholic Historical Review* 53 (July 1967): 194–216.

Ettenheim, Sarah C. *How Milwaukee Voted, 1848–1980.* 2nd ed. Milwaukee: University of Wisconsin, 1980.

Evans, Ellen L. *The Cross and the Ballot: Catholic Political Parties in Germany, Switzer-land, Austria, Belgium and the Netherlands, 1785–1985*. Boston: Humanities Press, 1999.

Evjue, William T. *A Fighting Editor*. Madison: Wells Printing Company, 1968.

Falk, Karen. "Public Opinion in Wisconsin during World War I." *Wisconsin Magazine of History* 25 (June 1942): 389–407.

"Federal Power to Prosecute Violence against Minority Groups." *Yale Law Journal* 57 (March 1948): 855–73.

Feldman, Egal. "Prostitution, the Alien Woman and the Progressive Imagination, 1910–1915." *American Quarterly* 19 (Summer 1967): 192–206.

Fink, Gary M. *The Fulton Bag and Cotton Mills Strike of 1914–1915: Espionage, Labor Conflict, and New South Industrial Relations*. Ithaca, NY: ILR Press, 1993.

Finnegan, John P. "The Preparedness Movement in Wisconsin, 1914–1917." Master's thesis, University of Wisconsin, 1961.

Foss, Robert H. "Theodore Kronshage, Jr." *Wisconsin Magazine of History* 26 (June 1943): 414–25.

Frooman, Jack. "The Wisconsin Peace Movement 1915–1919." Master's thesis, University of Wisconsin, 1949.

Garraty, John A. *Henry Cabot Lodge: A Biography*. New York: Knopf, 1968.

Genini, Ronald. "Industrial Workers of the World and Their Fresno Free Speech Fight, 1910–1911." *California Historical Quarterly* 53 (Summer 1974): 100–114.

Gentry, Curt. *J. Edgar Hoover: The Man and the Secrets*. New York: W. W. Norton, 1991.

Gere, Anne Ruggles. *Intimate Practices: Literacy and Cultural Work in U.S. Women's Clubs, 1880–1920*. Urbana: University of Illinois Press, 1997.

Gerstle, Gary. "Liberty, Coercion, and the Making of Americans." *Journal of American History* 84 (September 1997): 524–58.

Gibbs, Christopher C. *The Great Silent Majority: Missouri's Resistance to World War I*. Columbia: University of Missouri Press, 1988.

Gill, Gillian. *Mary Baker Eddy*. Reading, MA: Perseus Books, 1998.

Glad, Paul W. *The History of Wisconsin*. Vol. 5: *War, a New Era, and Depression, 1914–1940*. Madison: State Historical Society of Wisconsin, 1990.

Goldstein, Robert J. *Political Repression in Modern America from 1870 to the Present*. Cambridge, MA: Schenkman Publishing, 1978.

Gordon, Marsha. "Onward Kitchen Soldiers: Mobilizing the Domestic during World War I." *Canadian Review of American Studies* 29 (1999): 61–87.

Green, James R. *Grass-Roots Socialism: Radical Movements in the Southwest, 1895–1943*. Baton Rouge: Louisiana State University Press, 1978.

Gregory, John G., ed. *History of Milwaukee, Wisconsin*. Vols. 3 and 4. Chicago: S. J. Clarke Publishing Company, 1931.

Gregory, Thomas Watt. "Address of T. W. Gregory." *Proceedings of the Twenty-First Annual Session of the North Carolina Bar Association.* Edited by Thomas W. Davis. Raleigh, NC: Edwards and Broughton, 1920.

Grubbs, Frank L., Jr. *The Struggle for Labor Loyalty: Gompers, the A. F. of L., and the Pacifists, 1917–1920.* Durham, NC: Duke University Press, 1968.

Guide to Wisconsin Newspapers, 1833–1957. Compiled by Donald E. Oehlerts. Madison: State Historical Society of Wisconsin, 1958.

Gurda, John, *The Making of Milwaukee.* Milwaukee: Milwaukee County Historical Society, 1999.

Gutfeld, Arnon. "The Ves Hall Case, Judge Bourquin, and the Sedition Act of 1918." *Pacific Historical Review* 37 (May 1968): 163–78.

Gutman, Herbert G. "The Tompkins Square 'Riot' in New York City on January 13, 1874: A Re-examination of Its Causes and Its Aftermath." *Labor History* 6 (Winter 1965): 44–70.

Hamilton, Shane. "A Victor without Peace: Victor Berger and Socialist Opposition to World War I." Unpublished research paper, 1996, available at http://us.history.wisc.edu/hist102/bios/html/berger.html.

Harries, Meirion, and Susie Harries. *The Last Days of Innocence: America at War, 1917–1918.* New York: Vintage Books, 1998. First published 1997 by Random House.

Harris, Charles H. III, and Louis R. Sadler. "The 1911 Reyes Conspiracy: The Texas Side." *Southwestern Historical Quarterly* 83 (April 1980): 325–48.

Harvard Encyclopedia of American Ethnic Groups. Edited by Stephan Thernstrom. Cambridge, MA: Belknap-Harvard University Press, 1980.

Hawley, Ellis W. *The Great War and the Search for a Modern Order: A History of the American People and Their Institutions, 1917–1933.* 2nd ed. New York: St. Martin's Press, 1992.

Haynes, Robert V. *A Night of Violence: The Houston Riot of 1917.* Baton Rouge: Louisiana State University Press, 1976.

Heale, M. J. *American Anticommunism: Combating the Enemy Within, 1830–1970.* Baltimore: Johns Hopkins University Press, 1990.

Hickey, Donald R. "The Prager Affair: A Study in Wartime Hysteria." *Journal of the Illinois State Historical Society* 62 (Summer 1969): 117–34.

Higham, John. *Strangers in the Land: Patterns of American Nativism, 1860–1925.* 1955. New Brunswick, NJ: Rutgers University Press, 1992.

Hill, Robert A. "'The Foremost Radical among His Race:' Marcus Garvey and the Black Scare, 1918–1921." *Prologue* 16 (Winter 1984): 215–31.

History of Milwaukee City and County. Vol. 2. Chicago: S. J. Clarke Publishing Company, 1922.

Hobson, Barbara Meil. *Uneasy Virtue: The Politics of Prostitution and the American Reform Tradition.* New York: Basic Books, 1987.

Hofstadter, Richard. *The Age of Reform: From Bryan to F.D.R.* New York: Vintage, 1955.

Holter, Darryl. "Labor Spies and Union-Busting in Wisconsin, 1890–1940." *Wisconsin Magazine of History* 68 (Summer 1985): 243–65.

Horowitz, Helen Lefkowitz. "Victoria Woodhull, Anthony Comstock, and Conflict over Sex in the United States in the 1870s." *Journal of American History* 87 (September 2000): 403–34.

Hughes, Charles Evans. *The Autobiographical Notes of Charles Evans Hughes.* Edited by David J. Danelski and Joseph S. Tulchin. Cambridge, MA: Harvard University Press, 1973.

Hyde, Charles K. "Undercover and Underground: Labor Spies and Mine Management in the Early Twentieth Century." *Business History Review* 60 (Spring 1986): 1–27.

Irvin, Benjamin. "Tar, Feathers, and the Enemies of American Liberties, 1768–1776." *New England Quarterly* 76 (June 2003): 197–238.

Jensen, Joan M. *The Price of Vigilance.* Chicago: Rand McNally, 1968.

Johnson, Neil M. "The Patriotism and Anti-Prussianism of the Lutheran Church—Missouri Synod, 1914–1918." *Concordia Historical Institute Quarterly* 39 (October 1966): 99–118.

Joseph, Ted. "The United States vs. H. Miller: The Strange Case of a Mennonite Editor Convicted of Violating the 1917 Espionage Act." *Mennonite Life* 30 (September 1975): 14–18.

Judd, Richard W. *Socialist Cities: Municipal Politics and the Grass Roots of American Socialism.* Albany: State University of New York Press, 1989.

Kaczorowski, Robert J. *The Politics of Judicial Interpretation: The Federal Courts, Department of Justice and Civil Rights, 1866–1876.* New York: Oceana, 1985.

Karson, Marc. *American Labor Unions and Politics, 1900–1918.* Carbondale: Southern Illinois University Press, 1958.

Kazal, Russell A. *Becoming Old Stock: The Paradox of German-American Identity.* Princeton: Princeton University Press, 2004.

Keith, Jeannette. "The Politics of Southern Draft Resistance, 1917–1918: Class, Race, and Conscription in the Rural South." *Journal of American History* 87 (March 2001): 1335–61.

Kennedy, David M. *Over Here: The First World War and American Society.* New York: Oxford University Press, 1982. First published 1980 by Oxford University Press.

Kester, Randall B. "The War Industries Board, 1917–1918: A Study in Industrial Mobilization." *American Political Science Review* 34 (August 1940): 655–84.

Kitchen, Martin. "The German Invasion of Canada in the First World War." *International History Review* 7 (May 1985): 245–60.

Kivisto, Peter. *Immigrant Socialists in the United States: The Case of Finns and the Left.* Rutherford, NJ: Farleigh Dickinson University Press, 1984.

Klueter, Howard R., and James J. Lorence. *Woodlot and Ballot Box: Marathon County in the Twentieth Century.* Wausau, WI: Marathon County Historical Society, 1977.

Knock, Thomas J. *To End All Wars: Woodrow Wilson and the Quest for a New World Order.* New York: Oxford University Press, 1992.

Koch, John B. "Friedrich Bente on World War I in *Lehre und Wehre.*" *Concordia Institute Historical Quarterly* 42 (August 1969): 133–35.

Kohn, Stephen Martin. *American Political Prisoners: Prosecutions under the Espionage and Sedition Acts.* Westport, CT: Praeger, 1994.

König, Paul. *Voyage of the Deutschland: The First Merchant Submarine.* New York: Hearst's International Library, 1916.

Korman, Gerd. *Industrialization, Immigrants, and Americanizers: The View from Milwaukee, 1866–1921.* Madison: State Historical Society of Wisconsin, 1967.

Kornweibel, Theodore, Jr. *"Investigate Everything": Federal Efforts to Compel Black Loyalty during World War I.* Bloomington: Indiana University Press, 2002.

———. *"Seeing Red": Federal Campaigns against Black Militancy, 1919–1925.* Bloomington: Indiana University Press, 1999. First published 1998 by Indiana University Press.

Koppes, Clayton. "The Kansas Trial of the IWW, 1917–1919." *Labor History* 16 (Summer 1975): 338–58.

Kreuter, Kent, and Gretchen Kreuter. *An American Dissenter: The Life of Algie Martin Simons, 1870–1950.* Lexington: University Press of Kentucky, 1969.

La Follette, Fola. *Robert M. La Follette.* Vol. 2. New York: Hafner, 1971. First published 1953 by Macmillan.

La Follette, Robert M. "Consult the People!" *La Follette's Magazine* 8 (May 1916): 1.

———. "Take the Profit Out of War." *La Follette's Magazine* 7 (February 1915): 2.

Larson, Simeon. *Labor and Foreign Policy: Gompers, the AFL, and the First World War, 1914–1918.* Rutherford, NJ: Fairleigh Dickinson University Press, 1975.

Levy, Alan Howard. "The American Symphony at War: German-American Musicians and Federal Authorities during World War I." *Mid-America: An Historical Review* 71 (January 1989): 5–13.

Lincoln, W. Bruce. *Passage Through Armageddon: The Russians in War and Revolution.* New York: Oxford University Press, 1994. First published 1986 by Simon and Schuster.

Link, Arthur S. "That Cobb Interview." *Journal of American History* 72 (June 1985): 7–17.

———. *Wilson: Confusions and Crises, 1915–1916.* Princeton: Princeton University Press, 1964.

———. *Wilson: The Struggle for Neutrality, 1914–1915.* Princeton: Princeton University Press, 1960.

Linkh, Richard M. *American Catholicism and European Immigrants, 1900–1924.* New York: Center for Migration Studies, 1975.

Lissak, Rivka Shpak. *Pluralism and Progressives: Hull House and the New Immigrants, 1890–1919*. Chicago: University of Chicago Press, 1989.

Livermore, Seward W. *Politics Is Adjourned: Woodrow Wilson and the War Congress, 1916–1918*. Middletown, CT: Wesleyan University Press, 1966.

Lorence, James J. "'Dynamite for the Brain': The Growth and Decline of Socialism in Central and Lakeshore Wisconsin, 1910–1920." *Wisconsin Magazine of History* 66 (Summer 1983): 250–73.

———. "The Ethnic Impact of Wilson's War: The German-American in Marathon County, 1912–1916." *Transactions of the Wisconsin Academy of Sciences, Arts and Letters* (1978): 113–23.

———. "Socialism in Northern Wisconsin, 1910–1920: An Ethno-Cultural Analysis." *Mid-America: An Historical Review* 64 (October 1982): 25–51.

Lubove, Roy. "The Progressives and the Prostitute." *Historian* 24 (May 1962): 308–30.

Luebke, Frederick C. *Bonds of Loyalty: German-Americans and World War I*. De-Kalb: Northern Illinois University Press, 1974.

Manley, Robert N. "Language, Loyalty and Liberty: The Nebraska State Council of Defense and the Lutheran Churches, 1917–1918." *Concordia Historical Institute Quarterly* 37 (April 1964): 1–16.

Margulies, Herbert F. *The Decline of the Progressive Movement in Wisconsin, 1890–1920*. Madison: State Historical Society of Wisconsin, 1968.

———. "The Election of 1920 in Wisconsin: The Return to 'Normalcy' Reappraised." *Wisconsin Magazine of History* 41 (Autumn 1957): 15–22.

Maxwell, Robert S. *Emanuel L. Philipp: Wisconsin Stalwart*. Madison: State Historical Society of Wisconsin, 1959.

McAdoo, William G. *Crowded Years: The Reminiscences of William G. McAdoo*. Boston: Houghton Mifflin, 1931.

McCartin, Joseph A. *Labor's Great War: The Struggle for Industrial Democracy and the Origins of Modern American Labor Relations, 1912–1921*. Chapel Hill: University of North Carolina Press, 1997.

McCormick, Charles H. *Seeing Reds: Federal Surveillance of Radicals in the Pittsburgh Mill District, 1917–1921*. Pittsburgh: University of Pittsburgh Press, 1997.

Men of Milwaukee: A Biographical and Photographic Record of Business and Professional Men of Milwaukee. Milwaukee: Aetna Press, 1930.

Merriman, Scott A. "'An Intensive School of Disloyalty': The C. B. Schoberg Case under the Espionage and Sedition Acts in Kentucky during World War I." *Register of the Kentucky Historical Society* 98 (Spring 2000): 179–204.

Mershart, Ronald V. *Century: 1889–1989: A Memorial of 100 Years of Christian Community*. Superior, WI: Cathedral of Christ the King, 1989.

Miller, Sally M. "Casting a Wide Net: The Milwaukee Movement to 1920." In *Socialism in the Heartland: The Midwestern Experience, 1900–1925*, edited by Donald T. Critchlow, 18–45. Notre Dame, IN: University of Notre Dame Press, 1986.

———. "Socialist Party Decline and World War I: Bibliography and Interpretation." *Science & Society* 31 (Winter 1970): 398–411.

———. *Victor Berger and the Promise of Constructive Socialism, 1910–1920.* Contributions in American History 24. Westport, CT: Greenwood Press, 1973.

Mink, Gwendolyn. *The Wages of Motherhood: Inequality in the Welfare State, 1917–1942.* Ithaca, NY: Cornell University Press, 1995.

Moore's Who Is Who in Wisconsin. Los Angeles: Moore's Who is Who Publications, 1960.

Morn, Frank. *"The Eye That Never Sleeps": A History of the Pinkerton National Detective Agency.* Bloomington: Indiana University Press, 1982.

Mücke, Hellmuth von. *The Emden.* Translated by Helene S. White. Boston: Ritter and Company, 1917.

Murphy, Paul L. *World War I and the Origin of Civil Liberties in the United States.* New York: W. W. Norton and Co., 1979.

Murray, Robert K. *Red Scare: A Study in National Hysteria, 1919–1920.* Minneapolis: University of Minnesota Press, 1955.

Muzik, Edward J. "Victor L. Berger: Congress and the Red Scare." *Wisconsin Magazine of History* 47 (Summer 1964): 309–18.

Neely, Mark E. *The Fate of Liberty: Abraham Lincoln and Civil Liberties.* New York: Oxford University Press, 1991.

———. *Southern Rights: Political Prisoners and the Myth of Confederate Constitutionalism.* Charlottesville: University Press of Virginia, 1999.

Nelson, Clifford L. *German-American Political Behavior in Nebraska and Wisconsin, 1916–1920.* Lincoln: University of Nebraska, 1972.

Nelson, Robert H. *Zoning and Property Rights: An Analysis of the American System of Land-Use Regulation.* Cambridge: MIT Press, 1977.

Niven, Penelope. *Carl Sandburg: A Biography.* New York: Charles Scribner's Sons, 1991.

Nohl, Frederick. "The Lutheran Church—Missouri Synod Reacts to United States Anti-Germanism during World War I." *Concordia Historical Institute Quarterly* 35 (July 1962): 49–66.

O'Brian, John Lord. "Changing Aspects of Freedom." *The John Randolph Tucker Lectures Delivered before the School of Law of Washington and Lee University.* Lexington, VA: Washington and Lee University, 1952.

———. "Civil Liberty in War Time." *New York State Bar Association Proceedings of the Forty-Second Annual Meeting Held at New York, January 17–18, 1919.* Albany: Argus, 1919.

———. *The Reminiscences of John Lord O'Brian.* New York: Oral History Research Office, Columbia University, 1972.

———. "Restraints upon Individual Freedom in Times of National Emergency." *Cornell Law Quarterly* 26 (June 1941): 523–36.

Official Catholic Directory. New York: P. J. Kenedy and Sons, 1917–20.

O'Keefe, Thomas M. "*America,* the *Ave Maria* and the *Catholic World* Respond to the First World War, 1914–1917." *Records of the American Catholic Historical Society of Philadelphia* 94 (1983): 101–15.

Olds, Frank Perry. "'Kultur' in American Politics." *Atlantic Monthly* (September 1916): 382–91.

Olson, Frederick I. "The Milwaukee Socialists, 1897–1941." PhD diss., Harvard University, 1952.

———. "Victor Berger: Socialist Congressman." *Transactions of the Wisconsin Academy of Sciences, Arts, and Letters* 58 (1970): 27–38.

O'Reilly, Kenneth. *"Racial Matters": The FBI's Secret File on Black America, 1960–1972.* New York: Free Press, 1989.

Papen, Franz von. *Memoirs.* Translated by Brian Connell. London: Andre Deutsch, 1952.

Penton, M. James. *Apocalypse Delayed: The Story of Jehovah's Witnesses.* 2nd ed. Toronto: University of Toronto Press, 1997.

Peterson, H. C., and Gilbert C. Fite. *Opponents of War, 1917–1918.* Madison: University of Wisconsin Press, 1957.

Pfeifer, Michael J. *Rough Justice: Lynching and American Society, 1874–1947.* Urbana: University of Illinois Press, 2004.

Pienkos, Donald. "Politics, Religion and Change in Polish Milwaukee, 1900–1930." *Wisconsin Magazine of History* 61 (Spring 1978), 179–209.

Polenberg, Richard. *Fighting Faiths: The Abrams Case, the Supreme Court, and Free Speech.* New York: Penguin, 1989. First published 1987 by Viking Penguin.

Power, Garrett. "Advocates at Cross-Purposes: The Briefs on Behalf of Zoning in the Supreme Court." *Journal of Supreme Court History* 2 (1997): 79–87.

Powers, Richard Gid. *Secrecy and Power: The Life of J. Edgar Hoover.* New York: Free Press, 1987.

Preston, William, Jr. *Aliens and Dissenters: Federal Suppression of Radicals, 1903–1933.* 2nd ed. Urbana: University of Illinois Press, 1994.

Raat, W. Dirk. *Revoltosos: Mexico's Rebels in the United States, 1903–1923.* College Station: Texas A&M University Press, 1981.

Rabban, David M. *Free Speech in Its Forgotten Years.* New York: Cambridge University Press, 1997.

Reese, William J. "'Partisans of the Proletariat': The Socialist Working Class and the Milwaukee Schools, 1890–1920." *History of Education Quarterly* 21 (Spring 1981): 3–50.

Reeves, Thomas C. *The Life and Times of Joe McCarthy: A Biography.* New York: Stein and Day, 1982.

Register of the Department of Justice and the Courts of the United States. Washington: Government Printing Office, 1917–19.

Reinders, Robert C. "Daniel W. Hoan and the Milwaukee Socialist Party during the First World War." *Wisconsin Magazine of History* 36 (Autumn 1952): 48–55.

Rintelen, Captain von [Franz Rintelen von Kleist]. *The Dark Invader: Wartime*

Reminiscences of a German Naval Intelligence Officer. 1933. Introduction by Reinhard R. Doerries. London: Frank Cass, 1998.

Rood, Justin. "FBI Proposes Building Network of U.S. Informants." ABC News *The Blotter.* 25 July 2007, available at http://blogs.abcnews.com/theblotter/2007/07/fbi-proposes-bu.html.

Rosenfeld, Susan. "Organizational and Day-to-Day Activities." In *The FBI: A Comprehensive Reference Guide,* edited by Athan G. Theoharis with Tony G. Poveda, Susan Rosenfeld, and Richard Gid Powers, 205–47. Phoenix, AZ: Oryx Press, 1999.

Scheiber, Harry N. *The Wilson Administration and Civil Liberties 1917–1921.* Ithaca, NY: Cornell University Press, 1960.

Schedel, John R. "A Rhetorical Study of Editorials in Wisconsin Newspapers during the Anti-German Movement, 1916–1918." PhD diss., University of Nebraska, 1982.

Scheidt, David L. "Some Effects of World War I on the General Synod and General Council." *Concordia Historical Institute Quarterly* 43 (May 1970): 83–92.

Schmidt, Regin. *Red Scare: FBI and the Origins of Anticommunism in the United States.* Copenhagen: Museum Tusculanum Press, 2000.

Schrecker, Ellen. *Many Are the Crimes: McCarthyism in America.* Princeton: Princeton University Press, 1998.

———. *No Ivory Tower: McCarthyism and the Universities.* New York: Oxford University Press, 1986.

Sealander, Judith. "Violent Group Draft Resistance in the Appalachian South during World War I." *Appalachian Notes* 7 (1979): 1–12.

Sellars, Nigel Anthony. *Oil, Wheat, and Wobblies: The Industrial Workers of the World in Oklahoma, 1905–1930.* Norman: University of Oklahoma Press, 1998.

Sessions, Gene. "Espionage in Windsor: Clarence H. Waldron and Patriotism in World War I." *Vermont History* 61 (1993) 133–55.

Shannon, David A. *The Socialist Party of America: A History.* Chicago: Quadrangle Paperbacks, 1967. First published 1955 by Macmillan.

Simons, A. M. "The Future of the Socialist Party." *New Republic* 9 (2 December 1916): 118–20.

Singerman, Robert. "The American Career of the *Protocols of the Elders of Zion.*" *American Jewish History* 71 (September 1981): 48–78.

Smith, James Morton. *Freedom's Fetters: The Alien and Sedition Laws and American Civil Liberties.* Ithaca, NY: Cornell University Press, 1963. First published 1956 by Cornell University Press.

Smith, Robert M. "Industrial Espionage Agencies: Capital's Ineffective or Deadly Anti-Union Weapon?" *Mid-America: An Historical Review* 80 (Summer 1998): 93–121.

———. "Spies against Labor: Industrial Espionage Agencies, 1855–1940." *Labor's Heritage* 5 (Summer 1993): 64–77.

Spence, Robert B. "K. A. Jahnke and the German Sabotage Campaign in the United States and Mexico, 1914–1918." *Historian* 59 (Fall 1996): 89–112.

Steele, Richard W. "Fear of the Mob and Faith in Government in Free Speech Discourse, 1919–1941." *American Journal of Legal History* 38 (January 1994): 55–83.

Steinberg, Jonathan. *Why Switzerland?* 2nd ed. New York: Cambridge University Press, 1996.

Sterling, David L. "The 'Naïve Liberal,' the 'Devious Communist' and the Johnson Case." *Ohio History* 78 (Spring 1969): 94–103.

Stevens, John D. "Suppression of Expression in Wisconsin during World War I." PhD diss., University of Wisconsin, 1967.

Stevens, Michael E., and Ellen D. Goldlust-Gingrich, eds. *The Family Letters of Victor and Meta Berger, 1894–1929*. Madison: State Historical Society of Wisconsin, 1995.

Still, Bayrd. *Milwaukee: The History of a City*. Madison: State Historical Society of Wisconsin, 1948.

Stokesbury, James L. *A Short History of World War I*. New York: William Morrow and Company, 1981.

Taft, Philip. "The Federal Trials of the IWW." *Labor History* 3 (Winter 1962): 57–91.

Tagore, Rabindranath. *Nationalism*. New York: Macmillan, 1917. Reprint, Westport, CT: Greenwood Press, 1973.

Talbert, Roy, Jr. *Negative Intelligence: The Army and the American Left, 1917–1941*. Jackson: University Press of Mississippi, 1991.

Thelen, David P. *Robert M. La Follette and the Insurgent Spirit*. Madison: University of Wisconsin Press, 1985. First published 1976 by Little, Brown, and Company.

Theoharis, Athan G., and John Stuart Cox. *The Boss: J. Edgar Hoover and the Great American Inquisition*. Philadelphia: Temple University Press, 1988.

Thwaites, Reuben Gold, ed. *The University of Wisconsin: Its History and Alumni*. Madison: J. N. Purcell, 1900.

Tolnay, Stewart E., and E. M. Beck. *A Festival of Violence: An Analysis of Southern Lynchings, 1882–1930*. Urbana: University of Illinois Press, 1995.

Trattner, Walter I. "Julia Grace Wales and the Wisconsin Plan for Peace." *Wisconsin Magazine of History* 44 (Spring 1961): 203–13.

Tuchman, Barbara J. *The Zimmermann Telegram*. New York: Bantam, 1971. First published 1958 by Viking.

Ueberhorst, Horst. "Turners and Social Democrats in Milwaukee: Five Decades of Cooperation (1910–1960)." Lecture given at the research institute of the Friedrich Ebert Endowment, Bonn, March 26, 1980. Translated by Joseph Hahn. Milwaukee: privately printed, 1983.

Unger, Nancy C. *Fighting Bob La Follette: The Righteous Reformer*. Chapel Hill: University of North Carolina Press, 2000.

United States Census Bureau. *Thirteenth Census of the United States.* Washington, D.C.: Government Printing Office, 1913.

———. *Fourteenth Census of the United States.* Washington, D.C.: Government Printing Office, 1922.

Vaughn, Stephen. *Holding Fast the Inner Lines: Democracy, Nationalism, and the Committee on Public Information.* Chapel Hill: University of North Carolina Press, 1980.

Vonnegut, Kurt. *Slapstick: or, Lonesome No More!* New York: Delacorte Press, 1976.

Wachman, Marvin. *History of the Social-Democratic Party of Milwaukee, 1897–1910.* Urbana: University of Illinois Press, 1945.

Waligorski, Ann Shirley. "Social Action and Women: The Experience of Lizzie Black Kander." Master's thesis, University of Wisconsin, 1970.

Walker, Samuel. *In Defense of American Liberties: A History of the ACLU.* New York: Oxford University Press, 1990.

Weinberg, Carl R. *Labor, Loyalty, and Rebellion: Southwestern Illinois Coal Miners and World War I.* Carbondale: Southern Illinois University Press, 2005.

Weinstein, James. "Anti-War Sentiment and the Socialist Party, 1917–1918." *Political Science Quarterly* 74 (June 1959): 215–39.

———. *The Decline of Socialism in America, 1912–1925.* Introduction by James Weinstein. New Brunswick, NJ: Rutgers University Press, 1984. First published 1967 by Monthly Review Press.

———. "The Socialist Party: Its Roots and Strength, 1912–1919." *Studies on the Left* 1 (Winter 1960): 5–27.

Weissman, Norman. "A History of the Wisconsin State Journal since 1900." Master's thesis, University of Wisconsin, 1951.

Wesser, Robert F. *Charles Evans Hughes: Politics and Reform in New York, 1905–1910.* Ithaca, NY: Cornell University Press, 1967.

Wiebe, Robert H. *The Search for Order 1877–1920.* New York: Hill and Wang, 1995. First published 1967 by Hill and Wang.

Williams, David. "The Bureau of Investigation and Its Critics, 1919–1921: The Origins of Federal Political Surveillance." *Journal of American History* 68 (December 1981): 560–79.

Williamson, Joel. *A Rage for Order: Black-White Relations in the American South since Emancipation.* New York: Oxford University Press, 1986.

Wilson, Woodrow. *The Papers of Woodrow Wilson.* Edited by Arthur S. Link et al. 69 vols. Princeton: Princeton University Press, 1966–94.

———. "Spurious versus Real Patriotism in Education." *School Review* 7 (December 1899): 599–620.

———. "State of the Union Message." (7 December 1915) Lexis-Nexis Primary Sources in U.S. Presidential History.

Wisconsin Blue Book. Madison: Democrat Printing Company, 1917, 1919.

Wisconsin Memorial Day Annual. Madison, 1909, 1913, 1915, 1916.

Wittke, Carl. *The German-Americans and the World War.* Columbus, OH: Ohio State Archaeological and Historical Society, 1936.

——. *The German-Language Press in America.* Lexington: University of Kentucky Press, 1957.

Woodward, C. Vann. *Tom Watson, Agrarian Rebel.* New York: Galaxy-Oxford University Press, 1965. First published 1938 by The Macmillan Company.

Woods, Arthur. "The Problem of the Black Hand." *McClure's Magazine* 33 (May 1909): 40–47.

Wreszin, Michael. *Oswald Garrison Villard: Pacifist at War.* Bloomington: Indiana University Press, 1965.

Wright, Steven L. "Alfred Bettman: The Making of a Civil Libertarian, 1917–1929." *War & Society* 17 (October 1999): 59–79.

Wust, Klaus G. *Zion in Baltimore, 1755–1955: The Bicentennial History of the Earliest German-American Church in Baltimore, Maryland.* Baltimore: Zion Church of the City of Baltimore, 1955.

Zangrando, Robert L. *The NAACP Crusade against Lynching, 1909–1950.* Philadelphia: Temple University Press, 1980.

Zecker, Robert. "The Activities of Czech and Slovak Immigrants during World War I." *Ethnic Forum* 15 (1995): 35–54.

Zeiger, Susan. "She Didn't Raise Her Boy to Be a Slacker: Motherhood, Conscription, and the Culture of the First World War." *Feminist Studies* 22 (Spring 1996): 7–39.

——. "Teaching Peace: Lessons from a Peace Studies Curriculum of the Progressive Era." *Peace & Change* 25 (January 2000).

Index